KU-279-908

KU-279-908

Glorious Crocheted Sweaters

A CIP catalogue record for this book
is available from the British Library

Published in 1991 by David & Charles plc
Brunel House Newton Abbot Devon

© 1989 Altamont Press.

Photos and Instructions © Ariadne/Eska Tijdscriften,
Utrecht, Holland.
English Translation by Networks, Inc.
English Translation © 1988 Altamont Press.

ISBN 0-7153-9953-5

All Rights Reserved.

Every effort has been made to ensure that all
information in this book is accurate. However, due to
differing conditions, yarns, and individual crocheting
skills, the publisher cannot be responsible for any
injuries, losses, or other damages which may result
from the use of the information in this book.

Printed and bound in Hong Kong

Glorious Crocheted Sweaters

Edited by Nola Theiss

A DAVID & CHARLES CRAFT BOOK

Expert Assistants and Advisors:
    Diane Murphy, Janet Stollnitz, Patricia Syslo,
    Kay Wisniewski, Terry Zalenski
Editor: Dawn Cusick
Art Director: Rob Pulleyn
Production: Dawn Cusick
Typesetting: Diana Deakin
Drawings:
    Thom Boswell, John Koosner, Sarah Warren

Table of Contents

Introduction

As a craft, crochet has developed quite differently in North America and Europe.

Crochet is a typically American craft, perhaps best exemplified by the afghan. Crocheted afghans are in countless homes combining warmth and texture and a colourful handmade touch to any room. Even the sets of television shows, trying to create a home-like atmosphere, frequently have a crocheted afghan folded neatly over the back of a couch or chair. Afghans can be carefully planned and executed; or, as is more often the case, they can be made in a spontaneous burst of creativity using leftover pieces of scrap yarn with the pattern created as the project progresses.

In a sense, crochet is the craft most closely akin to the family traditions of patchwork quilts and early knitting. It is a skill taught by a relative or friend or by the next-door neighbour to a child who is fascinated by the flash of a crochet hook at work. A crocheter determined to learn new stitches usually learns them from another crocheter or by examining samples of work she admires.

Lacking a written literature, crochet in America has relied on folk tradition for subsistence — handed down, literally, from one generation to the next. American crocheters, like early quilters, enjoy the challenge of making something whole from leftover scraps, often producing unique colour combinations. The items American crocheters produce are usually quite functional — such as an afghan or baby blanket — and are often presented as gifts to celebrate important occasions.

European crochet is quite different. Because knitting is so popular in Europe, crocheters usually lack the helpful next-door neighbour for instruction, relying instead on written directions. Most crocheters in Europe are also fervent knitters, so it's not unusual for them to use knitted borders and edgings in their crochet work.

European knitters have long taken pride in the fashionable garments they produce, and are willing to invest in quality materials. European crocheters, eager to create their own fashionable garments with their craft, have designed new crochet stitches that, when combined with quality yarns and patterns, make truly glorious sweaters.

If you, too, feel limited in crocheting only afghans and baby blankets or don't feel particularly experienced in crocheting fashionable garments, **Glorious Crocheted Sweaters** will be a revelation. Like most crochet projects, these garments can be made quickly and do not require extensive knowledge.

We recommend you seek out an experienced crocheter if you need help with some of the stitches.

All of the patterns are labelled with their level of difficulty. Projects marked with a single star are recommended for the novice; projects with two stars for the intermediate crocheter who is eager to try something new; and projects with three stars for the advanced crocheter ready for a challenge.

We have also divided the patterns into four chapters. The novice crocheter would probably do well to start with the first chapter, SIMPLE STITCHES, SIMPLE STRIPES, and will be amazed at how fashionable crocheted sweaters can be. The second chapter, COLOUR, is very colourful indeed. Beautiful jacquard patterns, bold geometrics and plaids, and unusual techniques of crocheting around contrasting strands of yarn make this a fascinating chapter. The third chapter, RELIEF STITCHES, highlights texture. By working around the post of the stitches in previous rows, all sorts of ridges, basketweaves, cables and lattices are achieved. This chapter is the most three-dimensional and most akin to knitting. The fourth chapter, PATTERN STITCHES, contains a vast array of stitches, most of which are not difficult, but give a unique look to the garments. Work your way through the book from beginning to end or choose garments by level of difficulty from all four chapters. For a quick reference we have included a brief description of the most commonly used stitches.

As an added note, we have been referring to the crocheter as female, although we realize that crochet, along with other crafts, can be enjoyed by anyone, regardless of gender. We hope our readers will be inspired to embark on a voyage of glorious crocheting.

Nola Theiss

Stitches and Techniques

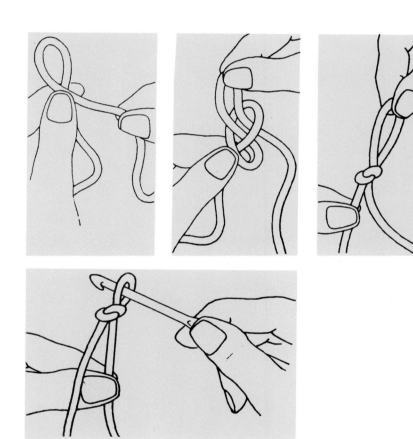

Making a Slip Knot

When following the instructions, it is very important to read carefully and to pay attention to the position of the hook at all times. Make a sample tension to learn the stitch and check measurements and tension (more about this later). Often you will be called upon to place the hook at the back or front of the work; but remember, unless specified, always insert the hook in the front of the stitch under both loops and work from right to left. Frequently, it will be necessary to skip stitches and then come back to them. Position of the hook is very important in this case because you must know whether to work in front or in back of the stitches worked after the skipped stitches. Use the photos as a guide.

Asterisks

The asterisk, *, is used in crochet as a repeat sign. All instructions included between two asterisks are to be repeated the total number of times indicated.

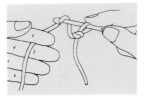
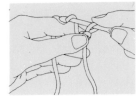

Yarn over (yo)

Technically a yarn over is not really a stitch in itself, but no crochet stitch is possible without it. Wrap the yarn around the hook from back to front to form a loop. Depending on the stitch, a number of yarn overs are formed and drawn through loops. In essence, this is crochet — a very simple process that no machine can duplicate.

Chain Stitch (ch)

Starting the chain (ch), make a slip knot; insert the hook from right to left through the loop. With the hook in front of the yarn, wrap the yarn around the hook from back to front. With the hook pointing down, draw a new loop through the loop on the hook. One chain stitch has been completed.

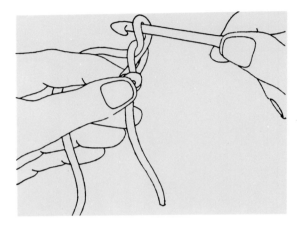
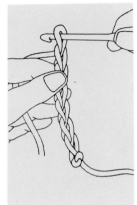

Slip Stitch (sl st) or Single Crochet (sc)

Insert hook into chain or stitch; wrap the yarn over the hook from back to front; draw a loop through both the chain or stitch and the loop on the hook. One slip stitch has been completed.

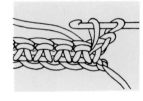
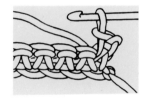

Double Crochet (dc)

Insert hook into the second chain from the hook. Wrap the yarn around the hook from back to front. Draw the yarn through the chain making two loops on the hook. Wrap the yarn around the hook from back to front and draw the yarn through the two loops on the hook. One double crochet stitch has been completed. Continue by inserting the hook in the next chain. After the last stitch, chain two and turn; insert the hook into the first stitch to begin the next row.

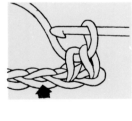

Shrimp Stitch or Crab Stitch

This stitch is used frequently as a finishing edge on necklines and other borders. It is worked like double crochet, but worked in the opposite direction that is, left to right, instead of right to left. Keep the right side of the work facing you as you work. If shrimp stitch is worked correctly, it

will feel as if you are working backwards. If it feels like you are doing double crochet, you have probably turned the work and you *are* doing double crochet.

Half-Treble Crochet (htr)

Wrap the yarn around the hook from back to front; insert the hook into the third chain from the hook; wrap the yarn over the hook and draw the yarn through the chain making three loops on the hook. Wrap the yarn around the hook from back to front and draw through the three loops on the hook. One half-treble crochet stitch has been completed. Continue by wrapping the yarn around the hook and inserting the hook in the next chain. After the last stitch, chain two and turn; wrap the yarn over the hook; insert the hook in the first stitch to begin the next row.

Treble Crochet (tr)

Wrap the yarn around the hook from back to front; insert the hook into the fourth chain from the hook; wrap the yarn over the hook and draw the yarn through the chain making three loops on the hook. Wrap the yarn over the hook and draw it through two loops; wrap the yarn over the hook again and draw the yarn through the last two loops completing the stitch. Continue by repeating the sequence in each chain stitch. After the last stitch, chain three and turn; insert the hook in the second stitch to begin the next row.

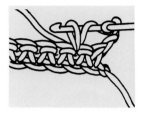
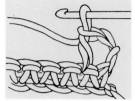

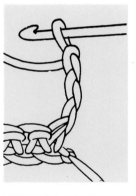
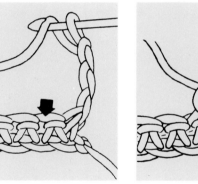

Double Treble Crochet (dtr)

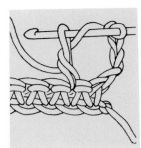

Wrap the yarn around the hook from back to front twice and insert the hook in the fifth chain from the hook. Wrap the yarn over the hook and draw a loop through the chain stitch making four loops on the hook. Wrap the yarn over the hook and draw the yarn through two loops; wrap the yarn over the hook and draw the yarn through 2 more loops; wrap the yarn over the hook again and draw the yarn through last two loops completing the stitch. Continue by repeating the sequence in each chain. After the last stitch, chain four and turn; insert the hook into the second stitch to begin the next row.

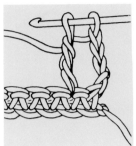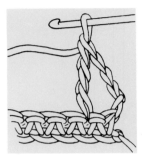

Afghan Stitch

Using an afghan crochet hook, make a chain equal to the desired number of stitches plus two.

Row 1: Insert the hook into the second chain from the hook, wrap the yarn over the hook and draw a loop through the chain. Continue by wrapping the yarn over the hook pulling a loop through each chain in the row. Do not turn the work — always work with the right side facing you.

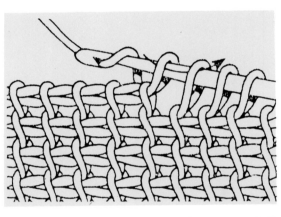

Row 2: The next row is worked by wrapping the yarn over the hook and pulling a loop through the first loop on the hook. Wrap the yarn over the needle and draw a loop through the next two loops on the hook. Repeat until there is one loop left on the hook. The remaining loop forms the first stitch of the next row.

Row 3: Skip the first vertical loop in the row below and insert the hook from right to left through the second vertical loop. Wrap the yarn over the needle and draw the loop through making two loops on the hook. Continue across the row. Note: insert the hook through the center of the last loop leaving two strands of yarn at the edge.

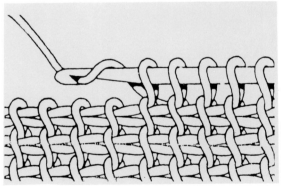

Row 4: Same as row 2.

Repeat rows 3 and 4 until desired length is reached.

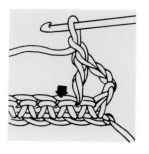

Filet Stitch

There are many versions of the filet stitch, but this is the most common. To make beautiful motifs, fill in the desired squares with one st.

Row 1: *1 Tr, ch 2*, rep * to * across.

Row 2 and all foll rows: Ch 4 to turn (beg of first square). Always work 1 tr in tr of previous row, ch above ch of previous row.

Relief Stitches

All relief stitches are the same: basically one inserts the hook around the post, that is the length of the stitch found in a previous row, and work whichever stitch one desires. The texture depends on the stitch, which previous row is worked, and whether the stitch is worked on the back or front of the work. We've listed a few variations to give you the general idea.

Front Relief Dc

Worked in dc by working around the post of the st below. For front relief sts, insert hook from right to left around the post of the indicated st at front of work. Yo, and draw through loop, yo and draw through both loops.

Back Relief Dc

Worked in dc by working around the post of the st below. For back relief sts, insert hook from right to left around the post of the indicated st at back of work. Yo, and draw through loop, yo and draw through both loops.

Front Relief Tr

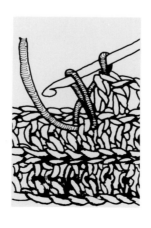

Worked in tr by working around the post of the st of the previous row. Yo over hook, insert hook from right to left around the post of the indicated st at front of work. Yo, and draw through loop, yo and continue as you would a tr.

Back Relief Tr

Worked in tr by working around the post of the st of the previous row. Yo over hook, insert hook from right to left around the post of the indicated st at back of work. Yo, and draw through loop, yo and continue as you would a tr.

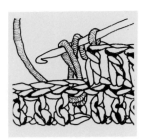

Border Stitches

Most American crocheters are not accustomed to the term border stitch. The first and last stitches, usually the chain at the beg of the row and the last st of the row, are considered as border stitches by Europeans because they are worked into the seams and are not part of the pattern. They are worked in the same colour as adjoining stitches in most cases. On jacquard patterns, they are usually not included on the chart. When border stitches are used, some explanation will be given in the pattern. Often when joining seams, one sews or crochets between the border stitch and the adjoining stitch.

Many of the patterns use a knitted ribbing rather than a crochet edging. We have included a description of all the stitches used here, as well as some alternatives. Again, a glance at other crochet reference books will provide you with even more ideas. Feel free to substitute your own preferred edgings. Knitted ribbings are more elastic, but don't let a knitted edge stop you from making a design; crochet your edgings instead.

1/1 ribbing:

Row 1: *K1, p1*. Rep * to * across.
Row 2 and all foll rows: Work sts as established in previous row, by knitting the stitches which were purled in the previous row and look flat on the second row, and purling the stitches which were knitted in the previous row and have a loop next to the needle.

2/2 ribbing:

Row 1: *K2, p2*. Rep * to * across.
Row 2 and all foll rows: Work sts as established in previous row.

Crochet Ribbing - Post stitch

ribbing (double crochet).
Worked on an even number of stitches. The idea is always to work a back relief post st in a front relief post stitch of the previous row so alternate ridges are formed on the back and front of work.

Row 1: 1 Dc in each ch.
Row 2: Ch 1 (= 1 border st) *1 front relief dc, 1 back relief dc*, 1 dc in last space (= 1 border st).
Row 3: Ch 1, *1 back relief dc, 1 front relief dc*, 1 dc in last space.
Repeat Rows 2 and 3.

Post Stitch Ribbing
(treble crochet).
Same as single crochet post st with longer posts.

Row 1: 1 Tr in each st.
Row 2: Ch 2 (= 1 border st) *1 front relief tr, 1 back relief tr*, rep * to * across row, end with 1 front relief tr, 1 htr (= 1 border st).
Row 3: Ch 2, *1 back relief tr, 1 front relief tr*, rep * to * across row, end with 1 back relief tr, 1 hdc.
Always rep rows 2 and 3.

Crochet Ribbing - Ridge stitch ribbing

Note: Ridges are formed horizontally, and when turned sideways, form ribbing. Chain desired depth of ribbing. When used as ribbing on a garment, the ridge stitch is usually crocheted separately to the desired length and then attached to the garment.

Row 1: Skip 1 ch, *1 dc in each ch*, ch 1, turn.
Row 2: *1 dc in back loop of each st*, ch 1 turn.
Repeat Row 2 for the pattern.

Helpful Notes

Notes on Establishing Tension

The correct tension is important for the proper size of a garment. If you are used to making afghans only, it may not have mattered if the finished piece was a few inches bigger or smaller than you planned. Those inches can be critical on a garment, so be careful. Each pattern has a specific tension — the number of stitches and rows that equal a 4 in. (10 cm) square. It is important to crochet a sample square using the yarn and hook size specified before starting the garment. If your square measures less than 4 in. (10 cm) try a larger hook size. If your square measures larger than 4 in. (10 cm) try a smaller hook size. Be sure to measure your swatch on a flat surface and avoid stretching it.

Increasing

To make a single increase, work two stitches in one stitch. To make a double increase, work three stitches in one stitch. You may want to work in the back loop for one increase and the front loop for the next. To add more stitches at the end of a row, make an additional chain stitch for each additional stitch needed plus the required number of turning chain stitches. On the next row, crochet a pattern stitch in each added chain. Some of the patterns give specific directions for increasing in that pattern stitch. We recommend you follow them or experiment with your own method. The goal is to make as smooth an edge as possible and to get the correct number of stitches.

Decreasing

To decrease a single stitch, insert the hook in a stitch, draw through a loop, insert the hook into the next stitch, draw through a loop. Wrap the yarn over the hook; draw the yarn through all three loops.

To decrease two stitches in dc or half treble crochet, insert the hook in a stitch, draw through a loop, skip the next stitch, insert the hook in the following stitch, draw through a loop. Wrap the yarn over the hook; draw the yarn through all three loops — this is called slip stitching across stitches and is the most common way to decrease at the beginning of a row. To decrease at the end of a row, work across until you have the specified number of sts unworked at the end of row. Turn and continue as directed across the next row. Be sure to work the correct number of turning chains to begin the following row. To avoid a staircase effect at the edge, you may wish to leave one fewer st, unworked than specified, then slip st across the first st of the following row to give a slanted edge.

Reversing Shapings

Although both sides of a neckline are generally shaped the same, keep in mind that they're the mirror image of each other. Usually, the directions will be very specific for the right side of the neckline and then say to reverse shapings for the left side. This simply means that the shapings that were worked at the beginning of the row will now be worked at the end of the row and vice versa. If you slip stitched across six sts at the beginning of a row on the right edge, work to the last six sts of the row and leave them unworked and so on. Increases will also be worked on the opposite edge on the second half.

On a cardigan, directions will only be given for one half of the front and you will reverse the instructions so that the two fronts will correspond in shaping. Keep the completed half nearby so that you do not forget which half you are working on.

Jacquard charts or pattern stitch motifs also may reverse pattern placement from one side of the front to the other or from the back to the front.

The directions may tell you to work the chart beginning at the left edge for the back and to begin the chart from the right edge on the front so that the motifs will match at the side seams. Always try to visualize the finished garment as you work and the logic of the design will guide you.

Yarns and substitutions

When possible, the names of specific yarns have been included in the directions for the garment. For the best results, please use those yarns. Always choose a comparable yarn when making a substitution. When it was not possible to name a specific yarn, a description of the type, weight, and yardage has been given to help you choose an appropriate yarn.

Making Buttonholes
Horizontal buttonholes:

Double crochet: at desired location for buttonhole, crochet chain stitches equal to length needed for buttonhole. Skip the corresponding number of stitches in the previous row; continue with double crochet. On following row, work the same number of stitches across the chained sts.

Knitted buttonholes:

On the right side of the work row, cast off the desired number of stitches. Work to the end of the row. On the wrong side of the work row, work to where you have cast off stitches. Cast onto the right hand needle the number of stitches that were cast off. Continue working to end of row.

Finishing Techniques
Blocking and pressing:

Check the yarn label before proceeding. Always heed the recommendation of the yarn manufacturer. Most crocheted garments need very little blocking. If it is necessary to block, block the individual sections of the garment separately. Using the correct measurements, draw an outline of the finished section on heavy paper. Place the paper on a flat surface padded with several soft towels. Using rustproof pins, pin the crocheted piece to the paper. Carefully work the piece to the correct size and shape. Cover the piece with a very damp cloth. Following the yarn manufacturer's recommendations you may either use the steam method or simply weight down the piece. **Steam method —** keep the weight of the iron above the work and gently steam the piece. Remove the damp cloth and leave the piece in position to dry thoroughly. **Weight method —** place additional towels on top of the very damp cloth and then place a wooden board on top of the towels. Leave all in place until the piece is completely dry.

Joining Methods

The pieces of a garment may be joined together using several methods.

Backstitch: Pin the right sides of the pieces together. Use a yarn or tapestry needle and the yarn used in crocheting the pieces. Work from right to left, using small, even stitches, inserting the needle back through the pieces at the point where it emerged on the previous stitch, bringing the needle through to the front slightly to the left of where it went into the fabric.

Slip stitch: Pin the right sides of the pieces together. Using a crochet hook and yarn, insert the hook through both pieces of the garment and draw a loop through the fabric and the loop on the hook. Repeat until the seam is completed.

Invisible weaving (vertical): Lay the edges to be joined next to one another, right side up. Using a yarn needle and yarn, insert the needle up through the lower half of the end stitch on one piece, draw through the thread through. From the front insert the needle through the upper half of the edge stitch on the other piece, draw the yarn through. Continue inserting the needle through alternate sides.

Invisible weaving (horizontal): This is used on the final row-edges. Lay the edges to be joined next to one another.

Using a yarn needle and yarn, insert the needle between the front and the back loops of the edges.

Crochet seams: Hold two pieces with right sides together unless specified otherwise. Insert hook through both thicknesses and draw up loop. Insert hook in next stitch and draw up loop, yo and draw through both loops. Continue along seam.

Tips on Using Two or More Colours

Double crochet: using the first colour, work to the last stitch in one colour. Insert the hook in the next stitch, wrap the yarn over the hook and draw through a loop through. Drop the first colour to the wrong side of the work and with the second colour, wrap the yarn over the hook and draw through a loop through. It is important to always change to a different colour in the same manner.

Half treble crochet: yarn colours in half treble crochet are changed in the same manner as double crochet. Always work the last wrap over the hook with the new colour so that the stitch before the new colour is completed with the new colour.

Double colourwork: the new colour is also used to complete the previous stitch before starting the stitch with the changed colour. The colour not being used is carried across the top of the previous row and the new row is worked over it making the fabric reversible. Do not draw through the new coloured yarn too tightly when using it again or it will distort your work.

Blocks of colour: When using two colours alternately across a row, they can be carried along the wrong side of work when not in use as described above. If you are using large blocks or isolated motifs, separate balls or bobbins are needed for each section. The bobbins or balls of yarn hang at the back of the work and the colours are changed by dropping the first colour to the back and using the second colour to wrap the yarn over

the hook to complete a stitch and start the new stitch with the second colour. Either weave the ends in or work over the ends when you change to a new colour.

Changing yarns: The directions given above apply to changing yarns as well as changing the colours of threads.

Hooks

Crochet hooks are made of plastic, coated aluminum, steel and wood in a range of sizes. The three sizing systems are the U.S. system, the British system, and the metric system. Since all of these patterns were originally worked with metric size hooks, we are including an interchange chart for metric-U.S.-U.K. size hooks. If possible, we tested the yarn on a U.S. sized hook; thus you may sometimes find that there is a slight discrepancy between the chart interchanges and the ones given in the instructions, or that another chart in another book is slightly different. In any case, you should use the chart as a guide only and always check your tension and change hooks accordingly.

Metric	U.S.	U.K.
2.5	B/1	12
3	C/2	11
3.25	D/3	10
3.5	E/4	9
4	F/5	8
4.5	G/6	7
5	H/8	6
5.5	I/9	5
6	J/10	4
7	K/10.25	2

Steel hooks are generally used with lightweight yarns and threads and for finer, lacy work. Aluminium and plastic hooks are used with most popular weight yarns. Wood hooks are usually found only in the larger and longer lengths. A special hook called an afghan hook is made of aluminium and has a straight shaft with a knob or cap at one end and a hook at the other. They are sized like the aluminium and plastic hooks.

Throughout the text all dimensions have
been given in inches and in centimetres.
For the sake of clarity, however, dimensions
on diagrams are given in centimetres only.

SUCCESS WILL REWARD YOUR EFFORTS IN THIS COAT OF PUTTY AND OATMEAL TWEED. COLLAR, CUFFS AND BUTTONBANDS ARE ALSO CROCHETED FOR A FIRM FINISH THAT HOLDS ITS SHAPE THROUGH YEARS OF WEAR.

TWEED COAT

SIZE

Women's size Large, bust 36-38 in. (91.5 - 97 cm). Finished bust measurement: 51¼ in. (130.5 cm), length: 41½ in. (105 cm), sleeve seam: 17½ in. (45 cm).

MATERIALS

35 skeins bulky weight yarn (approx. 75 yds (68.5 m) per 50 g skein) colour grey. Crochet hooks U.S. sizes H/8 and K/10.5 (U.K. sizes 6 and 2) (Metric sizes 5 and 7) or size needed to obtain tension.
3 buttons. **To save time, take time to check tension!**

TENSION

9 dc and 11 rows = 4 in. (10 cm).

STITCHES

Chain stitch (ch), single crochet (sc), double crochet (dc), treble crochet (tr).
Pattern stitch: Row 1: Dc across.
Row 2: 1 dc in the dc in the row below, *1 dc in the foll dc, 1 dc in the dc in the row below *, rep * to * across.
Row 3: 1 dc, *1 dc in the dc in the row below, 1 dc*, rep * to * across. Rep rows 2 to 3.

BODY

With larger hook, ch 125 + ch 2 (counts as first dc). Work in pat st.
Row 1: Work first dc in the 4th ch from the hook, dc across = 125 dc.
Row 2: 6 dc = left border, 113 sts of pat st, 2nd row of pat st, 6 dc = right border.
Row 3: 6 dc, 113 sts of pat st, 3rd row of pat st, 6 dc = right border.

Continue as established for 27½ in. (70 cm). Make 3 buttonholes on right border, beg when piece measures 21½ in. (55 cm), then spacing 2 more buttonholes about 6 in. (15 cm) apart. At right border, work 3 dc, ch 3, skip 3, continue across border. On foll row, work 3 dc in ch-3 sp. Mark center 55 sts. Work across first 33 sts as established, turn, leaving last 2 sts before marker unworked. *Sc over first st, work to end of row. Turn, work 1 row straight.* Work * to * 17 times more. With right side facing, sc over first 7 sts, work across, turn. Sc over first st, work to last st or row, turn, leaving last st unworked. *Sc over first st, work to end of row, turn. Work across to last st, turn, leaving last st unworked*, work * to * twice. Fasten off. Join yarn to first marker and *sc over first st, work to end of row*, rep * to * 40 times total. Work 1 row across rem 15 sts, then fasten off. Join yarn 2 sts from 2nd marker for left front. Work to end of row, turn. Work to last st, turn, leaving last st unworked. Continue by rev shapings of right front.

SLEEVES

With larger hook, ch 27 + ch 2. Work 3¼ in. (8 cm) in dc, then continue in pat st. Inc 1 st at each edge of every 4th row 10 times = 47 sts. When piece measures 19 in. (49 cm) from beg, shape raglans. *Sc over first st, work to last st, leave last st unworked*, rep * to * 40 times. Work across 7 sts. Fasten off.

POCKET

With larger hook, ch 15 + ch 2 to turn. Work first dc in 4th ch from hook. Work pat st over 15 sts for 5½ in. (14 cm). End with 1¼ in. (3 cm) of dc. Fasten off.

FINISHING

Block pieces to indicated measurements. Sew raglan seams. Fold sleeve borders to inside and sl st in place. Sew side and sleeve seams. With smaller hook, work 1 row of dc around neck, continue in dc for 6¼ in. (16 cm). Fasten off. Fold collar in half to inside and sew to first row of collar. Work 1 row of dc along collar ends, front edges and lower edge of body as foll: with smaller hook, beg at top of collar end, work 1 dc in each dc, 3 dc in corner, work 1 dc in each row along front, then 3 dc in corner. Change to larger hook and work in dc in each st and 3 dc in corner, along lower edge. Change to smaller hook, work 3 dc in corner, work in dc along front edge, work 3 dc in corner, work 1 dc in each dc along collar end. Fasten off. Sew the pockets to each front placed 16½ in. (42 cm) from lower edge and 6 in. (15 cm) from front edges. Sew on buttons.

PIECES

SLEEVE

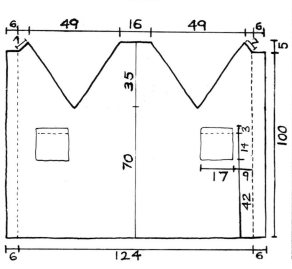

BRIGHT CRAYON STRIPES MAKE THIS PULLOVER A REAL ATTENTION-GETTER. THE WELL-BEHAVED MOHAIR BLEND IS AS EASY AS ABC TO CROCHET.

CRAYON STRIPED PULLOVER

SIZE

Women's Medium (Large, X Large), bust 33-35 (36-38, 39-42) in. - 84-89 (91.5-97, 99-107) cm. Finished bust measurement: 40 (45, 48) in. - 102 (114, 122) cm., length 28¼ in. (72 cm), sleeve seam 18¾ in. (48 cm).

MATERIALS

10 (11, 12) skeins mohair-blend bulky yarn — approx. 111 yds (100 m) per 50 g skein) colour black, 1 skein each colour red, gold, blue, green. Crochet hook U.S. size 1/9 (U.K. size 5) (Metric size 5.5) or size needed to obtain tension. Knitting needles U.S. size 7 (U.K. size 7) (Metric size 4.5).
To save time, take time to check tension!

TENSION

12 tr and 8½ rows = 4 in. (10 cm)

STITCHES

Double crochet (dc), treble crochet (tr), chain stitch (ch).
1/1 ribbing: Row 1: *K1, p1*, rep * to * across.
Row 2: Work sts as they appear.

Stripe pattern: *3 rows of tr in black, 1 row of dc in green, 3 rows of tr in black, 1 row of dc in red, 3 rows of tr in black, 1 row of dc in blue, 3 rows of tr in black, 1 row of dc in gold.* Rep these 16 rows for stripe pattern. Beg each row of tr with ch 3 as the first st. Beg each row of dc with ch 1 for the first st.

BACK

With knitting needles and black, cast on 84 (90, 96) sts and work 2¾ in. (7 cm) in 1/1 ribbing. Cast off loosely. With crochet hook and black, crochet 62 (68, 74) tr along cast off row of ribbing. Continue by foll stripe pattern until piece measures 28¼ in. (72 cm) from beg. End with 1 row of dc in green and 3 rows of tr in black. Fasten off.

FRONT

Work same as back.

SLEEVES

With knitting needles and black, cast on 44 sts and work 2¾ in. (7 cm) in 1/1 ribbing. Cast off loosely. With crochet hook and black, crochet 44 tr along cast off row of ribbing. Continue in stripe pattern, beg with 3 rows of tr in black and 1 row of dc in blue. At each edge of every row of dc, inc 1 st 8 times. You now have 60 sts. End with 1 row of dc in red and 3 rows of tr in black. When sleeve measures 21½ in. (48 cm), fasten off.

FINISHING

Sew shoulder seams over 5½ (6¼, 6½) in. - 14 (16, 17) cm. Sew sleeves to armholes, matching centre of sleeve with shoulder seams. Sew side and sleeve seams.

VELVETY STRIPED PULLOVER

SIZE

Women's Small, Medium (Large, X Large), bust 30-35 (36-42) in. - 76-89 (91.5-107) cm. Finished bust measurement: 39½ (47) in. - 100 (120) cm, length 28¼ in. (72 cm), sleeve seam 18¾ in. (48 cm).

MATERIALS

2 (3) skeins worsted weight, mohair-blend yarn (approx. 190 yds (173 m) per 50 g skein) colour dark grey-blue, 2 skeins each colour purple, dark blue, and light grey-blue. Crochet hook U.S. size F/5 (U.K. size 8) (Metric size 4) or size needed to obtain tension. Knitting needles U.S. size 4 (U.K. size 9) (Metric size 3.5).
To save time, take time to check tension!

TENSION

14 tr and 6 rows = 4 in. (10 cm)

STITCHES

Chain (ch), double crochet (dc), treble crochet (tr).
Stripe pattern: Work in tr as foll:
Row 1: dark grey-blue.
Row 2: light grey-blue.
Row 3: dark grey-blue.
Rows 4 to 6: purple.
Row 7: dark grey-blue.
Row 8: light grey-blue.
Row 9: dark grey-blue.
Rows 10 to 12: dark-blue.
Rep these 12 rows for the stripe pattern. Beg each row with ch 3 which counts as the first tr. Let the unused strands hang at the edges and carry them along the sides to be used in pattern repeat. Note: Some colours will hang at both edges.
1/1 ribbing: *K1, p1*, rep * to * across.

BACK

With knitting needles and dark grey-blue, cast on 70 (84) sts and work 2¾ in. (7 cm) in 1/1 ribbing. Cast off loosely. With crochet hook and dark grey-blue, work 1 dc in each cast off st. Then work in tr, working 12 rows of stripe pattern 3 times total, end with first 3 rows. Fasten off.

FRONT

Work same as back.

SLEEVES

With knitting needles and dark grey-blue, cast on 40 sts and work 2¾ in. (7 cm) in 1/1 ribbing. Cast off loosely.
With crochet hook and dark grey blue, work 54 dc along cast off row of ribbing, working 2 dc in 14 sts evenly spaced across row. Work in tr, 12 rows of stripe pattern twice total. **At the same time,** inc 1 tr at each edge of every 3rd row 8 times = 70 tr. (Work 2 trs in each edge tr.) End with 1 row of dark grey-blue. Fasten off.

FINISHING

Block pieces to indicated measurements. Sew shoulder seams over 5½ (6½) in. - 14 (17) cm. With dark grey-blue, work 1 row of dc around neck. Fasten off. Sew sleeves to armholes, matching centre of sleeve with shoulder seams. Sew side and sleeve seams.

FRONT-BACK

14-16-17 23-25-27 14-16-17

65

51-57-61

SLEEVE

50

14

7

28

35

SLEEVE

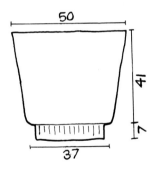

50

41

7

37

FRONT-BACK

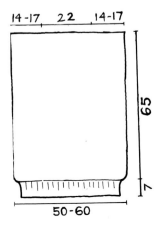

14-17 22 14-17

65

7

50-60

VELVETY VIOLET, BLUE, AND GREY; SIMPLE STRIPES FORM A SUMPTUOUS LOOK. EASY TO CROCHET, THIS PULLOVER IS A SURE-FIRE SUCCESS, EVEN FOR BEGINNERS.

⭐⭐
⭐

MARITIME STRIPES HIT

THE BEACHES IN A BIG WAY WITH
THIS POLO-COLLARED PULLOVER.
MINIATURE VERSIONS COME IN
BOATNECK AND POLO STYLES. A
MATCHING BEACH BAG IS THE
PERFECT ACCESSORY FOR
WATERSIDE EXCURSIONS.

WOMAN'S POLO PULLOVER

SIZE

Woman's Small (Medium, Large), bust 33-35, (36-38, 39-42) in. - 84-89 (91.5-97, 99-107) cm. Finished bust measurements: 37½ (40, 41½) in. - 96 (101, 106) cm, length: 23¼ (23½, 24) in. - 59 (60, 61) cm, sleeve seam: 11¾ in. (30 cm).

MATERIALS

4 (5, 6) skeins "Mayflower Helarsgarn" (100% cotton - approx. 88 yds (80 m) per 50 g skein) each colour pink, purple and gold, 2 skeins colour white.
Crochet hook U.S. size F / 5 (U.K. size 8) (Metric size 4) or size needed to obtain tension. Knitting needles U.S. size 6 (U.K. size 8) (Metric size 4). 3 buttons. **To save time, take time to check tension!**

TENSION

16 dc and 19 rows = 4 in. (10 cm).

STITCHES

Chain (ch), single crochet (sc), double crochet (dc), half treble crochet (htr).
Stripe pattern: Dc as foll: *2½ in. (6 cm) purple, 2½ in. (6 cm) gold, 2½ in. (6 cm) pink*, rep * to *. When changing colours, work the last loop of the last st with the colour of the next st. Hold the unused yarn against the wrong side of work.

When inserting hook, work around the unused yarn so that the new sts hold it against the work. Work the border sts in the same colour as the adjacent st in pat. Ch 3 at the beg of each row (= 1 border st).
1/1 ribbing: Row 1: *K1, p1*. Rep * to * across.
Row 2 and all foll rows: Work sts as established in previous row.

BACK

With knitting needles and white, cast on 77 (81, 85) sts and work 2¾ in. (7 cm) 1/1 ribbing. With purple, knit 1 row on right side of work. Cast off loosely. With crochet hook, work 1 dc in every st of cast off row of ribbing. Work in stripe pat until piece measures 22½ (22¾, 23¼) in. - 57 (58, 59) cm from beg. Mark the centre 19 (23, 27) sts. Work each shoulder separately. Beg at right edge of right side of work row, work to last 2 sts before marker, turn, leaving 2 sts unworked. Sc over 2 sts, ch 1, then work to end of row = 25 dc. Work until piece measures 23¼ (23½, 24) in. - 59 (60, 61) cm from beg, fasten off. Beg 2 sts from 2nd marker, work to end of row = 25 dc. Turn, ch 1, and work to 2 sts from end of row. Work until same measurement as first shoulder. Fasten off.

FRONT

Work same as back until piece measures 14½ in. (37 cm) from beg. Divide work as foll: with right side facing, work 41 (43,

23

45) dc and work for 6 in. (15 cm), then shape neck. Work to last 8 (10, 12) sts, ch 1, turn, leaving these sts unworked. *Work next row. On foll row, work to last 2 sts before end of row at neck edge, ch 1, turn.* Rep * to * 4 times total = 25 dc. Work until piece measures 23¼ (23½, 24) in. - 59 (60, 61) cm from beg, fasten off.

Work 2nd part the same for 6 in. (15 cm), then shape neck. At neck edge, sc over the first 3 (5, 7) sts. Then at neck edge of every 2nd row, sc 2 sts 4 times = 25 dc. Work until piece measures 23¼ (23½, 24) in. - 59 (60, 61) cm from beg, fasten off.

SLEEVES

With knitting needles and white, cast on 48 (51, 54) sts and work 2½ in. (6 cm) in 1/1 ribbing. With pink, knit 1 row on right side of work. Cast off loosely. With crochet hook, work 1 dc in each cast off st. Continue in striped pat, beg with pink. Inc 1 st at each edge of every 2nd row 11 times. (For each inc, work 2 dc in each edge st.) You now have 70 (73, 76) dc. When sleeve measures 11¾ in. (30 cm) from beg, fasten off.

FINISHING

Block pieces to indicated measurements. With knitting needles and white, pick up and knit 30 sts along right side of front opening and work in 1/1 ribbing. **At the same time,** when border measures 1/2 in. (1.5 cm), make 3 buttonholes as foll: work 3 sts, cast off 2 sts, work 9 sts, cast off 2 sts, work 9 sts, cast off 2 sts, work 3 sts. On the foll row, cast on 2 sts over cast off sts. Cast off when border measures 1¼ in. (3 cm). Sew shoulder seams. With knitting needles and white, pick up and knit 75 (85, 95) sts around neck, beg and end 1/2 in. (1.5 cm) from front edges. Work 3¼ in. (8 cm.) of 1/1 ribbing. Cast off. Sew sleeves to side seams, matching centre of sleeve with shoulder seam. Sew side and sleeve seams. Sew on buttons.

SLEEVE

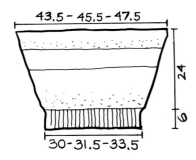

43.5 - 45.5 - 47.5

24

6

30 - 31.5 - 33.5

FRONT-BACK

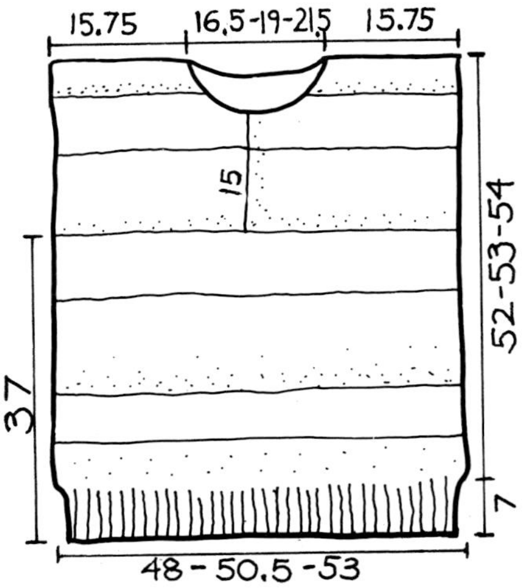

15.75   16.5 -19 -215   15.75

15

37

52 - 53 - 54

7

48 - 50.5 - 53

CHILD'S PULLOVER

SIZE

Child's size 4 (6, 8) years, chest 23 (25, 27) in. - 58.5 (63.5, 69) cm. Finished chest measurements: 27½ (29, 30½) in. - 70 (74, 78) cm, length: 15¼ (17, 18½) in. - 39 (43, 47) cm, sleeve seam: 5 (6, 6½) in. - 13 (15, 17) cm.

MATERIALS

2 (2, 3) skeins
2 (2, 3) skeins Mayflower Helasgarn (100% cotton - approx. 88 yds (80 m) per 50 g skein) each colour gold, green and pink, 1 skein colour white. Crochet hook U.S. size F/5 (U.K. size 8) (Metric size 4) or size needed to obtain tension. Knitting needles U.S. size 6 (U.K. size 8) (Metric size 4). 6 buttons. **To save time, take time to check tension!**

TENSION

16 dc and 19 rows = 4 in. (10 cm.)

STITCHES

**Chain (ch),
single crochet (sc),
double crochet (dc).
Stripe pattern:** Dc as foll: *1¾ (2, 2¼) in. - 4.5 (5, 5.5) cm pink, 1¾ (2, 2¼) in. -4.5 (5, 5.5) cm gold, 1¾ (2, 2¼) in. - 4.5 (5, 5.5) cm green*, rep * to * Ch 1 to turn at beg of each row. When changing colours, work the last loop of the last st with the colour of the next st. Hold the unused yarn against the wrong side of work. When inserting hook, work around the unused yarn so that the new sts hold it against the work.

Work the border sts in the same colour as the adjacent st in pat.
1/1 ribbing: Row 1: *K1, p1*. Rep * to * across.
Row 2 and all foll rows: Work sts as established in previous row.

BACK

With knitting needles and white, cast on 56 (59, 62) sts and work 1¾ (2, 2¼) in. - 4.5 (5, 5.5) cm in 1/1 ribbing. Knit 1 row on right side of work in pink, cast off. With crochet hook, work 1 dc in each st of cast off row of ribbing. Continue in stripe pat until piece measures 8½ (9½, 10¼) in. - 22 (24, 26) cm from beg. Sc over 5 sts, ch 1, work to last 5 sts, turn, leaving last 5 sts unworked = 46 (49, 52) dc. Continue until piece measures 14 (15¾, 17¼) in. - 36 (40, 44) cm from beg. Fasten off. With knitting needles and white, knit 1 row on right side of work, inc 8 sts evenly spaced across row. Work 1¼ in. (3 cm) in 1/1 ribbing. Cast off centre 20 (23, 26) sts. Working each half separately, work 1¼ in. (3 cm) more in 1/1 ribbing. Cast off.

FRONT

Work same as back until upper ribbing measures 1/2 in. (1.5 cm), then shape buttonholes as foll: *work 3 sts, cast off 2 sts*, work * to * 3 times total, then work to last 15 sts: *cast off 2 sts, work 3 sts*, work * to * 3 times total. On foll row, cast on 2 sts over cast off sts. When border measures 1¼ in. (3 cm), cast off all sts.

SLEEVES

With knitting needles and white, cast on 38 (40, 42) sts and work 1 (1¼, 1¾) in. - 2.5 (3, 3.5) cm in 1/1 ribbing. Knit 1 row in gold on right side of work. Cast off. With crochet hook, work 1 dc in each st of cast off row of ribbing, then work in stripe pat, beg with gold stripe. Inc 1 dc at each edge every 1/2 in. (1.5 cm) 5 (7, 9) times. (Work 2 dc in each edge st.) You now have 48 (54, 60) dc. When sleeve measures 6¼ (7¼, 7¾) in. - 16 (18, 20) cm, fasten off.

FINISHING

Block pieces to indicated measurements. Lap the front border over the top 1¼ in. (3 cm) of upper ribbing of back and baste in place. Sew sleeves to armholes, matching centre of sleeve with shoulder seams. Sew side and sleeve seams. Remove basting and sew on buttons.

SLEEVE

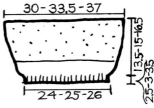

30 - 33.5 - 37

13.5-15-16.5

25-3-3.5

24 - 25 - 26

FRONT   BACK

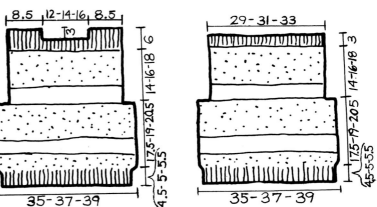

8.5   12 -14 -16   8.5   29 - 31 - 33

3

6

14-16-18

17.5 -19 -205

4.5 - 5 -5.5

35 - 37 - 39

3

14-16-18

17.5 -19 -205

4.5-5-5.5

35 - 37 - 39

CHILD'S POLO PULLOVER

SIZE

Child's size 4 (6, 8) years, chest 23 (25, 27) in. - 58.5 (63.5, 69) cm. Finished chest measurements: 27½ (29, 30½) in. - 70 (74, 78) cm, length: 15¼ (17, 18½) in. - 39 (43, 47) cm, sleeve seam: 5 (6, 6½) in. - 13 (15, 17) cm.

MATERIALS

2 (2, 3) skeins "Mayflower Helarsgarn" (100% cotton - approx. 88 yds (80 m) per 50 g skein) each colour green, red and purple, 1 skein colour white.
Crochet hook U.S. size F/5 (U.K. size 8) (Metric size 4) or size needed to obtain tension. Knitting needles U.S. size 6 (U.K. size 8) (Metric size 4). 3 buttons. **To save time, take time to check tension!**

TENSION

16 dc and 19 rows = 4 in. (10 cm).

STITCHES

**Chain (ch),
single crochet (sc),
double crochet (dc).
Stripe pattern:** Dc as foll: *1¾ in. (4 cm) green, 1¾ in. (4 cm) red, 1¾ in. (4 cm) purple*, rep * to *. Beg each row with ch 1. When changing colours, work the last loop of the last st with the colour of the next st. Hold the unused yarn against the wrong side of work. When inserting hook, work around the unused yarn so that the new sts

hold it against the work. Work the border sts in the same colour as the adjacent st in pat.
1/1 ribbing: Row 1: *K1, p1*. Rep * to * across.
Row 2 and all foll rows: Work sts as established in previous row.

BACK

With knitting needles and white, cast on 56 (59, 62) sts and work 2 in. (5 cm) in 1/1 ribbing. Knit 1 row in green on right side of work. Cast off loosely. With crochet hook and green, work 1 dc in each st of cast off row. Work in stripe pat until piece measures 8½ (9½, 10¼) in. - 22 (24, 26) cm from beg. Sc over first 5 sts, ch 1, work to last 5 sts of row, turn, leaving last 5 sts unworked. Work rem 46 (49, 52) dc until piece measures 15 (17, 18½) in. - 39 (43, 47) cm from beg, fasten off.

FRONT

Work same as back until piece measures 9½ (10½, 11¾) in. - 24 (27, 30) cm from beg, divide work as foll: right side facing, work 21 (22, 24) dc. Work straight for 4 in. (10 cm). Then work to 3 (3, 4) sts before neck edge, turn. Sc over 2 (3, 3) sts, ch 1, work to end of row, turn. Work to 1 (0, 0) st before end of row, turn. When piece measures 15 (17, 18½) in. - 39 (43, 47) cm from beg, fasten off. Work 2nd part for 4 in. (10 cm), then, right side facing, sc over 3 (3, 4) sts at neck edge, ch 1, work to end of row, work to last 7 (8, 8) sts. Work until piece measures 15 (17, 18½) in. - 39 (43, 47) cm from beg, fasten off.

SLEEVES

With knitting needles and white, cast on 38 (40, 42) sts and work 1¼ in. (3 cm) in 1/1 ribbing. Knit 1 row in red on the right side of work. Cast off loosely. With crochet hook, work 1 dc in each st of cast off row of ribbing, then work in stripe pat, beg with red. At each edge every ½ in. (1.5 cm), inc 1 st 5 (7, 9) times = 48 (54, 60) dc. When piece measures 6¼ (7¼, 7¾) in. - 16 (18, 20) cm from beg, fasten off.

FINISHING

Block pieces to indicated measurements. Sew shoulder seams. With knitting needles and white, pick up and knit 22 sts along left edge of front opening and work 1 in. (2.5 cm) of 1/1 ribbing. **At the same time,** when border measures 1/3 in. (1 cm), make 3 buttonholes as foll: work 2 sts, cast off 2 sts, work 6 sts, cast off 2 sts, work 6 sts, cast off 2 sts, work 2 sts. On the foll row, cast on 2 sts over cast off sts. Cast off in ribbing. With knitting needles and white, pick up and knit 51 (61, 71) sts around neck, beg and end ½ in. (1.5 cm) from each edge of front opening. Work 2½ in. (6 cm) in 1/1 ribbing. Cast off loosely. Sew sleeves to armholes, matching centre of sleeve with shoulder seams and sewing top 1¼ in. (3 cm) of sleeve to armhole edge. Sew side and sleeve seams. Sew on buttons.

BAG

MATERIALS

3 skeins of "Mayflower Cotton 8" (100% cotton - approx. 180 yds (164 m) per 50 g skein) colour gold.
Crochet hook U.S. size C/2 (U.K. size 11) (Metric size 3).

TENSION

10 squares and 10 rows = 4 in. (10 cm).

STITCHES

**Chain (ch),
double crochet (dc),
treble crochet (tr).
Filet st:** *Ch 2, skip 2, 1 tr*, rep * to * across.

BAG

Ch 180 and join with sl st in round. **Round 1:** Ch 5, 1 tr in the 3rd ch from hook, *ch 2, skip 2 ch, 1 tr in the foll ch*, rep * to *, end with ch 2, skip 2 ch, 1 sc in the 3rd ch from the beg. **Round 2:** Ch 5, *1 tr in the tr in the round below, ch 2, skip 2*, rep * to *, end with 1 sc in the 3rd ch from the hook. Always rep the 2nd round until piece measures 25½ in. (65 cm). Fasten off.

FINISHING

Ch cord 59 in. (150 cm) long and thread through squares at each edge. Knot ends tog.

Filet stitch bags can be made in different sizes and shapes and are perfect for beachwear. When worked in fancy yarns and lined, they also make attractive evening bags.

FRONT-BACK

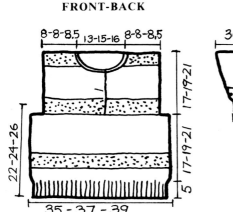

8-8-8.5 | 13-15-16 | 8-8-8,5
22-24-26
17-19-21
5
17-19-21
35 - 37 - 39

SLEEVE

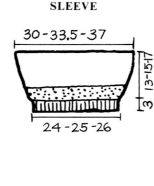

30 - 33.5 - 37
13-15-17
3
24 - 25 - 26

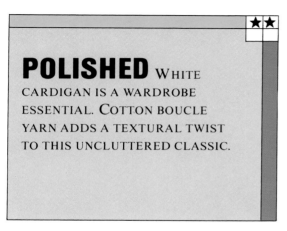

★★

POLISHED WHITE CARDIGAN IS A WARDROBE ESSENTIAL. COTTON BOUCLE YARN ADDS A TEXTURAL TWIST TO THIS UNCLUTTERED CLASSIC.

WHITE CARDIGAN

SIZE

Woman's Small (Medium, Large), bust 30-32 (33-35, 36-38) in. - 76-81.5 (84-89, 91.5-97) cm. Finished bust measurements: 39½ (43, 47½) in. - 101 (110, 121) cm, length: 22¾ (23¼, 23½) in. - 58 (59, 60) cm, sleeve seam: 17¾ in. (45 cm).

MATERIALS

11 (12, 13) skeins sport weight boucle yarn (approx. 143 yds (131 m) per 50 g skein) colour white.
Crochet hook U.S. size F/5 (U.K. size 8) (Metric size 4) or size needed to obtain tension. Knitting needles U.S. size 3 (U.K. size 10) (Metric size 3). 7 buttons. Stitch holders.
To save time, take time to check tension!

TENSION

10 motifs (20 sts) and 17 rows = 4 in. (10 cm).

STITCHES

Chain (ch),
single crochet (sc),
double crochet (dc),
half treble crochet (htr).
Pattern st: Worked on a foundation row of dc.
Row 1: Ch 2 to turn (= 1 border st), *in 1 dc: 1 htr, 1 dc; skip 1 dc*, rep * to *, end with 1 htr in the last st (= 1 border st).
Row 2: Ch 2 to turn, * in the dc of the previous row: work 1 htr, 1 dc; skip 1 st*, rep * to *, end with 1 htr around the turning ch of the previous row. Repeat rows 1 and 2.
1/1 ribbing: Row 1: *K1, p1*. Rep * to * across.
Row 2 and all foll rows: Work sts as established in previous row.

BACK

With knitting needles, cast on 102 (112, 122) sts and work 2 in. (5 cm) in 1/1 ribbing. Cast off. With crochet hook, work 1 dc in each st across cast off row = 102 (112, 122) dc. Continue in pat st across = 50 (55, 60) motifs with 1 border st at each edge. When piece measures 11¾ in. (30 cm) above ribbing, shape armholes. Sc over 2 motifs, work to last 2 motifs and turn, leave last 2 motifs unworked. Work 1 row straight, then sc over first 1 (2, 2) motifs, work to last 1 (2, 2) motifs, leave last 1 (2, 2) motifs unworked. Work 1 row straight. *Sc over first motif, then work to last motif on row, turn, leaving last motif unworked. Work 1 row straight.* Work * to * twice total = 40 (43, 48) motifs. Work straight until armhole measures 8 (8¼, 8½) in. -20 (21, 22)

cm. Mark the centre 10 (11, 12) motifs. Sc over first 4 (4, 5) motifs, work to first marker, turn. Work to end of row. Sc over first 4 (4, 5) motifs, work to 3 motifs before first marker, leave last 3 motifs unworked, turn. Work to end of row. Sc over first 4 (5, 5) motifs. Fasten off. Join yarn to 2nd marker and work 2nd half to correspond.

RIGHT FRONT

With knitting needles, cast on 58 (62, 68) sts and work in 1/1 ribbing. When border measures 1/3 in. (1 cm), make 1 buttonhole. Cast off the 5th and 6th sts from the right edge. On foll row, cast on 2 sts over cast off sts. Continue in 1/1 ribbing until piece measures 2 in. (5 cm) from beg. Make a 2nd buttonhole above previous one. Work 1 row straight, then place 9 sts at right edge on holder. Work 49 (53, 59) dc over the rem sts = 24 (26, 29) motifs. When piece measures 11¾ in. (30 cm) above ribbing, shape armhole. Work to last 2 motifs of row, turn, leave last 2 motifs unworked. Work 1 row straight, turn, work to last 1 (2, 2) motifs, turn, leave last 1 (2, 2) motifs unworked. Work 1 row straight. Turn. *Work to last motif on row, turn, leaving last motif unworked. Work 1 row straight.* Work * to * twice total = 19 (20, 23) motifs. Work straight until armhole measures 6

(6¼, 6¼) in. -15 (16, 16) cm, shape neck. Sc over first 2 (2, 3) motifs, work to end of row. Turn, work to end of row. Sc over first 2 motifs. Work to end of row, turn. Now at right edge of every 2nd row, sc over first motif. **At the same time,** when piece measures 8 (8¼, 8½) in. -20 (21, 22) cm, shape shoulder. With right side facing, work to last 4 (4, 5) motifs, turn, leave last 4 (4, 5) motifs unworked. Sc over first 4 (4, 5) motifs, work to end of row, turn. Work to last 4 (5, 5) motifs. Fasten off.

LEFT FRONT

Work same as right front, rev shapings and omitting buttonholes.

SLEEVE

With knitting needles, cast on 44 (46, 48) sts and work 2 in. (5 cm) in 1/1 ribbing. Cast off. With crochet hook, work dc across, working 2 dc in 8 (10, 12) sts evenly spaced across = 52 (56, 60) sts. Work in pat st = 25 (27, 29) motifs + 1 border st at each edge. Inc 1 st at each edge of every 4th row 13 times. Work inc sts in pat st as you inc = 38 (40, 42) motifs. When piece measures 15¾ in. (40 cm), shape cap. Sc across first 2(3, 3) motifs, work to last 2 (3, 3) motifs of row, turn, leave last 2 (3, 3) motifs unworked. Sc across first 2 motifs, work to last 2 motifs of row, turn, leave last 2 motifs unworked. *Sc over first

motif of row, work to last motif, turn, leaving last motif unworked*. Rep * to * 14 times. Sc over first 2 (2, 3) motifs, work to last 2 (2, 3) motifs, turn, leave last 2 (2, 3) motifs unworked. Sc over first 3 motifs, work to last 3 motifs, turn. Work across rem 8 motifs. Fasten off.

FINISHING

Block pieces to indicated measurements. With knitting needles, pick up 9 sts from holder at left edge. Inc 1 st at centre edge and work in 1/1 ribbing. Work until ribbing, slightly stretched, reaches to neck. Dec 1 st at centre edge and place sts on holder. Work right front border the same, making 4 buttonholes as previous ones spaced about 3½ in. (9 cm) apart along front edge, allowing for the 7th buttonhole on neck edge. Cast off. Sew shoulder seams. With crochet hook, work 1 row of dc along neck edge, fasten off. Then with knitting needles, pick up 9 sts from holder, 2 sts from each dc, 9 sts from 2nd holder = 105 (109, 111) sts. Work 1¼ in. (3 cm) of 1/1 ribbing, making last buttonhole above previous ones when border measures ½ in. (1.5 cm). Cast off. Set in sleeves. Sew side and sleeve seams. Sew borders to fronts. Reinforce buttonholes. Sew on buttons.

1/2 BACK

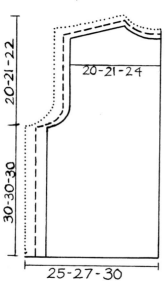

20-21-22

20-21-24

30-30-30

25-27-30

1/2 FRONT

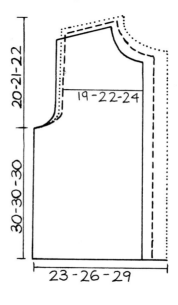

20-21-22

19-22-24

30-30-30

23-26-29

1/2 SLEEVE

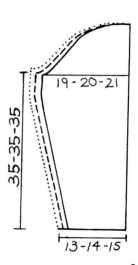

35-35-35

19-20-21

13-14-15

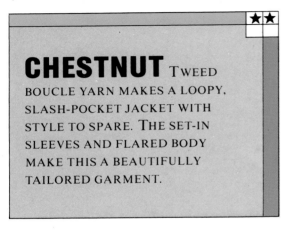

CHESTNUT TWEED

BOUCLE YARN MAKES A LOOPY, SLASH-POCKET JACKET WITH STYLE TO SPARE. THE SET-IN SLEEVES AND FLARED BODY MAKE THIS A BEAUTIFULLY TAILORED GARMENT.

TWEED BOUCLE JACKET

SIZE

Woman's Medium (Large, X Large), bust 33-35 (36-38, 39-42) in. - 84-89 (91.5-97, 99-107) cm + 2 in. (5 cm) front border overlap. Finished bust measurements: 39¾ (41¾, 43¾) in. - 101 (106, 111) cm. length: 28 (28¼, 28¾) in. - 71 (72, 73) cm, sleeve seam: 18½ in. (47 cm).

MATERIALS

27 (29, 31) skeins bulky boucle yarn (approx. 40 yds (36 m) per 50 g skein) colour brown tweed. Crochet hook U.S. size J/10 (U.K. size 4) (Metric size 6) or size needed to obtain tension. 3 buttons. **To save time, take time to check tension!**

TENSION

8.5 htr and 7 rows = 4 in. (10 cm).

STITCHES

Chain (ch), single crochet (sc), double crochet (dc), half treble crochet (htr).

BACK

Ch 50 (52, 54) + ch 1. Work 1 dc in the 2nd ch from hook, then work in dc across. Continue in htr, beg each row with ch 2. Work straight for 4 in. (10 cm). *Sc over first st, htr to last st, turn, leaving last st unworked. Work 3 rows straight.* Work * to * 4 times = 42 (44, 46) htr. When piece measures 19 in. (48 cm), shape arm-holes. Sc over first 2 (2, 3) sts, work to last 2 (2, 3) sts, turn, leave last 2 (2, 3) sts unworked. Sc over first 2 sts, work to last 2 sts, turn, leave last 1 (2) sts unworked = 34 (35, 36) htr. Work until armhole measures 8¼ (8½, 9) in. - 21 (22, 23) cm. Mark centre 10 (11, 12) sts. Sc over first 5 sts, work to first marker, turn. Sc over first 2 sts. Work to end of

row. Turn. Sc over first 5 sts. Fasten off. Work 2nd half to correspond.

RIGHT FRONT

Ch 28 (30, 32) + ch 1, and work 1 row of dc. Continue in htr. Work straight for 4 in. (10 cm). *Then with right side facing, work to last st, turn, leaving last st unworked. Work 2 rows straight.* Work * to * 4 times = 20 (22, 24) htr. **At the same time**, when piece measures 6½ in. (17 cm) from beg, shape pocket. With right side facing, work 13 htr at right edge, then work rem sts for 6¼ in. (16 cm). Leave these stitches unworked. Now work 13 sts at right edge for 6¼ in. (16 cm). Rejoin all sts and work across. **At the same time**, make 1 buttonhole at right edge when piece measures 8 in. (20 cm) as foll: work 3 sts, skip 2 sts and ch 2 over skipped sts. Space 2 other buttonholes 6 in. (15 cm) apart. On foll row work 2 sts in ch-2 sp. When piece measures 19 in. (48 cm), shape armhole and shawl collar. At right edge, inc 1 htr, work to last 2 (2, 3) sts, turn, leave last 2 (2, 3) sts unworked. Sc over first 2 sts, work to end of row, turn. **At the same time**, at right edge every 2 in. (5 cm), inc 1 st 3 more times. Work until armhole measures 8¼ (8½, 9) in. - 21 (22, 23) cm. With right side facing, work to last 4 (4, 5) sts, turn, leave last 4 (4, 5) sts unworked. Sc over

first 5 sts, work to end of row. Continue on rem sts, working the 6 sts at shoulder edge in dc on right side of work rows. Work the same sts in htr on wrong side of work rows. (This will make the shoulder edge shorter than the neck edge.) When the shoulder edge of collar measures 3¼ in. (8 cm) from shoulder, fasten off.

LEFT FRONT

Work same as right front, rev shapings and omitting buttonholes.

SLEEVES

Ch 35 (36, 37) + ch 1, and work 1 row of dc. Continue in htr, beg each row with ch 2 until sleeve measures 18½ in. (7 cm) from beg, then shape cap. Sc over 3 sts, work to last 3 sts, turn, leave last 3 sts unworked. Sc over 2 sts, work to last 2 sts, turn, leave last 2 sts unworked. *Sc over first st, work to last st, turn, leaving last st unworked.* Rep * to * 7 (8, 9) times. Sc over 3 (2, 2) sts, work to last 3 (2, 2) sts, turn, leave last 3 (2, 2) sts unworked. Work over rem 5 (6, 5) sts. Fasten off.

POCKET BORDER AND LININGS

Along centre edge of pockets, work 3 rows of dc. Fasten off. Join edge to lower edge of pocket opening and ch 8. Work in htr. After 1½ in. (4 cm), sc over first st of every row. When piece measures 4 in. (10 cm), fasten off. Sew pocket linings and border ends in place.

FINISHING

Block pieces to indicated measurements. Sew shoulder seams. Set in sleeves. Sew side and sleeve seams. Sew back seam of collar and sew to back neck. Reinforce buttonholes. Buttons: make a chain long enough to go around each button and sc to join in ring. Work 8 dc in this ring, insert button and work in rounds of dc until piece covers the button. Break yarn and thread through sts to gather. Sew to front.

When sewing pocket linings to inside of fronts, take care to sew through back loops of stitches only so that the outline of the pocket doesn't show on the right side of your work.

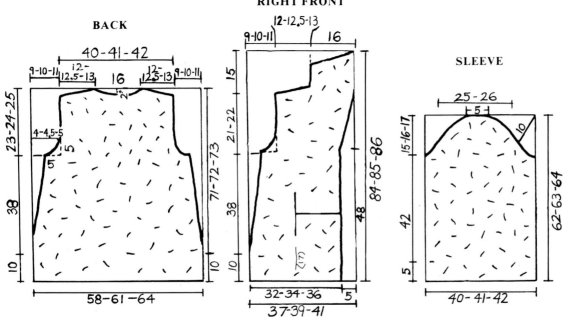

BACK

RIGHT FRONT

SLEEVE

★★

SCORE BIG POINTS BY MAKING THIS CHILD'S PULLOVER WITH CHECKERED STITCH IN HIS TEAM COLOURS.

CHILD'S CHECKERED PULLOVER

SIZE

Child's size 4 (6, 8, 10) years, chest 23 (25, 27, 28½) in. - 58.5 (63.5, 69, 72.5) cm. Finished chest measurements: 27½ (29½, 31½, 33½) in. - 70 (75, 80, 85) cm, length 15¾ (17, 18¼, 19) in. - 41 (44, 48, 50) cm, sleeve seam 13½ (13¾, 15, 16¼) in. - 27 (30, 33, 36) cm.

MATERIALS

5 (5, 6, 7) skeins worsted weight yarn (50 g skein) colour dark blue, 3 (4, 5, 6) skeins colour red. Crochet hook U.S. size E/4 (U.K. size 9) (Metric size 3.5) or size needed to obtain tension. Knitting needles U.S. size 4 (U.K. size 9) (Metric size 3.5).
To save time, take time to check tension!

TENSION

16 dc and 15½ rows = 4 in. (10 cm).

STITCHES

Chain (ch), single crochet (sc), double crochet (dc), half treble crochet (htr).
Block st: Rows 1-4: Ch 1 to turn (does not count as first st), *4 dc in red, 4 dc in dark blue*. Rep * to * across row. Use a separate ball of yarn for each section of colour. When changing colours, work the last loop of the last st. Do not carry unused yarn across wrong side of work. Work 4 rows in established colours.
Rows 5-8: Ch 1 to turn, *4 dc in dark blue, 4 dc in red*. Rep * to * across row. Alternate colours by working opposite colour of previous row for 4 rows. Always rep these 8 rows.
1/1 ribbing: Row 1: *K1, p1*. Rep * to * across.
Row 2 and all foll rows: Work sts as established in previous row.

BACK

With knitting needles and dark blue, cast on 56 (60, 64, 68) sts and work 2¾ in. (7 cm) 1/1 ribbing. Cast off.
With crochet hook, work 1 dc in each st of bound off row of ribbing, then work in block st: You will have 14 (15, 16, 17) block motifs. Work until piece measures 9¾ (10¾, 11¾, 12) in. - 25 (27.5, 30, 31) cm from beg. Sc over 2 block motifs at right edge, work to last 2 blocks, turn and continue in block motif on the rem 10 (11, 12, 13) block motifs = 40 (44, 48, 52) dc. Work in dc until piece measures 6 (6¼, 6½, 7) in. - 15 (16, 17, 18) cm from beg of armhole. With the colour of the next st, mark centre 16 (16, 18, 18) dc. Then shape shoulder: sc over 4 (5, 5, 6) dc, then work 8 (9, 10, 11) dc in block st. Ch 1 and turn. Work 4 (5, 5, 5) dc. Fasten off. Join yarn to 2nd armhole edge and work by rev shapings. Fasten off.

FRONT

Beg front same as back, but beg block motif with dark blue so that the block motif will continue when side seams are joined. Work same as back until armhole measures 4¾ (5, 5, 5½) in. - 12 (13, 13, 14) cm. Then shape neck: mark the centre 8 (8, 10, 12) dc. Work dc at right edge as foll: work to 2 dc from marker. Turn, sc over first st, work in block st to end of row. With right side facing, work to 1 dc from end of row. Ch 1, turn. Work dc to end of row. When armhole

measures 6 (6¼, 6½, 7) in. - 15 (16, 17, 18) cm, work shoulder shapings same as back. Work 2nd half by rev shapings.

SLEEVES

With knitting needles and dark blue, cast on 40 (42, 46, 48) sts and work 1½ (1½, 2, 2) in. - 4 (4, 5, 5) cm in 1/1 ribbing. Cast off. With crochet hook, work in 1 dc in each st of cast off row, then continue in block st, centring the pat as foll: 0 (1, 2, 3) dc in dark blue, 3 (4, 4, 4) dc in red, then work *4 dc in dark blue, 4 dc in red*, rep * to * across, end with 4 dc in dark blue, 3 (4, 4, 4) dc in red, 0 (1, 2, 3) dc in dark blue. Inc 1 dc at each edge of every 6th (6th, 8th, 8th) row 4 times. (For each inc, work 2 dc in each dc at edge.) You now have 48 (50, 54, 56) dc. When piece measures 10½ (11¾, 13, 14¼) in. - 27 (30, 33, 36) cm from beg, work 2 in. (5 cm) straight, then fasten off.

FINISHING

Sew shoulder seams for 3/4 in. (2 cm) from armhole edges. Sew sleeves to armholes, matching centre of sleeve with shoulder seams and sewing top 2 in. (5 cm) of sleeve seam to armhole edges of body. Sew side and sleeve seams. With knitting needles and dark blue, pick up and knit 21 (21, 23, 23) sts along back neck and work 2¾ in. (7 cm) in 1/1 ribbing. Cast off. With knitting needles and dark blue, pick up and knit 27 (27, 29, 31) sts along front neck and work 2¾ in. (7 cm) in 1/1 ribbing. Cast off. Fold neckband in half to inside and slip stitch in place. With crochet hook and dark blue, work 2 rows of dc along each back shoulder edge. Fasten off. On the front shoulder edge, make 4 buttonholes evenly spaced across row. For each buttonhole, ch 2 and skip 2 sts. Sew on buttons.

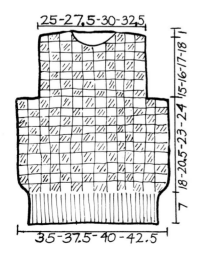

FRONT-BACK

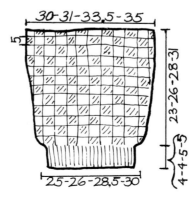

SLEEVE

★★

STEAL THE SHOW AT THE NEXT BABY SHOWER WITH THIS NURSERY RHYME SWEATER. THE SHEEP MOTIF IS SIMPLE TO MAKE.

NURSERY RHYME PULLOVER

SIZE

Child's size: 6 (9, 12, 18) months. Finished chest measurements: 21¼ (22, 22¾, 23½) in - 54 (56, 58, 60) cm, length 10¼ (10½, 11, 11½) in. - 26 (27, 28, 29) cm, sleeve seam 7 (7½, 8, 8¼) in. - 18 (19, 20, 21) cm.

MATERIALS

2 (2, 3, 3) skeins baby weight yarn (approx. 183 yds (167 m) per 50 g skein) colour light green, 2 skeins colour light blue, 1 skein colour white, small amount of light grey for eyes. Crochet hook U.S. size B/1 (U.K. size 12) (Metric size 2.5) or size needed to obtain tension. Knitting needles U.S. size 1 (U.K. size 12) (Metric size 2.5). 6 buttons. **To save time, take time to check tension!**

TENSION

19 dc and 23½ rows = 4 in. (10 cm).

STITCHES

**Chain (ch),
single crochet (sc),
double crochet (dc),
half treble crochet (htr),
treble crochet (tr).
Bobble:** All in the same st: yo, insert hook and draw up loop 7 times, yo draw through all loops on hook.

SHEEP APPLIQUE

Ch 5, 1 dc in the 4th and 5th ch from hook = 1 foot, ch 12, 1 dc in the 4th and 5th ch from hook = 2nd foot.
Row 1: Ch 3, 1 bobble in the foot, *Ch 1, skip 1 ch, 1 bobble*, rep * to * 4 times, end with 1 tr. (The 5th bobble will come on top of the 2nd foot.)
Row 2: Ch 3, 1 bobble between the first ch and the bobble, *ch 1, 1 bobble between 2 bobbles of the previous row*, rep * to * 4 times, end with ch 1, 1 bobble between the last bobble and the tr, ch 1, 1 tr = 6 bobbles.
Row 3: Work same as the 2nd row, making 7 bobbles.
Row 4: Ch 3, 1 bobble between the first and the 2nd bobbles, *ch 1, 1 bobble between the next 2

bobbles*, work * to * 5 times = 6 bobbles. For the head, work 1 row of dc along the edge of the 4th, 3rd, and the 2nd rows, turn. Ch 4, then insert hook in the first st and work 1 dc, then 1 tr in the foll dc, 1 htr, 1 dc, then ch 7, 1 dc in the 3rd ch from the hook, 1 htr, 2 tr, 1 dc = ear, 1 dc in each of the last 2 dc.
Row 5: Ch 1, 5 bobbles worked between the 6 bobbles, working 1 tr between the bobbles instead of a ch 1 between the bobbles: 1 dc in the last tr of the border st of the 4th row, ch 7, 1 dc in the 7th ch from the hook, 3 dc. Break yarn and draw end through between the last bobble and the border st of the 4th row and sew to last 3 dc from the border st. Sew ears to body so they flap toward the front. Sheep may face left or right. Place ear on right side of work. Embroider an eye in grey.
1/1 ribbing: Row 1: *K1, p1*. Rep * to * across.
Row 2 and all foll rows: Work sts as established in previous row.
NOTE: Worked entirely in dc. Beg each row with ch 2.

BACK

With crochet hook and green, ch 51 (53, 55, 57) + ch 2. **Row 1:** 1 dc in the 4th ch from the hook = 49 (51, 53, 55) dc + 1 border st at each edge = 51 (53, 55, 57) sts. Work straight until piece measures 4¾ (5, 5¼, 5½) in. - 12.5 (13, 13.5, 14) cm. Continue in blue until piece measures 9 (9¼, 9¾, 10¼) in. - 23 (24, 25, 26) cm from beg. Fasten off.

FRONT

Work same as back until piece measures 8¼ (8½, 9, 9¼) in. - 21 (22, 23, 24) cm. Mark centre 9 (9, 11, 11) sts. Work to first marker, sc over first st on foll row. Sc over 1 st at neck edge, wrong side facing 3 times total. When piece measures 9½ (9¾, 10¼, 10½) in. - 24 (25, 26, 27) cm, fasten off. Join yarn to 2nd marker and work to correspond to first half, rev shapings.

SLEEVES

With crochet hook and green (green, blue, green), ch 28 (30, 32, 34) + 2 ch to turn. **Row 1:** Work 1 dc in the 4th ch from the hook, 26 (28, 30, 32) dc + 1 border st at each edge = 28 (30, 32, 34) sts. Continue in dc. At each edge of every 4th row, work 2 dc in each st 6 times. **At the same time,**

change colours as foll: 2 (4, 0, 1) row in green, *4 rows in blue, 4 rows in green*, work * to * 4 (4, 5, 5) times, then work 1 (2, 0, 1) row in blue. When sleeve measures 6 (6¼, 6½, 7) in. - 15 (16, 17, 18) cm, fasten off 40 (42, 44, 46) dc.

FINISHING

Block pieces to indicated measurements. Make 3 sheep and sew to front. Along the lower edge of sleeves, with knitting needles and green, pick up and knit 28 (30, 32, 34) sts and work 1¼ in. (3 cm) in 1/1 ribbing. Cast off. Along lower edge of front and back, pick up and knit 46 (50, 52, 54) sts and work 1¼ in. (3 cm) in 1/1 ribbing. Cast off. With crochet hook and green along the upper edge of back, work 1 row of dc. Along front neck edge, work 1 row of dc in blue. Along the front shoulders and neck, work 1 row of dc in green, making 3 buttonholes evenly spaced on each shoulder. For each buttonhole, ch 2 and skip 2 dc of previous row. Lap the front shoulders over the back and baste in place. Sew the sleeves to side seams, matching centre of sleeve with shoulder seam. Sew the side and sleeve seams. Sew on buttons.

YELLOW FILET TOP

SIZE
Women's Small (Medium), bust 30-32 (33-35) in. - 76-81.5 (84-89) cm. Finished bust measurements: 39½ (42½) in. - 100 (110) cm, length 24½ in. (62 cm).

MATERIALS
8 (9) skeins "Neveda Valentine" (50% cotton, 50% acrylic - approx. 126 yds (115 m) per 50 g skein) colour yellow. Crochet hook U.S. size F/5 (U.K. size 8) (Metric size 4) or size needed to obtain tension. Knitting needles U.S. size 3 (U.K. size 10) (Metric size 3). **To save time, take time to check tension!**

TENSION
10 squares and 10 rows = 4 in. (10 cm).

STITCHES
Chain (ch), single crochet (sc), double crochet (dc), treble crochet (tr).
Filet stitch: Row 1: *1 Dc, ch 1*, rep * to * across.
Row 2 and all foll rows:

Ch 4 to turn (beg of first square). Always work 1 tr in tr of previous row, ch above ch of previous row.
1/1 ribbing: Row 1: *K1, p1*. Rep * to * across.
Row 2 and all foll rows: Work sts as established in previous row.

BACK
With knitting needles, cast on 76 (80) sts and work 2¾ in. (7 cm) in 1/1 ribbing. Cast off. With crochet hook, work dc in each cast off st across row, then work in filet st = 50 (55) squares. Work in filet st for 21½ in. (55 cm). Fasten off.

FRONT
Work same as back.

SLEEVES
Ch 81. Ch 4 to turn. Work in filet st, working first tr in 7th ch from hook = 40 squares. Work in filet st for 6 in. (15 cm). Fasten off.

FINISHING
Block pieces to indicated measurements. Sew shoulder seams, leaving centre 9¾ in. (25 cm) open for neck. Sew the sleeves to side seams, matching centre of sleeve with shoulder seams. Sew side and sleeve seams.

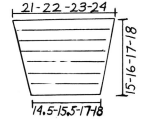

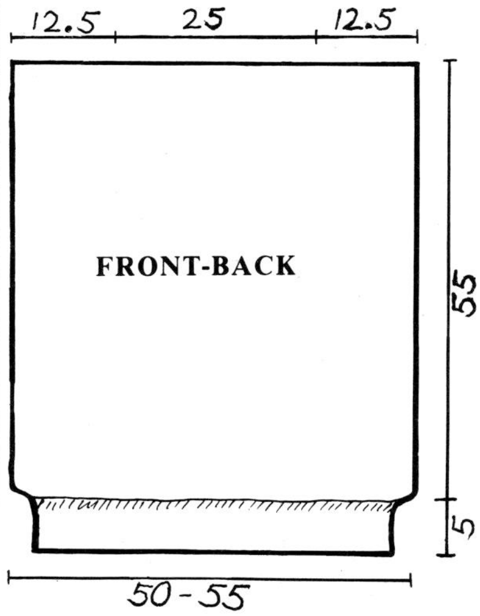

SLEEVE

21 - 22 - 23 - 24

15 - 16 - 17 - 18

14.5 - 15.5 - 17 - 18

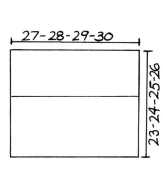

27 - 28 - 29 - 30

BACK

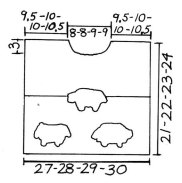

9,5 - 10 - 10 - 10,5   8 - 8 - 9 - 9   9,5 - 10 - 10 - 10,5

3

23 - 24 - 25 - 26

21 - 22 - 23 - 24

27 - 28 - 29 - 30

FRONT

12.5   25   12.5

FRONT-BACK

55

50 - 55

15

40

5

SLEEVE

FESTIVE Colours
celebrate the sunset in this
showoff jacket, an
extravagant display of
jacquard crochet. Long and
loose, it's styled for town or
travel.

JACQUARD JACKET

SIZE

Woman's Small (Medium, Large), bust 30-32 (33-35, 36-38) in. - 76-81.5 (84-89, 91.5-97) cm. Finished bust measurements: 42 (45, 47) in. - 106 (112, 118) cm, length: 27½ in. (70 cm), sleeve seam: 17 in. (43 cm).

MATERIALS

3 (4, 5) skeins kid mohair blend (approx. 135 yds (123 m) per 50 gr skein) colour dark green, 3 (3, 4) skeins colour lilac, 2 (2, 3) skeins colour dark rose, 2 skeins colour light green, 1 skein each colour purple, light rose and white. 8 buttons. Crochet hook U.S. size C/2 (U.K. size 11) (Metric size 3) or size needed to obtain tension. Knitting needles U.S. size 6 (U.K. size 8) (Metric size 4). 8 buttons. **To save time, take time to check tension!**

TENSION

18 tr and 9 rows = 4 in. (10 cm).

STITCHES

Chain (ch), single crochet (sc), treble crochet (tr).
Bobble: Work 5 tr in 1 st, keeping the last loop of each tr on hook, then draw the last loop through the first tr, yo and draw through the 2 loops.
Jacquard tr: Work in tr foll chart. Work each row ch 3 which counts as first tr = border st. When changing colours, always work the last loop of 1 st with the colour of the next st. Carry the yarn not in use loosely across wrong side of work, catching the yarn under the strand as you work in the new colour.
Stocking stitch: Knit 1 row on right side of work rows, purl 1 row on wrong side of work rows.
1/1 ribbing: Row 1: *K1, p1*. Rep * to * across.
Row 2 and all foll rows: Work sts as established in previous row.

BODY

With crochet hook and dark green, ch 187 (197, 207) + ch 3 (counts as first st). Work in tr foll jacquard chart. Centre point A (B, A). Work the first tr in the 5th ch from hook. Work 36 rows of chart. [Piece will measure 15¾ in. (40 cm) from beg.] Shape right front: Work 46 (48, 50) tr continuing in jacquard st. Shape raglans as foll: *work to last 2 sts, leave last 2 sts unworked, turn. Sc over the first st of row*. Work * to * 3 times. Work the last dec on the 42nd row. Fasten off. Work the centre 95 (101, 107) sts in jacquard st, working raglan dec at each edge of every row as foll: *sc over 2 sts, work to last 2 sts, leave last 2 sts unworked, turn. Sc over first st, work to last st, leave last st unworked, turn*, work * to * 3 times total. Fasten off after the 42nd row. Work the last 46 (48, 50) sts as on right front, rev raglan shapings. Fasten off.

SLEEVES

With dark green, ch 43 (47, 51) + ch 3 (counts as first st). Work in tr by foll chart, centring point A of chart. At each edge of every 2nd row inc 1 tr 16 times. (For inc, work 2 tr in each edge st.) You now have 75 (79, 83) tr. Work 36 rows. [Piece will measure 15¾ in. (40 cm) from beg.] Shape raglans: At each edge of every row, dec as on back. After the last dec, fasten off.

YOKE

Sew raglan seams taking in 1 tr at each raglan edge. Work across in tr. You now have 255 (273, 291) tr + 1 border st at each edge. Continue by foll chart. Dec as foll: **Row 1:** Dec 6 sts evenly spaced across row = 249 (267, 285) tr + 1 border st at each edge. **Row 2:** Work without dec. **Row 3:** Dec 18 (19, 20) sts by foll chart = 231 (248, 265) tr + 1 border st at each edge. **Rows 4 and 5:** Work without dec. **Row 6:** Dec 18 (19, 20) sts by foll chart = 213 (229, 245) tr + 1 border st at each edge. **Rows 7 and 8:** Work without dec. **Row 9:** Dec 36 (38, 40) sts by foll chart = 177 (191, 205) tr + 1 border st at each edge. **Row 10:** Work without dec. **Row 11:** Dec 36 (38, 40) sts by foll chart = 141 (153, 165) tr + 1 border st at each edge. **Row 12:** Work without dec. **Row 13:** Dec 36 (38, 40) tr by foll chart = 105 (115, 125) tr + 1 border st at each edge. **Rows 14 and 15:** Work without dec. **Row 16:** Dec 36 (38, 40) sts by foll chart = 69 (77, 85) sts + 1 border st at each edge. Fasten off.

FINISHING

With knitting needles and dark green, pick up and knit 70 (70, 86) sts around neck and work 1¼ in. (3 cm) of 1/1 ribbing. Cast off loosely. With knitting needles and dark green, pick up and knit 43 (47, 51) sts from lower edge of sleeves and work 1¼ in. (3 cm) of 1/1 ribbing. Cast off loosely. Sew side seams. With knitting needles and dark green, pick up and knit 187 (197, 207) sts along lower edge of body and work 2½ in. (6 cm) of 1/1 ribbing. Cast off loosely. With knitting needles and dark green, pick up and knit 130 sts along left front edge and work 1½ in. (3.5 cm) of 1/1 ribbing. Cast off loosely. Work same border on right front, but when border measures 1/2 in. (1.5 cm), make buttonholes as foll: beg at neck edge, work 2 sts, k2 tog, yo, *work 15 sts, k2 tog, yo*, work * to * 7 times, work 7 sts. Sew on buttons.

KEY TO CHART

⦿	= dark green
⦿	= light green
⬛	= dark pink
⊞	= light pink
◣	= purple
◺	= lilac
⬝	= white
◤	= bobble with purple
⊞	= bobble with light green

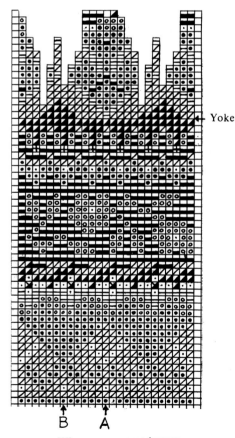

← Yoke

B A

When a square no longer is indicated on yoke, it indicates 1 decrease.

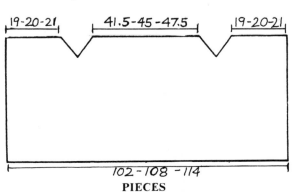

19-20-21   41.5-45-47.5   19-20-21

102-108-114

PIECES

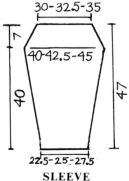

30-32.5-35

40-42.5-45

7

40

47

22.5-25-27.5

SLEEVE

SENSATIONAL
SPORTY BOATNECK TEAM
EMPLOYS ARROWHEAD STITCHES.
THESE SWEATERS ARE ALWAYS
READY FOR THE ACTIVE LIFE.

ARROWHEAD BOATNECK

SIZE

Woman's Small (Medium, Large), bust 30-32 (33-35, 36-38) in. - 76-81.5 (84-89, 91.5-97) cm. Finished bust measurements: 41½ (45¾ 47½) in. - 106 (114, 121) cm, length: 23½ in. (60 cm), sleeve seam: 17¼ in. (44 cm).

MATERIALS

6 (7, 7) skeins "Scheepjeswol Voluma" (85% acrylic, 15% kid mohair - approx. 209 yds (191 m) per 50 g skein) colour dark blue, 2 skeins colour blue and 1 skein colour light blue.
Crochet hook U.S. size E / 4 (U.K. size 9) (Metric size 3.5) or size needed to obtain tension. Knitting needles U.S. size 3 (U.K. size 10) (Metric size 3).
To save time, take time to check tension!

TENSION

19 htr and 14 rows = 4 in. (10 cm).

STITCHES

**Chain (ch),
single crochet (sc),
half treble crochet (htr).
Jacquard htr:** Work in htr by foll chart. Beg each row with ch 2 (counts as first htr). When changing colours, work the last st in 1 colour with the colour of next st. Carry the yarn not in use loosely across wrong side of work, catching the yarn under the strand as you work in the new colour.
1/1 ribbing: Row 1: *K1, p1*. Rep * to * across.
Row 2 and all foll rows: Work sts as established in previous row.

BACK

With crochet hook and dark blue, ch 103 (110, 117) + ch 2 (counts as first htr). **Row 1:** wrong side of work: 1 htr in the 4th ch from the hook, 1 htr in each ch = 103 (110, 117) htr. **Row 2:** right side of work: *2 htr in light blue, 1 htr in dark blue*, rep * to *. Continue in jacquard htr foll chart, working between points B and D. Then work dot pattern by rep rows between D and E for 34 rows, beg and end with 1 row of light blue dots, then work from point E to point H. Piece will measure 21½ in. (55 cm) with 77 rows. Fasten off.

FRONT

Work same as back.

SLEEVES

With dark blue, ch 56 (60, 64) + ch 2 (counts as first htr). Work jacquard htr by centring the chart and work from point A to point D. Work 30 rows of dot pattern (point D to E). The piece will measure about 11¾ in. (30 cm). Then work 12 rows from point E to point F, end with 1 row of light blue dots. **At the same time,** inc 1 st at each edge of every 4th row 13 times (work 2 htr in each edge st) = 82 (86, 90) htr. Piece will measure about 15¼ in. (39 cm) from beg. Fasten off.

FINISHING

Block pieces to indicated measurements. Sew shoulder seams, leaving centre 9 (9¼, 9¾) in. - 23 (24, 25) cm open for neck. Work 1 row of dc in dark blue around neck. Fasten off. With knitting needles and dark blue, pick up and knit 46 (48, 50) sts along lower edge of each sleeve and work 2 in. (5 cm) in 1/1 ribbing. Cast off loosely. With knitting needles and dark blue, pick up and knit 96 (100, 104) sts along lower edge of back and work 2 in. (5 cm) in 1/1 ribbing. Cast off loosely. Knit same ribbing along lower edge of front. Sew sleeves to side seams, matching centre of sleeve with shoulder seam. Sew side and sleeve seams.

CHILD'S ARROWHEAD BOATNECK

SIZE

Child's size 4 (6, 8, 10) years, chest 23 (25, 27, 28½) in. - 58.5 (63.5, 69, 72.5) cm. Finished chest measurements: 24½ (27, 30½, 33) in. - 62 (69, 77, 84) cm, length: 14 (15¼, 16½, 17¼) in. - 36 (39, 42, 44) cm, sleeve seam: 10½ (11¾, 13, 14) in. - 27 (30, 33, 36) cm.

MATERIALS

3 (4, 4, 5) skeins "Scheepjeswol Voluma" (85% acrylic, 15% kid mohair - approx. 209 yds (191 m) per 50 g skein) colour dark blue, 2 skeins colour blue and 1 skein colour light blue.
Crochet hook U.S. size E / 4 (U.K. size 9) (Metric size 3.5) or size needed to obtain tension. Knitting needles U.S. size 3 (U.K. size 10) (Metric size 3).
To save time, take time to check tension!

TENSION

19 htr and 14 rows = 4 in. (10 cm).

STITCHES

**Chain (ch),
half treble crochet (htr).
Jacquard htr:** Work in htr by foll chart. Beg each row with ch 2 (counts as first htr). When changing colours, work the last loop of the last stitch of 1 colour with the colour of next stitch. Carry the yarn not in use loosely across wrong side of work, catching the yarn under the strand as you work in the new colour.
1/1 ribbing: Row 1: *K1, p1*. Rep * to * across.
Row 2 and all foll rows: Work sts as established in previous row.

BACK

With crochet hook and dark blue, ch 61 (68, 75, 82) + ch 2 (counts as first htr). **Row 1:** Beg at point B (wrong side of work): 1 htr in the 4th ch from hook, 1 htr in each ch = 61 (68, 75, 82) htr. **Row 2:** right side of work: work jacquard htr by foll chart from point A to D, then work in dot pattern working from D to E [working stripe pattern foll chart 14 (18, 22, 26) rows, beg and end with 1 stripe of light blue]. Then work point E to G. You now have 45 (49, 53, 57) rows total and piece measures about 12½ (13¾, 15, 16) in. - 32 (35, 38, 40.5) cm. Fasten off.

FRONT

Work same as back.

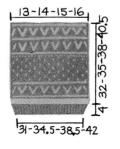

13-14-15-16

32-35-38-40.5

4

31-34.5-38.5-42

FRONT-BACK

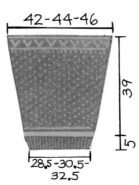

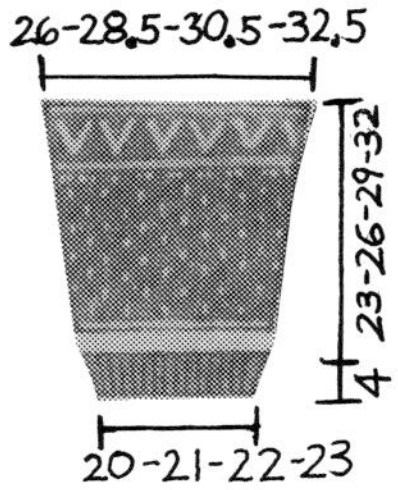

26-28.5-30.5-32.5

23-26-29-32

4

20-21-22-23

SLEEVE

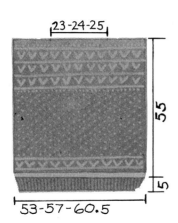

23-24-25

5.5

5

53-57-60.5

42-44-46

39

5

28.5-30.5-32.5

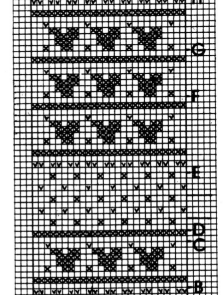

H
G
F
E
repeat
D
C
B
A
M
first row

SLEEVES

With crochet hook and dark blue, ch 40 (42, 44, 46) + ch 2 (counts as first htr). Work jacquard htr by centring chart. Work from point C to point D, then work 18 (22, 26, 30) rows of dot pattern D to E until piece is about 5½ (6½, 8, 9) in. - 14 (17, 20, 23) cm from beg, then work point E to F, ending with dark blue row. **At the same time,** inc 1 st at each edge of every 4th row 0 (1, 2, 3) times, inc 1 st at each edge of every 5th row 6 times. (For each inc, work 2 htr in each edge st.) You now have 52 (56, 60, 64) htr and piece will measure about 9 (9¾, 11½, 12½) in. - 23 (26, 29, 32) cm from beg. Fasten off.

FINISHING

Block pieces to indicated measurements. Sew shoulder seams, leaving centre 5 (5½, 6, 6¼) in. - 13 (14, 15, 16) cm open for neck. With crochet hook and dark blue, work 1 row of dc around neck. Fasten off. With knitting needles and dark blue, pick up and knit 32 (32, 34, 36) sts along lower edge of sleeve. Work 1½ in. (4 cm) in 1/1 ribbing. Cast off loosely. With knitting needles and dark blue, pick up and knit 58 (60, 62, 64) sts along lower edge of back. Work 1½ in. (4 cm) in 1/1 ribbing. Cast off loosely. Knit same ribbing on front. Sew sleeves to armholes, matching centre of sleeve with shoulder seams. Sew side and sleeve seams.

JACQUARD PULLOVER

SIZE

Woman's Medium / Large, bust 33-38 in. (84-97 cm). Finished bust measurement: 46½ in. (118 cm), length 24 in. (61 cm), sleeve seam 17¾ in. (45 cm).

MATERIALS

5 skeins mohair yarn (approx. 135 yds (123 m) per 50 g skein) colour black, 3 skeins colour light yellow and 2 skeins colour light pink. Crochet hook U.S. size H / 8 (U.K. size 6) (Metric size 3.5). Knitting needles U.S. size 10 (U.K. size 4) (Metric size 6) or size needed to obtain tension. **To save time, take time to check tension!**

TENSION

11 htr and 10 rows = 4 in. (10 cm).

STITCHES

Chain (ch), single crochet (sc), half treble crochet (htr). Jacquard htr: Work in htr by foll chart using single strand of yarn. The border sts are not shown on chart. Work border sts in the same colour as the adjacent yarn. Beg each row with ch 2 which counts as the first htr. When changing colours, work the last loop of the last st with the colour of the next st. Hold the unused yarn against wrong side of work. When inserting hook, work around the unused yarn so that the new sts hold it against the work. **1/1 ribbing:** Use double strand of yarn for knitting borders. **Row 1:** *K1, p1*. Rep * to * across. **Row 2 and all foll rows:** Work sts as established in previous row.

BACK

With knitting needles and double strand of black, cast on 66 sts and work 2 in. (5 cm) of 1/1 ribbing. Cast off loosely.
With crochet hook and single strand, work 1 row of htr in cast off row, by foll jacquard chart, inc 1 htr on first row = 67 htr. Work straight foll jacquard chart for 56 rows - 22 in. (56 cm). The total length from beg is 24 in. (61 cm). Fasten off.

FRONT

Work same as back until piece measures 20 in. (51 cm) - 51 rows of jacquard chart. Mark the centre 13 sts. Continue jacquard htr. Work to first marker, ch 2, turn. Work 1 row, ch 2, turn, then work to 3 htr before marker, leave 3 htr unworked. Turn, sc over 2 htr, ch 2. Work to end of row, ch 2, turn. Work to last htr, turn, leave last htr unworked, sc over 1 htr. Work to end of row = 56 rows of jacquard chart. Fasten off. Join yarn to 2nd marker, work to end of row. Ch 2, turn, work to last 3 htr, leave 3 htr unworked. Turn, sc over first 2 htr, ch 2, work to end of row. Then work to last htr. Turn, sc over first htr, ch 2, continue to end of row. Fasten off.

SLEEVES

With knitting needles and double strand of black, cast on 30 sts and work 2 in. (5 cm) of 1/1 ribbing. Cast off loosely.
With crochet hook and single strand, work htr in cast off row, by centring jacquard chart, and inc 1 htr on first row (work 31 htr + 1 border st at each edge) = 33 htr. Inc 1 htr in edge st of every 3rd row 10 times. Inc 1 htr at each edge of every 4th row, twice = 57 htr. To inc, work 2 htr in each edge st. Continue until sleeve measures 17¾ in. (45 cm) from beg. Fasten off.

FINISHING

Block pieces to indicated measurements. Sew 1 shoulder seam. With knitting needles and double strand of black, pick up and knit about 54 sts around neck and work 1½ in. (4 cm) of 1/1 ribbing. Cast off loosely. Sew 2nd shoulder and neckband seam. Sew sleeves to side seams, matching center of sleeve with shoulder seam. Sew side and sleeve seams.

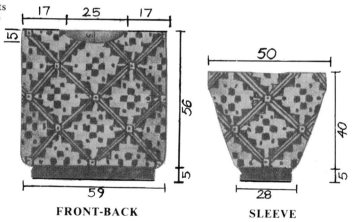

FRONT-BACK   **SLEEVE**

KEY TO CHART

= dark blue
= light blue
= blue

1etoer = first row
herhalen = repeat

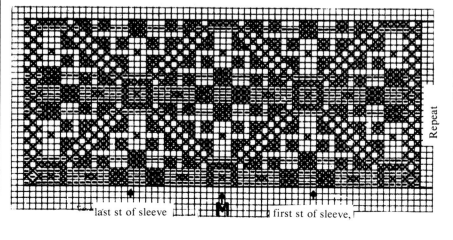

last st of sleeve   first st of sleeve,

Repeat

KEY TO CHART

= black
= yellow
= pink

LUXURIOUS MOHAIR ADDS A SOFT TOUCH TO ANY GARMENT. HERE, BLACK HAS BEEN SUPERIMPOSED ON THE PALEST PINK AND YELLOW FOR A STYLISH EFFECT.

FANCIFUL INTERACTION OF BLUES AND GREEN GIVES THESE JACQUARD PLAID SWEATERS THEIR COLOURFUL APPEAL.

CHILD'S JACQUARD CARDIGAN

SIZE
Child's size 8 (10, 12) years, chest 27 (28½, 30) - 69 (72.5, 76) cm. Finished chest measurements: 34 (36¼, 38¾) in. - 86 (92, 97) cm, length: 18 (19¼, 20¼) in. - 46 (49, 51) cm, sleeve seam: 13¼ (14, 15¼) in. - 34 (36, 39) cm.

MATERIALS
3 (4, 4) skeins bulky weight mohair yarn (approx. 110 yds (100 m) per 50 g skein) colour blue, 3 (3, 4) skeins colour green and 2 skeins colour light blue. Crochet hook U.S. size H/8 (U.K. size 6) (Metric size 5) or size needed to obtain tension. Knitting needles U.S. size 8 (U.K. size 6) (Metric size 5). 5 wooden buttons. **To save time, take time to check tension!**

TENSION
11½ htr and 9 rows = 4 in. (10 cm).

STITCHES
Chain (ch),
single crochet (sc),
half treble crochet (htr).
Jacquard htr: Work in htr by foll chart. When changing colours, work the last loop of the last st with the colour of the next st. Hold the unused yarn against the wrong side of work. When inserting hook, work around the unused yarn so that the new sts hold it against the work. Work the border sts in the same colour as the adjacent st in pat. Ch 2 at the beg of each row (= 1 border st).
1/1 ribbing: Row 1: *K1, p1*. Rep * to * across.
Row 2 and all foll rows: Work sts as established in previous row.

BODY
With knitting needles and green, cast on 110 (116, 122) sts and work 1 in. (2.5 cm) in 1/1 ribbing, then make 1 buttonhole 3 sts from right edge. Cast off 2 sts, work to end of row. On foll row, cast on 2 sts over cast off sts. Continue in ribbing until ribbing measures 2 in. (5 cm) from beg. Place 7 sts at each edge on a holder. Cast off rem sts. With crochet hook, work 96 (102, 108) htr across cast off sts of ribbing foll chart, inc 1 htr at each edge for border sts. (For inc, work 2 htr in each edge st) Work to armholes on chart - 10¾ (11½, 12) in. - 27 (29, 30.5) cm from beg. Now work in 3 parts. Work the first 24 (25, 26) htr for right front. Inc 1 st at armhole edge for border st. Work 12 (13, 14) rows over these 25 (26, 27) htr until piece measures 16 (17¼, 18) in. - 40.5 (43.5, 46) cm from beg, then shape neck. At right edge, sc over 3 sts, work to end of row, turn. Work to last 2 sts, turn, leave 2 sts unworked. Sc over first st and work to end of row, turn. Work to last st, turn, leaving last st unworked = 18 (19, 20) htr. After the 37th (40th, 42nd) row from ribbing, fasten off. Skip 3 sts from right front and work the foll 44 (48, 52) htr for the back by foll chart, inc 1 st at each edge for border sts = 46 (50, 54) htr. Work straight to same height as right front. Fasten off. Skip 3 sts from back and work left front same as right front, rev shapings.

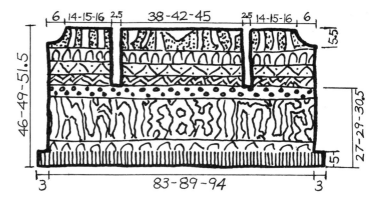

PIECES

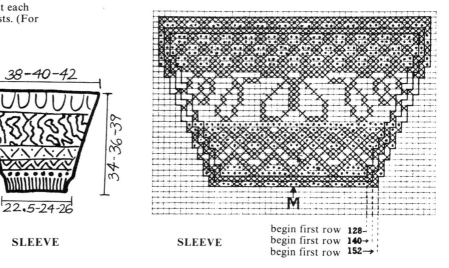

SLEEVE

SLEEVE

begin first row **128**
begin first row **140** →
begin first row **152** →

KEY TO CHART
⊠ = green
⊡ = light blue
☐ = blue

PIECES

begin first row **128** →
begin first row **140** →
begin first row **152** →

46

SLEEVES

With knitting needles and green, cast on 28 (30, 32) sts and work 2 in. (5 cm) in 1/1 ribbing. Cast off. With crochet hook, work 26 (28, 30) htr + 1 border st at each edge from cast off sts of ribbing. Work by foll chart for sleeve. Inc 1 st at each edge of every 2nd row once, inc 1 st at each edge of every 3rd row once (= 2 inc every 3 rows at each edge). (For each inc, work 2 htr in each edge st.) Work until you have 46 (48, 50) htr and 26 (28, 31) rows. Fasten off. Piece will measure 13½ (14¼, 15¼) in. - 34 (36, 39) cm.

FINISHING

Block pieces to indicated measurements. Front bands: With knitting needles and green, pick up 7 sts from left front holder and inc 1 st at inner edge and work in 1/1 ribbing. Work until band fits to neck. Place 7 sts on holder, dec border st. Work same band on right front, but make 3 buttonholes evenly spaced along band, allowing for 5th buttonhole on neckband. (Space buttonholes about 3¾ (4, 4¼) in. - 9.5 (10, 10.5) cm apart.) Sew bands to fronts. Sew shoulder seams. With knitting needles and green, pick up 53 (55, 57) sts around neck, including sts on holders and work 1/2 in. (1.5 cm) in 1/1 ribbing. Make 1 buttonhole above previous ones. Complete band until it measures 1¼ in. (3 cm) from beg. Cast off loosely. Sew sleeves to armholes, matching centre of sleeve with shoulder seams. Sew side and sleeve seams. Reinforce buttonholes and sew on buttons.

CHILD'S PLAID CARDIGAN

SIZE

Child's size 8 (10, 12) years, chest 27 (28½, 30) - 69 (72.5, 76) cm. Finished chest measurements: 34 (36¼, 38¾) in. - 86 (92, 98) cm, length: 19¼ (20¾, 22½) in. - 49 (53, 57) cm, sleeve seam: 13 (14½, 16) in. - 33 (37, 41) cm.

MATERIALS

4 (5, 5) skeins bulky weight mohair yarn (approx. 110 yds (100 m) per 50 g skein) colour green, 3 (3, 4) skeins colour blue, and 1 (2, 2) skeins colour light blue. Crochet hook U.S. size K / 10 (U.K. size 2) (Metric size 7) or size needed to obtain tension. Knitting needles U.S. size 10 (U.K. size 4) (Metric size 6). 5 wooden buttons.
To save time, take time to check tension!

TENSION

9½ tr and 7½ rows = 4 in. (10 cm).
1 motif between stripes = 4 in. (10 cm).

STITCHES

**Chain (ch),
single crochet (sc),
treble crochet (tr).**
Pattern stripes: Always use double strand. Beg each row with ch 3 (border st) and end with 1 dtr in the 3rd ch of the turning ch of previous row (border st). When changing colours, work the last st of one colour with colour of the next st. Work as foll: *3 rows green, 2 rows blue, 2 rows light blue, 2 rows blue, 3 rows green*, rep * to *.
Vertical lines: Work between the horizontal sts by slip stitching with double strand of yarn. Insert hook from front to back between sts, yo and pull through loop, insert hook in next row and continue as before. Beg at lower edge and work to top edge of each piece. Beg at centre back, work as foll: 3 lines green, *2 lines blue, 2 lines light blue, 2 lines blue, 6 lines green*, rep * to *.
1/1 ribbing: Row 1: *K1, p1*. Rep * to * across.
Row 2 and all foll rows: Work sts as established in previous row.

BODY

Worked in 1 piece, using double strand throughout. With knitting needles and double strand of blue, cast on 89 (95, 101) sts and work 1 in. (2.5 cm) of 1/1 ribbing. At right edge, work 2 sts, cast off 2 sts, work to end of row. On foll row, cast on 2 sts over cast off sts. Continue in ribbing until piece measures 2 in. (5 cm). Place 5 sts at each edge on holder. Cast off rem sts. With crochet hook and double strand of green, work 79 (85, 91) tr across cast off sts of ribbing and work in stripe pat, inc 1 st at each edge for border sts = 81 (87, 93) sts, leave last 2 sts unworked. Work 11¼ (12½, 13¾) in. - 29 (32, 34.5) cm from beg - 18 (20, 22) rows from top of ribbing. Now work in 3 parts. Work the first 21 (22, 23) sts for right front. Inc 1 st at armhole edge for border st. Work 12 (13, 14) rows over these 22 (23, 24) sts, then shape neck. At right edge, sc over 4 sts, work to end of row, turn. Work to last 2 sts. (For each inc, work 2 htr in each edge st.) Sc over first st and work to end of row, turn. Work to last st, turn, leaving last st unworked. After the 33rd (36th, 39th) row from ribbing, fasten off. Work the last 21 (22, 23) sts for right front by rev shapings. Work the centre 39 (43, 47) sts in stripe pat, inc 1 st at each edge = 41 (45, 49) sts. Continue until piece measures same as front shoulders. Fasten off.

SLEEVES

With knitting needles and double strand of blue, cast on 25 (25, 27) sts and work 2 in. (5 cm) in 1/1 ribbing. Cast off. With crochet hook work 23 (23, 25) tr + 1 border st at each edge from cast off sts of ribbing. Work in stripe pat. Inc 1 st at each edge of every 3rd row 7 (8, 8) times. You now have 39 (41, 43) sts and 21 (24, 27) rows. Fasten off. Piece will measure 13 (14½, 16) in. -33 (37, 41) cm.

FINISHING

Block pieces to indicated measurements. Work vertical lines on body, beg at centre back (3 rows green at centre). Work vertical lines on each sleeve. Front bands: With knitting needles and double strand of blue, pick up 5 sts from left front holder and inc 1 st at inner edge and work in 1/1 ribbing. Work until band fits to neck. Place 5 sts on holder, dec border st. Work same band on right front, but make 3 buttonholes evenly spaced along band, allowing for 5th buttonhole on neckband. [Space buttonholes about 4 (4¼, 4¾) in. - 10 (11, 12) cm apart.] Sew bands to fronts. Sew shoulder seams. With knitting needles and green, pick up and knit 57 (59, 61) sts total around neck, including sts on holder and work 1/2 in. (1.5 cm) in 1/1 ribbing. Make 1 buttonhole above previous ones. Complete band until it measures 1¼ in. (3 cm) from beg. Cast off loosely. Sew sleeves to armholes, matching centre of sleeve with shoulder seams. Sew side and sleeve seams. Reinforce buttonholes and sew on buttons.

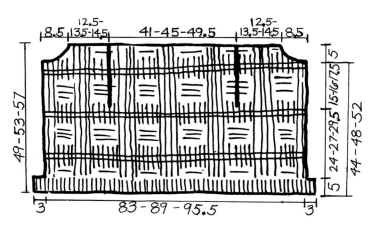

PIECES

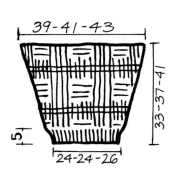

SLEEVE

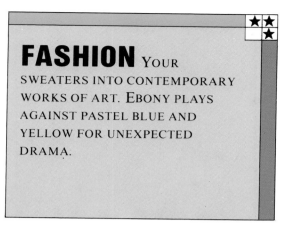

FASHION YOUR

SWEATERS INTO CONTEMPORARY
WORKS OF ART. EBONY PLAYS
AGAINST PASTEL BLUE AND
YELLOW FOR UNEXPECTED
DRAMA.

ARTWORK JACQUARD JACKET

SIZE

Woman's Small
(Medium, Large), bust
30-32 (33-35, 36-38) in. -
76-81.5 (84-89, 91.5-97)
cm. Finished bust
measurements: 43¼ (46,
49¼) in. - 110 (117, 125)
cm, length: 24½ in.
(62 cm), sleeve seam:
17¼ in. (44 cm).

MATERIALS

7 skeins sport weight
mohair (approx. 135 yds
(123 m) per 50 g skein)
colour black, 4 skeins
colour light yellow and 2
skeins colour light blue.
Crochet hook U.S. size
H/8 (U.K. size 6) (Metric
size 5) or size needed to
obtain tension. Knitting
needles U.S. size 10 (U.K.
size 4) (Metric size 6). 5
buttons. **To save time,
take time to check
tension!**

TENSION

14½ htr and 10 rows = 4
in. (10 cm).

STITCHES

**Chain (ch),
single crochet (sc),
half treble crochet (htr).
Jacquard htr:** Work in htr
by foll chart using single
strand of yarn. The
border sts are not shown
on chart. Beg each row
with ch 2 which counts as
first htr (= border). Work
the border sts in the same
colour as the adjacent st
in pat. When changing
colours, work the last
loop of the last st with the
colour of the next st.
Hold the unused yarn
against the wrong side of
work. When inserting
hook, work around the
unused yarn so that the
new sts hold it against the
work.

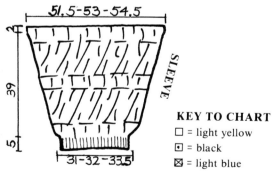

51.5-53-54.5

39

SLEEVE

5

31-32-33.5

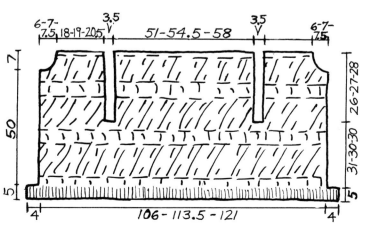

6-7-7.5 18-19-20.5 3.5 51-54.5-58 3.5 6-7-7.5

7

50

5

31-30-30 26-27-28 5

106 - 113.5 - 121

4   4

PIECES

1/1 ribbing: Use double
strand of yarn for knitted
borders. **Row 1:** *K1,
p1*. Rep * to * across.
Row 2 and all foll rows:
Work sts as established in
previous row.
NOTE: The body is
worked in 1 piece. All
jacquard is worked with a
single strand of yarn and
the ribbing is worked
with a double strand of
yarn.

BODY

With knitting needles and
double strand of black,
cast on 139 (147, 155) sts
and work in 1/1 ribbing.
When ribbing measures 1
in. (2.5 cm), make 1
buttonhole 3 sts from
right edge of work. For
buttonhole, cast off 2 sts.
On foll row, cast on 2 sts
over cast off sts. When
ribbing measures 2 in. (5
cm), place 7 sts at each
edge on stitch holders and
cast off rem sts. With
crochet hook and single
strand, work 2 htr in first
st of centre 125 (133, 141)
sts, work in htr across sts
by foll jacquard chart, inc
29 (32, 35) sts evenly
spaced across the first
row, end with 2 htr in last
st. For each inc, work 2
htr in 1 st of cast off row
= 156 (167, 178) htr.
Work by foll chart for 31
(30, 30) rows. Piece will
measure 14¼ (13¾, 13¾)

in. - 36 (35, 35) cm from
beg.
Divide work as foll for
armholes: work first 36
(39, 42) sts for right front,
working 2 htr in last st =
37 (40, 43) sts. Work for
19 (20, 20) rows by foll
chart. The armhole will
measure 7½ (8, 8) in. - 19
(20, 20) cm. Shape neck:
with right side facing, sc
over 3 (3, 4) sts, ch 2,
work htr to end of row.
On foll row, work to last
2 sts from end, leave last
2 sts unworked, turn. Sc
over 1 (2, 2) sts, ch 2 and
work htr to end of row.
On foll row, work to last
st from end, leave last st
unworked, turn. Sc over 1
st, ch 2, work to end of
row. Work to last st from
end, leave last st
unworked. Turn, work
rem 28 (30, 32) sts until
armhole measures 10¼
(10½, 10½) in. - 26 (27,
27) cm. Fasten off. (Note:
you will have worked 57
rows of chart - 3 repeats.)
Skip 5 htr from the right
front and work in htr
over 74 (79, 84) sts for the
back by foll chart, inc 1 st
at each edge for border
sts = 76 (81, 86) htr. Work
until armhole measures
10¼ (10½, 10½) in. - 26
(27, 27) cm. Fasten off.
Skip 5 htr from back and
work in htr over the last
36 (39, 42) htr, inc 1 st at
armhole edge = 37 (40,
43) htr by foll chart until

piece measures 7½ (8, 8)
in. - 19 (20, 20) cm. Shape
neck: Work to last 3 (3, 4)
sts, leave these sts
unworked, turn. Sc over 2
sts, ch 2 and work in htr
to end of row. Work next
row to last 1 (2, 2) sts,
leave 1 (2, 2) sts
unworked, turn, sc over 1
st, ch 2, work to end of
row. Turn, ch 2, work to
last st on row, leave last
st unworked, turn, work
to end of row. Turn, ch 2,
work to last st, leave st
unworked. Turn, work
rem 28 (30, 32) sts until
armhole measures 10¼
(10½, 10½) in. - 26 (27,
27) cm. Fasten off.

SLEEVES

With knitting needles and
double strand of black
cast on 28 (30, 32) sts and
work 2 in. (5 cm) of 1/1
ribbing. Cast off loosely.
With crochet hook and
single strand, work htr in
sts of cast off row by
centring jacquard chart,
inc 19 sts evenly spaced
across row = 47 (49, 51)
htr. *Inc 1 htr (work 2 htr
in each edge st) at each
edge of every 2nd row
once, inc 1 htr at each
edge of every 3rd row
once*, rep * to * 7 times.
Inc 1 htr at each edge of
every 2nd row once = 77
(79, 81) htr. Work until
sleeve measures 18¼ in. -
(46 cm) from beg. Fasten
off.

KEY TO CHART

□ = light yellow
⊡ = black
⊠ = light blue

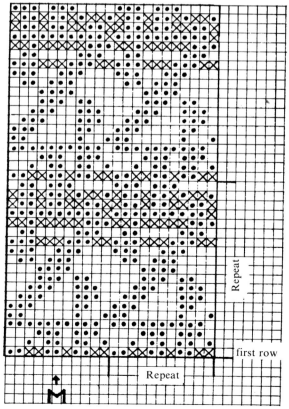

Repeat

first row

Repeat

49

FINISHING

With knitting needles and double strand of black, pick up 7 sts from left front and inc 1 st at inside edge and work until band, slightly stretched, reaches to neck. Place sts on holder. Work same band along right front, evenly spacing 3 button-holes as on lower ribbing along the band. [The last buttonhole will be on neckband. Buttonholes will be spaced about 5¼ in. (13.5 cm) apart.] Block pieces to indicated measurements. Sew bands to fronts. Sew shoulder seams. With knitting needles and double strand of black, pick up and knit about 71 (75, 79) sts along neck edge, including the sts from front bands. Work in 1/1 ribbing. When ribbing measures 3/4 in. (2 cm), make the 5th buttonhole above the previous buttonholes. When band measures 1½ in. (4 cm), cast off. Set in sleeves. Sew side and sleeve seams. Reinforce buttonholes and bind off. Sew on buttons.

HANDWOVEN

AMERICAN SOUTHWEST LOOK FOR THIS LONG JACKET OF SUBTLE DESERT COLOURS.

★★

DESERT JACKET

For the woven look, work the thin strand around a thick strand. During the work, on every row, lay the thick strands along the top of the underlying row and crochet by in-serting hook under the thick strand. Be sure to have the turning of the thick yarn showing on the wrong side of work. Check your tension as you work.

SIZE

Woman's Small (Medium, Large), bust 33-35 (36-38, 39-42) in. - 84-89 (91.5-97) cm. Finished bust measure-ments: 44 (47, 50½) in. - 112 (120, 128) cm, length: 31½ in. (80 cm), sleeve seam 15 in. (38 cm).

MATERIALS

8 (9, 10) skeins fingering weight alpaca yarn (approx. 206 yds (190 m) per 50 g skein) colour ecru and 9 (9, 10) skeins bulky yarn (approx. 110 yds (100 m) per 50 g skein) colour ecru. Crochet hook U.S. size B/1 (U.K. size 12) (Metric size 2.5) or size needed to obtain tension. Circular or double pointed knitting needles U.S. size 9 (U.K. size 5) (Metric size 5.5). **To save time, take time to check tension!**

TENSION

9 squares (1 dc + ch 3) and 11 rows = 4 in. (10 cm).

STITCHES

Chain (ch), single crochet (sc), double crochet (dc). 1/1 ribbing: Row 1: *K1, p1*. Rep * to * across. **Row 2 and all foll rows:** Work sts as established in previous row.

BACK

With alpaca, ch 204 (220, 236) and work in woven crochet st. Lay 3 strands of bulky yarn on the ch row and crochet around them with alpaca and Row 1: 1 sc in the 3rd ch from hook, *ch 3, skip 3, 1 dc in the foll ch*, rep * to *, end with 1 dc in the last ch = 50 (54, 58) squares and 1 border st at work in pat st. **each edge.** Row 2: Ch 2 (border st), 1 dc in the foll dc, *ch 3, 1 dc in the ch-3 sp,* rep * to *, end with ch 1, 1 dc in the foll dc, 1 sc in the turning of the thick yarn (border st). Always rep row 2. Work until piece measures 31½ in. (80 cm) from beg, then fasten off.

POCKETS

With alpaca, ch 68 (72, 76) and work in pat st = 16 (17, 18) squares + 1 border st at each edge. When piece measures 9¾ in. (25 cm), fasten off. Make 2.

RIGHT FRONT

With alpaca, ch 104 (112, 120), then work in pat st. After the first row, you will have 25 (27, 29) squares + 1 border st at each edge. Work even until piece measures 11¾ in. (30 cm). On foll row, work 4 (5, 5) squares, skip 16 (17, 18) squares, then substitute the squares of pocket (leaving border sts unworked), work rem 5 (5, 6) squares. Continue for 31½ in. (80 cm), then fasten off.

LEFT FRONT

Work same as right front, rev placement of pocket.

SLEEVES

With alpaca, ch 96 (104, 112) then work in pat st = 23 (25, 27) squares + 1 border st at each edge of first row. At beg of each row, inc 1 st 16 times. Inc 1 st at beg of every 4th and 5th row 5 times. Work inc as foll: at beg of 2nd row, ch 5, 1 dc in the 3rd ch from hook, ch 1, skip 1 ch, 1 dc in the foll ch, ch 3, 1 dc around the foll ch-sp and continue across as on row 3 of pat. Inc at the beg of 3rd row: ch 5, 1 dc in the 3rd ch from the hook, ch 3, skip 1 dc, 1 dc, ch 3, 1 dc around the ch-sp, continue across as on row 3 of pat. Work inc sts = 49 (51, 53) squares + 1 border st at each edge until piece measures 15 in. (38 cm) from beg. Fasten off.

FINISHING

Block pieces to indicated measurements. Sew shoulder seams over 7½ (8, 8¼) in. - 19 (20, 21) cm from armhole edge. Sew sleeves to side seams, matching centre of sleeve with shoulder seam. Sew side and sleeve seam. Sew pocket lining in place.

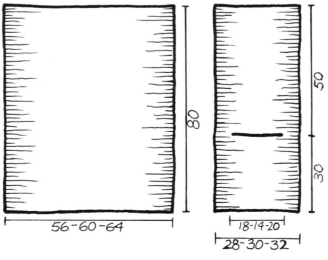

BACK 56-60-64 80

FRONT 18-14-20 28-30-32 50 30

SLEEVE 54.5-56.5-59 26-28-30 38

TRAVELLING

COMPANION IN GADABOUT PLAID IS A MEMORABLE SWEATER. THIS V-NECK VERSION TAKES SHAPE QUICKLY IN BULKY WEIGHT MOHAIR.

★ ★

V-NECK PLAID PULLOVER

SIZE

Woman's Small (X Large), bust 30-32 (39-42) in. - 76-81.5 (99-107) cm. Finished bust measurements: 41½ (52) in. - 105 (132) cm, length: 23½ in. (60 cm), sleeve seam: 16½ in. (42 cm).

MATERIALS

3 (4) skeins bulky mohair yarn (approx. 110 yds (100 m) per 50 g skein) colour blue, 5 skeins colour brown and 3 skeins colour green. Crochet hook U.S. size F/5 (U.K. size 8) (Metric size 4) or size needed to obtain tension. Knitting needles and circular needle U.S. size 8 (U.K. size 6) (Metric size 5). **To save time, take time to check tension!**

TENSION

13½ tr and 8 rows = 4 in. (10 cm).

STITCHES

Chain (ch), single crochet (sc), double crochet (dc), half treble crochet (htr). Jacquard pattern: Work in tr and dc by foll chart. When changing colours, work the last loop of the last st in 1 colour with the colour of the next st. Hold the unused yarn against the wrong side of work. When inserting hook, work around the unused yarn so that the new sts hold it against the work. Work the border sts in the same colour as the adjacent st in pat. Ch 3 at the beg of each row (= 1 border st). Stripes are crocheted on finished work.
1/1 ribbing: Row 1: *K1, p1*. Rep * to * across.
Row 2 and all foll rows: Work sts as established in previous row.

BACK

With knitting needles and blue, cast on 72 (90) sts and work 2½ in. (6 cm) in 1/1 ribbing. Cast off loosely. With crochet hook, work 1 st in each st of cast off row of ribbing by foll chart = 73 (91) tr. Work until piece measures 22½ in. (57.5 cm) from beg, shape neck. Mark centre 23 (25) sts. Work each side separately. With right side facing, work to last st before marker, leave last st unworked, turn. Work rem 24 (32) sts until piece measures 23¾ in. (60 cm) from beg, fasten off. For 2nd half, join yarn to 2nd marker and work across, turn. Work to 1 st before marker, turn, leaving 1 st unworked. Complete as first half.

FRONT

Work same as back until piece measures 15¼ in. (39 cm) from beg. Divide work in half leaving centre st unworked. Work each side separately. At neck edge of every row, dec 1 st. (At end of row, work·to last st, turn, leaving last st unworked. At beg of row, sc over first st.) Work until piece measures 23¾ in. (60 cm) from beg, fasten off. Work 2nd half to correspond by rev shapings.

SLEEVES

With knitting needles and blue, cast on 40 sts and work 2 in. (5 cm) in 1/1 ribbing. Cast off loosely. With crochet hook, work 51 tr (inc 11 sts evenly spaced) across cast off row by foll the chart. Inc 1 st at each edge every 2¼ in. (5 cm), 6 times = 63 sts. Continue until sleeve measures 16½ in. (42 cm) from beg. Fasten off.

FINISHING

Block pieces to indicated measurements. Work the vertical stripes on back, front and sleeves as foll: beg at lower edges and alternating blue and green stripes. On the first row, insert hook under the first ch from front to back, then draw through loop, insert hook in the foll row, yo and pull up loop and draw through loop on hook, continue in this way up the front and down the back on all sections. Fasten off. Sew shoulder seams. With circular knitting needle and blue, pick up and knit 120 sts around neck and work 1¼ in. (3 cm) in 1/1 ribbing. Work back and forth beg at centre front. Cast off loosely. Lap right side over left and sew in place. Sew sleeves to side seams, matching centre of sleeve with shoulder seam. Sew side and sleeve seams.

Border stitches are always worked in the same colour as the adjacent stitch. They will be sewn into the seam and are included so that all the stitches on the chart will show on finished work.

FRONT-BACK

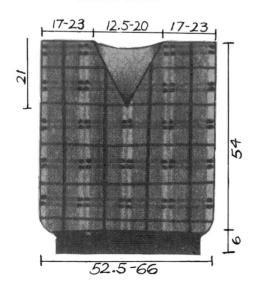

17-23   12.5-20   17-23

21

54

6

52.5-66

SLEEVE

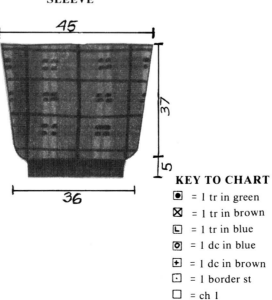

45

37

5

36

KEY TO CHART

⊙ = 1 tr in green
⊠ = 1 tr in brown
Ⓛ = 1 tr in blue
⊙ = 1 dc in blue
⊞ = 1 dc in brown
⊡ = 1 border st
☐ = ch 1

★★

TARTAN CARDIGAN IS WORKED IN ONE PIECE. MOHAIR TAKES A HIGHLAND FLING WITH TRADITIONAL COLOURS FOR SURPRISING RESULTS.

HIGHLAND TARTAN CARDIGAN

SIZE

Woman's Small
(X Large), bust 30-32
(39-42) in. - 76-81.5
(99-107) cm. Finished
bust measurements: 41½
(51½) in. - 105 (132) cm,
length: 23½ in. (60 cm),
sleeve seam: 17¾ in.
(45 cm).

MATERIALS

5 skeins mohair yarn
(approx. 110 yds (100 m)
per 50 g skein) colour
rust, 4 skeins colour red,
and 3 skeins colour blue.
Crochet hook U.S. size
F/5 (U.K. size 8) (Metric
size 4) or size needed to
obtain tension. Knitting
needles U.S. size 8 (U.K.
size 5) (Metric size 5). 8
leather buttons. **To save
time, take time to check
tension!**

TENSION

13½ tr and 8 rows in
jacquard pattern = 4 in.
(10 cm).

STITCHES

**Chain (ch),
single crochet (sc),
double crochet (dc),
half treble crochet (htr),
treble crochet (tr),
double treble crochet
(dtr).
Jacquard pattern:** Work
in tr and dc by foll chart.
When changing colours,
work the last loop of the
last st in 1 colour with the
colour of the next st.
Hold the unused yarn
against the wrong side of
work. When inserting
hook, work around the
unused yarn so that the
new sts hold it against the
work. Work the border
sts in the same colour as
the adjacent st in pat. Ch
3 at the beg of each row

(= 1 border st). The
vertical stripes are worked later on finished work.
1/1 ribbing: Row 1: *K1,
p1*. Rep * to * across.
Row 2 and all foll rows:
Work sts as established in
previous row.

BODY

Worked in 1 piece, beg
with left front. With red,
ch 36 (45) + ch 3 (counts
as the first st). Work 1 tr
in the 5th ch from hook,
continue by foll chart. (At
left edge, there will be 1
border st which will be
sewn in the seam.) Work
until piece measures 10¾
in. (27.5 cm) from beg. At
right edge, shape the
sleeve: inc 1 st once, inc 2
sts once, inc 1 st once, inc
10 sts 5 times = 90 (99)
sts. Work incs at beg of
row as foll: To make a
single inc, work 2 sts in 1
st. To make a double inc,
work 3 sts in 1 st. To add
more sts at the end of a
row, make an additional
chain st for each
additional st needed plus
the required number of
turning chain sts. On the
next row crochet a
pattern st in each added
chain. Work until piece
measures 18¼ in. (46.5
cm) from beg, then shape
neck. Right side facing,
work to last 6 (7) sts,
turn, leave last 6 (7) sts
unworked, sc over first 4
sts and work to end of
row, work to last st, turn,
leaving last st unworked.
Turn, sc over first st,
work to end of row.
Work rem 78 (85) sts for
3 rows, then inc 1 st at

left edge. Leave sts
unworked.
Work right front same as
left front, rev shapings.
Inc at left edge for sleeve
and dec at right edge for
neck. Work across left
front piece, ch 23 (25) for
neck, work across right
front piece = 181 (199) sts.
Continue until piece
measures 13¾ in. (34 cm)
measured along sleeve
end. With right side
facing, *sc across 10 sts at
beg of row, work to last
10 sts, turn, leave 10 sts
unworked.* Work * to *
5 times. Sc across first st,
work to last st, turn,
leaving last st unworked.
Sc across first 2 sts, work
to last 2 sts, turn, leaving
last 2 sts unworked. Sc
across first st, work to
last st, turn, leaving last
st unworked = 73 (91) sts.
Work straight for back until
piece measures a total of
62¼ in. (108 cm) from
beg. Fasten off.

FINISHING

Block piece to indicated
measurements. Crochet
vertical stripes as foll:
work from lower edge of
front. Alternately work
red and green stripes,
working over the ch sts of
jacquard chart. On the
first row, insert hook
under the first ch from
front to back, then draw
through loop, insert hook
in the foll row, yo and
pull up loop and draw
through loop on hook,

continue in this way up
the front and down the
back on all sections.
Fasten off.
With crochet hook and
red, work 40 dc along
lower edge of each sleeve.
Fasten off. With knitting
needles and red, pick up
and knit 1 st from each dc
and work 2 in. (5 cm) in
1/1 ribbing. Cast off
loosely. With crochet
hook and red, work 59 dc
along neck edge. Fasten
off. With knitting needles
and red, pick up and knit
1 st in each dc and work
1¼ in. (3 cm) of 1/1
ribbing. Cast off. Sew
side and sleeve seams.
With knitting needles and
red, pick up and knit 1 st
from every crocheted st
and work 2½ in. (6 cm) of
1/1 ribbing along lower
edge. Cast off. With
knitting needles and red,
cast on 6 sts and work in
1/1 ribbing until piece fits
along left front edge. Cast
off. Work same band for
right front, making 7
buttonholes as foll: place
the first 1¼ buttonhole
in. (3 cm) from lower
edge. For each
buttonhole work 2 sts, k2
tog, yo, work 2 sts. Make
6 more buttonholes
spaced about 2¾ in. (7
cm) apart, with the last
buttonhole at neckband
height. Sew on front
bands. Reinforce button-
holes, sew on buttons.

FRONT

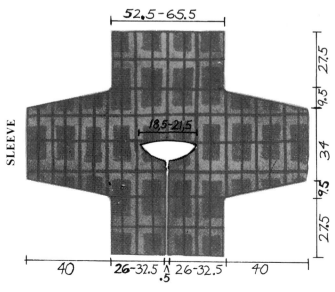

52.5-65.5

18.5-21.5

27.5

9.5

34

9.5

27.5

40

26-32.5

.5

26-32.5

40

SLEEVE

BACK

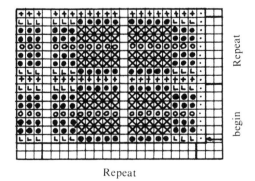

Repeat

begin

Repeat

KEY TO CHART

⊙ = 1 tr in rust

⊠ = 1 tr in green

⌴ = 1 tr in red

⊚ = 1 dc in red

⊕ = 1 dc in green

· = 1 border st

☐ = ch 1

55

SPARKLING Blends
of pastel colours are
crocheted in the beloved
afghan stitch to create this
charming pair of all cotton
sweaters.

CHILD'S PASTEL BOATNECK

SIZE

Child's size 6 (8, 10) years, chest 25 (27, 28½) in. -63.5 (69, 72.5) cm. Finished chest measurements: 32 (34, 36) in. - 81 (86, 91) cm, length: 15 (16½, 17½) in. - 38 (41, 45) cm, sleeve seam: 2 in. (5 cm).

MATERIALS

3 skeins "Mayflower Cotton 8" (100% cotton - approx. 180 yds (164 m) per 50 g skein) colour light rose, 2 skeins colour white, 1 skein each colour salmon, gold, green and light blue.
Afghan crochet hook U.S. size E/4 (U.K. size 9) (Metric size 3.5) or size needed to obtain tension. Knitting needles U.S. size 3 (U.K. size 12) (Metric size 2.5). Double pointed needles U.S. size 3 (U.K. size 12) (Metric size 2.5). **To save time, take time to check tension!**

TENSION

25 sts and 18 rows = 4 in. (10 cm) = 9 motifs.

STITCHES

Chain (ch), treble crochet (tr), double treble crochet (dtr).
Brocade afghan stitch: Use afghan crochet hook. Work on a chain base.
Row 1: Right side of work: with yarn at back of work, insert hook into 3rd ch from hook, yo and draw through loop. Work this way in each ch to end of row. (1 loop remains on hook from each ch.)
Row 2: Wrong side of work: with yarn at back of work, yo and draw hook through first loop, *yo and draw hook through 2 loops*, rep * to * across row. Work the last loop of the last st of the row with the colour of the next row. **Row 3:** Right side of work: the loop on the hook is the border st, *insert hook in first loop, pull through 1 loop = 1 drawn loop, 1 drawn loop, insert hook in next 2 loops, but do not draw through any loops = 2 sc, (carry yarn along wrong side of work); 2 drawn loops; insert hook in next loop, yo, draw through loop = tr, 1 tr (2 tr total), yo, insert hook in next loop, draw through loop, yo, draw through 2 loops = 1 dtr, 1 dtr = 2 dtr total, 2 tr*, rep * to * across, end by inserting hook in last st, yo and draw through loop. **Row 4:** Same as row 2. **Row 5:** Same as row 1. **Row 6:** Ch 1 (= border st), *2 tr, 2 dtr, 2 tr, 2 drawn loops, sc 2, 2 drawn loops. Rep rows 2 to 6.

Work in stripe pat as foll:
(Alternate 1 row of white between all colour rows.) 0 (2, 4) rows light rose, 0 (1, 1) rows salmon, 1 row gold, 1 row green, 4 rows light rose, 1 row salmon, 1 row green, 1 row light rose, 1 row light blue, 4 rows light rose, 1 row green, 1 row salmon, 4 rows light rose, 1 row salmon, 1 row gold, 1 row light blue, 1 row green, 1 row light rose, 1 row salmon, 3 (3, 4) rows light rose.
1/1 ribbing: Row 1: *K1, p1*, Rep * to * across.
Row 2 and all foll rows: Work sts as established in previous row.

BACK

With knitting needles and light rose, cast on 72 (78, 84) sts and work 2 in. (5 cm) in 1/1 ribbing. Cast off loosely. With afghan hook and white, pick p 104 (110, 116) sts across cast off sts of ribbing. Continue in brocade st, working first row in white. Work by foll chart, with 1 border st at each edge. Work from point A to C, 8 (9, 9) times, then work from point A to B, 1 (0, 1) time, 1 border st. Work until piece measures 9½ (10¼, 11) in. - 24 (26, 28) cm from beg and 17 (19, 21) brocade motifs are complete. On the foll

row, ch 12 sts at each edge and continue across 128 (134, 140) sts in brocade st until piece measures 14¾ (16½, 17½) in. - 38 (41.5, 45) cm, = total of 30 (33, 36) brocade motifs. End with the 2nd or 4th row of pat st, and 1 row salmon. Work 1 row of dc white, working 1 dc in each loop. Fasten off.

FRONT

Work same as back, working brocade st as foll: 1 border st, work from point B to C, 1 (0, 1) time, then work from point A to C, 8 (9, 9) times, 1 border st. End with 1 row of green, then work 1 row of dc in white, working 1 dc in each loop. Fasten off.

FINISHING

Block pieces to indicated measurements. Sew shoulder seams over 6 (6¼, 6½) in. - 15 (16, 17) cm. Sew side and underarm seams. Work 1 row of dc in white around sleeve ends and fasten off.

For stitch chart, see Child's Pastel Rib Neck

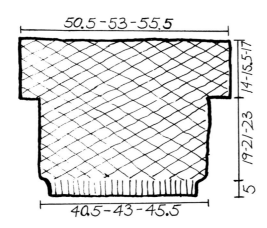

50.5 - 53 - 55.5
40.5 - 43 - 45.5
14 - 15.5 - 17
19 - 21 - 23
5

FRONT-BACK

CHILD'S PASTEL RIBNECK

SIZE

Child's size 1 (3, 5) years, chest 20 (22, 24) in. - 51 (56, 61) cm. Finished chest measurements: 24½ (26½, 28) in. - 62 (67, 72) cm, length: 11 (12½, 13) in. - 29 (32, 35) cm, sleeve seam: 2 in. (5 cm).

MATERIALS

2 skeins "Mayflower Cotton 8" (100% cotton - approx. 180 yds per 50 g skein) each colour white and sea green, 1 skein each colour salmon, gold, light pink, lilac and green. Afghan crochet hook U.S. size E/4 (U.K. size 9) (Metric size 3.5) or size needed to obtain tension. Knitting needles U.S. size 3 (U.K. size 12) (Metric size 2.5). Double pointed needles U.S. size 3 (U.K. size 12) (Metric size 2.5).

To save time, take time to check tension!

TENSION

25 sts and 18 rows = 4 in. (10 cm) = 9 motifs.

STITCHES

Chain (ch), single crochet (sc), double crochet (dc), double treble crochet (dtr).

Afghan stitch: Use afghan crochet hook. Work on a chain base. **Row 1:** Right side of work: with yarn at back of work, insert hook into 3rd ch from hook, yo and draw through loop. Work this way in each ch to end of row. (1 loop remains on hook from each ch.) **Row 2:** Wrong side of work: with yarn at back of work, yo and draw hook through first loop, *yo and draw hook through 2 loops*, rep * to * across row. **Row 3:** *With yarn at back of work, insert hook through vertical loop of 2nd st of previous row, yo and draw through 1 loop*, rep * to * across to end of row.

Brocade stitch: Use afghan crochet hook. Work on a chain base. **Row 1:** Right side of work: with yarn at back of work, insert hook into 3rd ch from hook, yo and draw through loop. Work this way in each ch to end of row. (1 loop remains on hook from each ch.) **Row 2:** Wrong side of work: with yarn at back of work, yo and draw hook through first loop, *yo and draw hook

through 2 loops*, rep * to * across row. Work the last loop of the row with the colour of the next row. **Row 3:** Right side of work: the loop on the hook is the border st, *insert hook in first loop, pull through 1 loop = 1 drawn loop, 1 drawn loop, insert hook in next 2 loops, but do not draw through any loops = 2 scs, (carry yarn along wrong side of work); 2 drawn loops; insert hook in next loop, yo, pull through loop = tr, 1 tr = 2 tr total, yo, insert hook in next loop, pull through loop, yo, draw through 2 loops = 1 dtr, 1 dtr = 2 dtr total, 2 tr*, rep * to * across, at end insert hook in last st, yo and pull through loop. **Row 4:** Same as row 1. **Row 5:** Same as row 2. **Row 6:** Ch 1 (= border st), *2 tr, 2 dtr, 2 tr, 2 drawn loops, sc 2, 2 drawn loops. Rep rows 2 to 6.

Work in stripe pat as foll: **(Alternate 1 row of white between all colour rows.)**

1 (3, 4) rows sea green, 1 row salmon, 1 row gold, 3 rows sea green, 1 row lilac, 1 row green, 1 row light rose, 3 rows sea green, 1 row salmon, 1 row lilac, 3 rows sea green, 1 row gold, 1 row sea green, 1 row light rose, 1 row salmon, 1 (2, 4) rows sea green. **1/1 ribbing: Row 1:** *K1, p1*. Rep * to * across. **Row 2 and all foll rows:** Work sts as established in previous row.

BACK

With smaller size knitting needles and sea green, cast on 60 (66, 72) sts and work 1½ in. (4 cm) in 1/1 ribbing. Cast off loosely. With afghan hook, pick up 80 (86, 92) sts across cast off sts of ribbing. Continue in brocade st, working first row in white. Work by foll chart, with 1 border st at each edge. Work from point A to C, 6 (7, 7) times, then work from point A to B, 1 (0, 1) time, 1 border st. Work until piece

measures 6¼ (7¼, 7¼) in. - 16.5 (18.5, 20.5) cm from beg and 11 (13, 15) brocade motifs are complete. On the foll row, ch 12 sts at each edge and continue across 104 (110, 116) sts in brocade st until piece measures 11 (12½, 12½) in. - 29 (32, 35) cm, = 22 (25, 28) brocade motifs. End with 2nd or 4th row of pat st. Work 1 row of dc in white, working 1 dc in each loop. Fasten off.

FRONT

Work same as back, working brocade st as foll: 1 border st, work from point B to C, 1 (0, 1) time, then work from point A to C, 6 (7, 7) times, 1 border st. Work until piece measures 10¼ (11½, 12¼) in. - 26.5 (29.5, 31.5) cm from beg and 20 (23, 26) brocade motifs have been worked. Mark centre 32 (34, 36) sts. Work to first marker, turn. At neck edge, sc across 3 sts, work to end of row. Turn, work to last 2 sts, leave unworked, turn. Continue in brocade st over the rem 31 (33, 35) sts until 22 (25, 28) motifs are complete, ending with 2nd or 4th row of brocade st. Work 1 row of dc as on back. Fasten off. Work 2nd shoulder to correspond.

FINISHING

Block pieces to indicated measurements. Sew shoulder seams. With double pointed needles and sea green, pick up and knit 96 (100, 104) sts around neck and work 4 rows in 1/1 ribbing. Cast off loosely. Sew side and sleeve seams. With sea green, work 1 row of dc around each sleeve end. Fasten off.

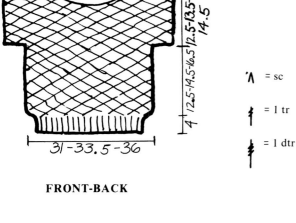

FRONT-BACK

17-17.5-18.5

12.5-13.5-14.5

4 12.5-14.5-16.5

31 - 33.5 - 36

$\wedge$ = sc

↑ = 1 tr

‡ = 1 dtr

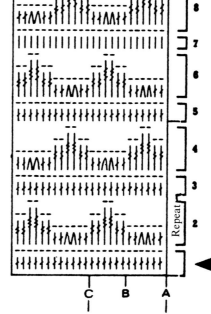

8

7

6

5

4

3

2

Repeat

C B A

Row 1 is on the right side of work row.

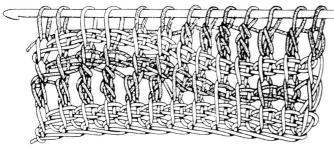

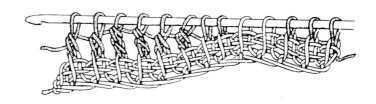

VERSATILE JACKET

WITH SHAWL COLLAR ESCORTS YOU IN STYLE. THIS PASTEL TWEED WILL TOP ALL YOUR SLACKS AND SKIRTS WITH A TOTALLY NEW LOOK.

★★

PASTEL TWEED JACKET

SIZE

Woman's Small (Medium, Large), bust 30-32 (33-35, 36-38) in. - 76-81.5 (84-89, 91.5-97) cm. Finished bust measurements: 44½ (46¾, 49) in. - 110 (116, 120) cm, length: 26¾ (27, 27½) in. - 68 (69, 70) cm, sleeve seam (with cuff): 17¾ in. (45 cm).

MATERIALS

10 (11, 12) skeins fingering weight yarn (approx. 143 yds (130 m) per 50 g skein) multicolour, 3 (4, 4) skeins sport weight mohair yarn (approx. 170 yds per 50 g skein) multicolour. Crochet hook U.S. size E/4 (U.K. size 9) (Metric size 3.5) or size needed to obtain tension. **To save time, take time to check tension!**

TENSION

8 squares and 19 rows = 4 in. (10 cm).

STITCHES

Chain (ch), single crochet (sc), double crochet (dc), half-treble crochet (htr).
Pattern stitch: Worked around a double strand of mohair. Work on a ch base. Lay the double strand of mohair over the chain base.
Row 1: Lay the double strand of mohair over the ch row and crochet around it. Work 1 dc in the 3rd ch from hook, *ch 2, skip 2 ch, 1 dc*, rep * to *, end with 1 dc in each of the last 2 ch.
Row 2: Lay the double strand of mohair over the last row, leaving a small loop at each edge. Ch 1 (border st), 1 dc, *ch 2, 1 dc*, rep * to *, end with 1 dc in the last dc and 1 dc in the turning ch (border st), Always rep the 2nd row. Be sure to check tension as you work. Beg each row with ch 1, 1 dc and end with 2 dc.

BACK

Ch 130 (136, 142) and work in pat st = 42 (44, 46) squares + 1 border st at each edge. Work until piece measures 16½ in. (42 cm). Sc over first 23 sts, work to last 23 sts, turn, leave last 23 sts unworked, work to end of row. Work 1 row straight. *Sc over first st, work to last st, turn, leaving last st unworked, turn and work to end of row. Work 1 row straight*. Work * to * 2 times total = 34 (36, 38) squares. Piece will measure 16¾ (17¾, 18¾) in. - 42.5 (45, 47.5) cm across. Work until armhole measures 9¼ (9¾, 10¼) in. - 24 (25, 26) cm. Mark the centre 8 squares. Work right shoulder as foll: sc over 3 (4, 5) squares, work to first marker, turn, work to end of row. Sc over first 4 squares, work to last square, turn, leaving last square unworked. Work to end of row. Sc over first 4 squares, work to last square, turn, leaving last square unworked. Work to end of row. Fasten off. For left shoulder, join yarn at 2nd marker and work to end of row. Sc over 3 (4, 5) squares, work to 2nd marker, turn. Sc over first square, work to end of row. Turn, sc over first 4 squares, work to end of row, turn. Sc over first square, work to end of row. Sc over first 4 squares, work to end of row, fasten off.

RIGHT FRONT

Ch 82 (85, 88). Work in pat st = 26 (27, 28) squares + 1 border st at each edge. Work until piece measures 15 in. (38 cm) from beg. At beg of right side of work rows, sc over 1 square 5 times as foll: work 6 squares, skip 1 square, (do not ch over), work next 2 dc. In the foll row, work these 2 dc tog. **At the same time**, after the 8th row from beg of neck dec, shape armhole as on back (work to end of row, leaving last 2 squares unworked, then at armhole edge of next 2 right side of work rows, leave 1 square unworked.) When armhole measures 9¼ (9¾, 10¼) in. - 24 (25, 26) cm, shape shoulder: sc over 3 (4, 5) squares, work to end of row, turn, and work to end of row. Turn, sc over first 4 squares, work to end of row, turn, work to end of row. Turn, sc over first 4 squares, work to end of row = 6 squares rem. Turn and work to end of row, ch 7, turn. Insert hook in the 3rd ch from hook and work 1 dc = 8 squares total. Work in pat st for 2¾ in. (7 cm). At beg of wrong side of work rows, sc over first 22 squares 4 times. Fasten off.

LEFT FRONT

Work same as right front, rev neck, armhole and shoulder shapings.

SLEEVES

Ch 76 (79, 82) and work in pat st = 24 (25, 26) squares + 1 border st at each edge. Work straight for 4 in. (10 cm). Then at each edge every 2¾ in. (7 cm), inc 1 square 5 times as foll: ch 1, 1 dc, ch 2, 1 dc in the foll dc, work to the last square; 1 dc, ch 2, 1 dc around the ch 2, 1 dc in the dc and 1 dc in the turning ch. Work these 34 (35, 36) squares until sleeve measures 19¾ in. (50 cm) from beg. Shape cap: *Sc over first 2 squares, work to last 2 squares, turn, leaving last 2 squares unworked, turn, sc over first square, work across to last square, turn, leaving last square unworked.* Rep * to * until you have 8 (9, 10) squares rem. Fasten off.

FINISHING

Block pieces to indicated measurements. Sew shoulder seams and sew collar seam. Sew collar to back neck. Work 1 row of htr around fronts and back neck edges, beg with ch 2 at lower edge of left front. Work 2 rows in pat st using 3 strands of mohair instead of 2 strands. Fasten off. Fold border in half to outside and sc in place. Set in sleeves. Sew side and sleeve seams. Fold lower 2 in. (5 cm) of sleeve to outside.

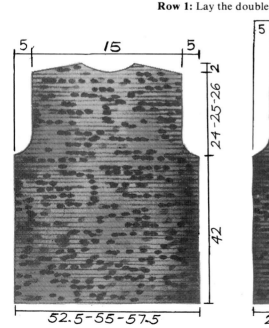

5 — 15 — 5
2
24-25-26
42
52.5-55-57.5

BACK

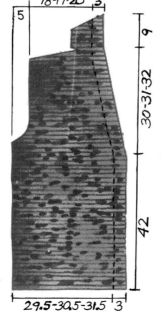

18-19-20 3
5
9
30-31-32
42
29.5-30.5-31.5 3

RIGHT FRONT

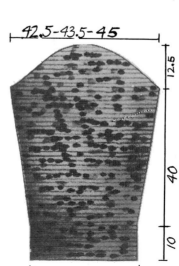

42.5-43.5-45
12.5
40
10
30-31-32.5

SLEEVE

ELEGANT PEWTER AND
ECRU COLLABORATE FOR THIS
CLASSIC ENSEMBLE. THE
CARDIGAN'S DIAGONAL LINES
FLATTER EVERY FIGURE.
COORDINATING PULLOVER IN
SILKY KID MOHAIR IS WORKED
FROM JACQUARD CHART.

MOHAIR CARDIGAN

SIZE

Woman's Small (Medium, Large, X Large), bust 30-32 (33-35, 36-38, 39-42) in. - 76-81.5 (84-89, 91.5-97, 99-107) cm. Finished bust measurements: 42½ (45½, 49, 52) in. - 108 (116, 124, 132) cm, length: 25½ in. (65 cm), sleeve seam 17 in. (43 cm).

MATERIALS

7 (7, 7, 8) skeins mohair blend bulky yarn (65% kid mohair, 29% mohair, 29% wool, 6% nylon - approx. 110 yds (100 m) per 50 g skein) colour light grey and 6 (6, 7, 7) skeins colour ecru. Crochet hook U.S. size F/5 (U.K. size 8) (Metric size 4) or size needed to obtain tension. Knitting needles U.S. size 7 (U.K. size 3) (Metric size 4.5). 7 grey buttons. **To save time, take time to check tension!**

TENSION

14 tr and 5½ rows = 4 in. (10 cm).

STITCHES

Chain (ch), single crochet (sc), double crochet (dc), treble crochet (tr).
Jacquard stitch: Centre the chart. When changing colours, work the last loop of the last st in 1 colour with the colour of the next st. Hold the unused yarn against the wrong side of work. When inserting hook, work around the unused yarn so that the new sts hold it against the work. Work the border sts in the same colour as the adjacent st in pat. Ch 3 at the beg of each row (= 1 border st).

1/1 ribbing: Row 1: *K1, p1*. Rep * to * across.
Row 2 and all foll rows: Work sts as established in previous row.

BACK

With crochet hook ch 77 (83, 89, 95). **Row 1 (size small and large):** Ch 3 with grey (= 1 border st), 1 tr with grey in the 5th ch from hook, *3 tr with ecru, 3 tr with grey*, work * to * 6 (7) times, 1 tr with ecru = centre st, **3 tr with grey, 3 tr with ecru**, work ** to ** 6 (7) times, 2 tr with grey.
Row 1 (size medium and X large): Ch 3 with ecru (= 1 border st), 1 tr with ecru in the 5th ch from hook, 3 tr with grey, *3 tr with ecru, 3 tr with grey*, work * to * 6 (7) times, 1 tr with ecru (= centre st), **3 tr with grey, 3 tr with ecru**, work ** to ** 6 (7) times, 3 tr with grey, 2 tr with ecru. **For all sizes:** Work 75 (81, 87, 93) tr + 1 border st at each edge in jacquard tr by centring chart. Work 33 rows. Fasten off.

LEFT FRONT

Ch 38 (41, 44, 47) + ch 3 in grey. **Row 1:** Work same as the first 38 (41, 44, 47) tr as on back (with 1 border st at each edge). The diagonals will go to the right. Work 30 rows, then shape neck. Work to last 9 (10, 11, 12) sts, turn — leave last 9 (10, 11, 12) sts unworked. Work the first 2 sts of foll row tog as foll: in next st, draw through loop, yo, draw through all loops on hook. Work to end of row. On foll row, work to last 2 sts and work 2 tog. Fasten off.

RIGHT FRONT

Work same as left front, rev neck shapings and working last 38 (41, 44, 47) tr as on back so that stripes shift toward left.

SLEEVES

Ch 47 (47, 49, 49) with grey. **Row 1:** Ch 3 with ecru (= 1 border st), 1 tr in the 5th ch from hook, then work 0 (0, 1, 1) tr with ecru, 3 tr in grey, *3 tr with ecru, 3 tr with grey*, work * to * 3 times, 1 tr in ecru (= centre st), **3 tr with grey, 3 tr with ecru**, work ** to ** 3 times, 3 tr with grey, 2 (2, 3, 3) tr with ecru = 45 (45, 47, 47) tr + 1 border st at each edge.
Continue jacquard tr by centring chart. Inc 1 tr at each edge of every 2nd row once, then inc 1 tr at each edge of 3rd row once = 4 incs every 3rd row. (For each inc, work 2 tr in each edge st.) Work until you have 69 (69, 71, 71) tr + 1 border st at each edge. Work 21 rows, piece will measure 15 in. (38 cm) from beg. Fasten off.

FINISHING

Block pieces to indicated measurements. With knitting needles and grey, pick up and knit 34 (34, 36, 36) sts from lower edge of each sleeve and work 2 in. (5 cm) in 1/1 ribbing. Cast off loosely. Sew shoulder seams. Sew sleeves to side seams, matching centre of sleeve with shoulder seams. Sew side and sleeve seams. Along lower edge with knitting needles and grey, pick up and knit 1 st in every st. Work 2 in. (5 cm) in 1/1 ribbing. Cast off. With knitting needles and grey, pick up and knit 1 st from every st and 2 sts from every row along neck and work 1 in. (2.5 cm) in 1/1 ribbing. Cast off loosely. With knitting needles and grey, pick up and knit 3 sts from every row along left front edge inside border st, and work 1 in. (2.5 cm) of 1/1 ribbing. Cast off loosely. Work the same band along right front, marking positions for 7 buttonholes. When band measures 1/3 in. (1 cm), make buttonholes. For each buttonhole, cast off 2 sts. On foll row, cast on 2 sts over cast off sts. Reinforce buttonholes. Sew on buttons.

center of row, pullover

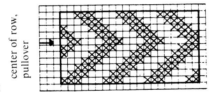

KEY TO CHART

☐ 1 tr in ecru, pullover
1 tr in gray, cardigan

☒ 1 tr in gray, pullover
1 tr in ecru, cardigan

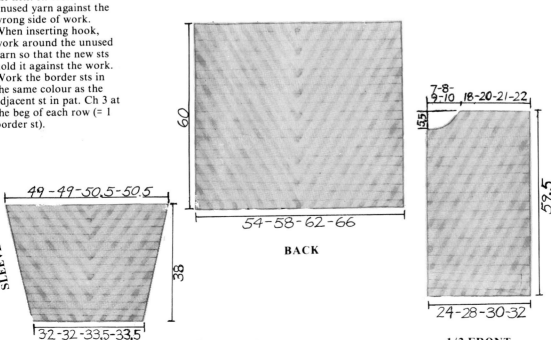

SLEEVE

49 - 49 - 50.5 - 50.5

38

32 - 32 - 33.5 - 33.5

60

54 - 58 - 62 - 66

BACK

7-8-9-10   18-20-21-22

5.5

59.5

24 - 28 - 30 - 32

1/2 FRONT

MOHAIR DIAGONAL PULLOVER

SIZE

Woman's Small (Medium, Large, X Large), bust 30-32 (33-35, 36-38, 39-42) in. - 76-81.5 (84-89, 91.5-97, 99-107) cm. Finished bust measurements: 42½ (45½, 49, 52) in. - 104 (112, 120, 128) cm, length: 21½ in. (55 cm), sleeve seam 16½ in. (42 cm).

MATERIALS

6 (6, 6, 7) skeins mohair blend bulky yarn - approx. 110 yds (100 m) per 50 g skein) colour light grey and 5 (5, 6, 6) skeins colour ecru. Crochet hook U.S. size F/5 (U.K. size 8) (Metric size 4) or size needed to obtain tension. Knitting needles U.S. size 7 (U.K. size 7) (Metric size 4.5). **To save time, take time to check tension!**

TENSION

14 tr and 5½ rows = 4 in. (10 cm).

STITCHES

Chain (ch), single crochet (sc), double crochet (dc), treble crochet (htr).
Jacquard stitch: Centre the chart. When changing colours, work the last loop of the last st of 1 colour with the colour of the next st. Hold the unused yarn against the wrong side of work. When inserting hook, work around the unused yarn so that the new sts hold it against the work. Work the border sts in the same colour as the adjacent st in pat. Ch 3 at the beg of each row (= 1 border st).
1/1 ribbing: Row 1: *K1, p1*. Rep * to * across.
Row 2 and all foll rows: Work sts as established in previous row.

BACK

Worked in 1 piece beg at lower edge of sleeve. With crochet hook and grey, ch 53. **Row 1:** Ch 3 with ecru (= 1 border st), 1 tr with ecru in the 5th ch from hook, *3 tr with grey, 3 tr with ecru*, work * to * 4 times total, 1 tr with grey (= centre st), **3 tr with ecru, 3 tr with grey**, work ** to ** 4 times total, 2 tr with ecru. You now have 51 tr with 1 border st at each edge. Continue by foll chart. (Beg with the 2nd row, at each edge of every row, inc 1 st 19 times = 20 rows = 14½ in. (37 cm) from beg.) For each inc, work 2 tr in each edge st. You now have 89 tr + 1 border st at each edge. Work separately, make 2 chains in grey by chaining 25 sts. Join to each edge of sleeve. Work 1 border st, then 24 tr over ch, 91 tr over sleeve, 24 tr over 2nd ch, 1 border st = 139 tr + 1 border st at each edge. Work 6 (7, 8, 9) rows of chart.
Shape Neck: Work 70 tr, turn. Work 7 rows, dec at neck edge of each row as foll: at end of row, work to last st, turn, leaving last st unworked, sc across the first st of the next row. Work 1 row without dec = centre row of pullover which is the 35th (36th, 37th, 38th) row from beg. Piece will measure 25 (25½, 26, 26¾) in. - 63 (65, 67, 69) cm from beg.

Continue in jacquard pat by rev order of diagonals, that is, shift the right diagonals to the left by 1 st every row and shift the left diagonals to the right by 1 st every row. (See photo and small chart.)
At the same time, inc 1 st at neck edge of next 7 rows by working 2 sts in edge st of every row. Work back the same as front, rev shapings, then work 6 (7, 8, 9) rows straight across all sts. Work centre 91 sts for sleeve (89 tr + 1 border st at each edge), (leave 25 sts at each edge unworked), dec 1 st at each edge of every row until you have 51 sts with border st at each edge. Piece will measure 50 (51, 52, 53½) in. - 126 (130, 134, 138) cm from beg. Fasten off.

FINISHING

Block piece to indicated measurements. Along the lower edge of each sleeve, work 32 (34 36, 38) dc with grey. Fasten off. With knitting needles, pick up and knit 1 st from every dc and work 2 in. (5 cm) in 1/1 ribbing. Cast off. With knitting needles and grey, around lower edge of back and front, pick up and knit 1 st from the edge tr next to the border sts of every row and work 2 in. (5 cm) in 1/1 ribbing. Cast off loosely. With knitting needles, grey, pick up and knit 1 st from every row (inside the border st) along the back neck edge and 3 sts along each shoulder and work 3/4 in. (2 cm) in 1/1 ribbing. Mark the centre 3 sts. On every row, work the centre 3 sts as foll: sc 2 tog knitwise, k1, psso. Cast off. Work same border on front neck. Lap front band over back and sew in place. Sew side and sleeve seams.

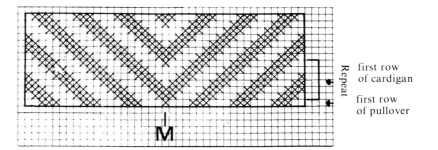

first row of cardigan

first row of pullover

M

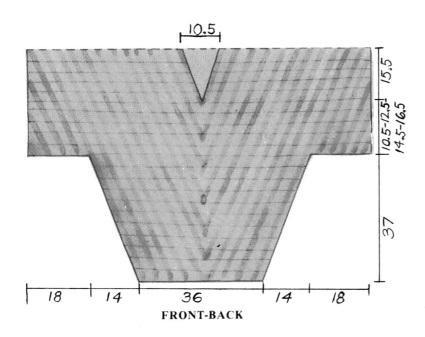

10.5

15.5

10.5-12.5

14.5-16.5

37

18   14   36   14   18

FRONT-BACK

PRIMARY APPEAL OF RED, YELLOW AND BLUE ENSURE THIS SWEATER'S POPULARITY FOR SCHOOL OR WEEKENDS. OVERSIZE LOOK IS JUST RIGHT FOR YOUNG JUNIORS.

★★

CHILD'S GEOMETRIC PULLOVER

SIZE

Child's size 8 (10, 12) years, chest 27 (28½, 30) in. - 69 (72.5, 76) cm. Finished chest measurements: 31½ (34, 36½) in. - 80 (86, 93) cm, length: 18 (19¾, 21¼) in. - 46 (50, 54) cm, sleeve seam: 12¾ (14, 15) in. -32 (35, 38) cm.

MATERIALS

8 (9, 10) skeins worsted weight yarn (approx. 80 yds (73 m) per 50 g skein) colour gold, 5 skeins colour black, 3 (4, 4) skeins colour blue and 1 skein colour red. Crochet hook U.S. size F/5 (U.K. size 8) (Metric size 4) or size needed to obtain tension. Knitting needles U.S. size 6 (U.K. size 8) (Metric size 4). **To save time, take time to check tension!**

TENSION

15 htr and 10 rows in jacquard pat = 4 in. (10 cm).

STITCHES

Chain (ch), half treble crochet (htr). Jacquard htr: Foll the chart in htr. When changing colours, work the last loop of the last st of one colour with the colour of the next st. Hold the unused yarn against the wrong side of work. When inserting hook, work around the unused yarn so that the new sts hold it against the work. Work the border sts in the same colour as the adjacent st in pat. Beg each row with ch 2, which counts as the first htr.

2/2 ribbing: Row 1: *K2, p2*. Rep * to * across. **Row 2 and all foll rows:** Work sts as established in previous row.

BACK

With knitting needles and black, cast on 70 (74, 78) sts and work in 2/2 ribbing as foll: 1 row black, 2 rows red, 2 rows black, 2 rows red, 2 rows black, 2 rows red, 2 rows black. Cast off. With crochet hook and black, work 62 (66, 72) htr across the cast off row of ribbing. Continue by foll chart 1, beg at point A (B, C). Work until piece measures 16½ (18¼, 19¾) in. - 42 (46, 50) cm from beg. Fasten off. With knitting needles and black, pick up and knit 78 (86, 94) sts along last row of crochet. Then work in 2/2 ribbing as foll: 3 rows black, 2 rows red, 2 rows black, 2 rows red and 2 rows in black. Cast off in black.

FRONT

Work same as back.

SLEEVES

With knitting needles and black, cast on 30 (34, 38) sts and work ribbing same as back. Cast off. With crochet hook, work 65 (71, 79) htr across cast off row of ribbing and work by centring chart 2 (centre is at point G). Inc 1 st at each edge of every 2nd row 12 (14, 15) times. (For each inc, work 2 htr in each edge st.) Work inc in jacquard htr. You now have 59 (65, 71) htr. Work until piece measures 12¾ (14, 15) in. - 32 (35, 38) cm from beg. Fasten off.

FINISHING

Block pieces to indicated measurements. Sew shoulder seams, leaving centre 8 (8¼, 8¾) in. - 20 (21, 22.5) cm open for neck. Sew sleeves to armholes, matching centre of sleeve with shoulder seams. Sew side and sleeve seams.

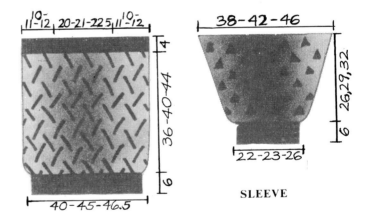

FRONT-BACK

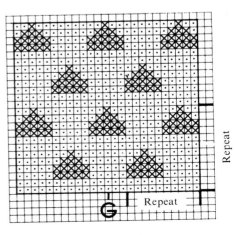

SLEEVE

KEY TO CHART
☐ = gold
⊠ = black
⊡ = blue

F E D   Repeat   A B C
G

Chart 1

G   Repeat

Chart 2

68

STACCATO SLASHES
AND DOTS PUNCTUATE THIS
PULLOVER. EASY FIT MEANS IT'S
SURE TO BE A HIT WITH KIDS.

CHILD'S RED PULLOVER

SIZE

Child's size 8 (10, 12) years, chest 27 (28½, 30) in. - 69 (72.5, 76) cm. Finished chest measurements: 32½ (35, 37½) in. - 83 (89, 96) cm, length: 18¾ (20¼, 21¾) in. - 47 (51, 55) cm, sleeve seam: 13½ (14¾, 15¾) in. - 34 (37, 40) cm.

MATERIALS

8 (9, 10) skeins worsted weight yarn (approx. 80 yds (73 m) per 50 g skein) colour red, 4 (4, 5) skeins colour black. Crochet hook U.S. size F/5 (U.K. size 8) (Metric size 4) or size needed to obtain tension. Knitting needles U.S. size 4 (U.K. size 8) (Metric size 4). **To save time, take time to check tension!**

TENSION

15 htr and 10 rows in jacquard htr = 4 in. (10 cm).

STITCHES

Chain (ch), half treble crochet (htr).
Jacquard htr: Foll the chart in htr. When changing colours, work the last loop of the last st of 1 colour with the colour of the next st. Hold the unused yarn against the wrong side of work. When inserting hook, work around the unused yarn so that the new sts hold it against the work. Work the border sts in the same colour as the adjacent st in pat. Beg each row with ch 2, which counts as the first htr.
2/2 ribbing: Row 1: *K2, p2*. Rep * to * across.
Row 2 and all foll rows: Work sts as established in previous row.

BACK

With knitting needles and black, cast on 74 (78, 82) sts and work in 2/2 ribbing as foll: 1 row black, 2 rows red, 2 rows black, 2 rows red, 2 rows black, 2 rows red, 2 rows black. Cast off. With crochet hook and black, work 64 (68, 74) htr across the cast off row of ribbing. Continue by foll chart 1. Work until piece measures 17½ (19, 20½) in. - 44 (48, 52) cm from beg. Fasten off with knitting needles and black, pick up and knit 82 (90, 98) sts along last row of crochet. Then work in 2/2 ribbing as foll: 2 rows black, 2 rows red, 2 rows black and 2 rows red. Cast off in black.

FRONT

Work same as back.

SLEEVES

With knitting needles and black, cast on 34 (38, 42) sts and work ribbing same as back. Cast off. With crochet hook, work 38 (40, 44) htr across cast off row of ribbing. Continue work by foll chart 2. Inc 1 st at each edge of every 2nd row 12 (14, 15) times. (For each inc, work 2 htr in each edge st.) Work inc in jacquard htr. You now have 62 (68, 74) sts. Work until piece measures 13½ (14¾, 15¾) in. - 34 (38, 42) cm from beg. Fasten off.

FINISHING

Block pieces to indicated measurements. Sew shoulder seams, leaving centre 8½ (8¾, 9¼) in. - 21 (22.5, 24) cm open for neck. Sew sleeves to armholes, matching center of sleeve with shoulder seams. Sew side and sleeve seams.

Here is the perfect opportunity to use up "leftover" yarn. Make the back, front, sleeves, even ribbing using contrasting colours of yarn, but always work the motifs and stripes in the same colour to unify the entire design.

KEY TO CHART
☐ = red
☒ = black

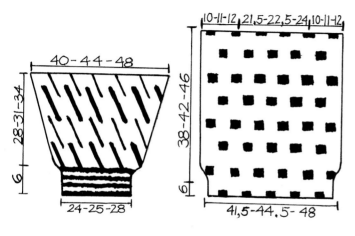

SLEEVE   FRONT-BACK

Repeat

Chart 1

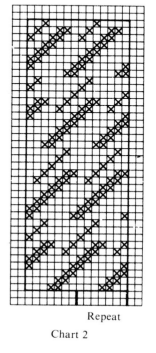

Repeat

Chart 2

VIVID Autumn images form when burnished copper, rust and gold mohair are blended. The cardigan features spacious pockets and a designer flair.

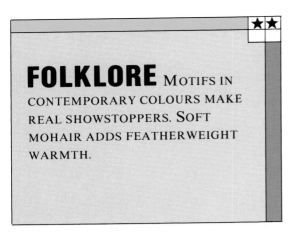

FOLKLORE MOTIFS IN CONTEMPORARY COLOURS MAKE REAL SHOWSTOPPERS. SOFT MOHAIR ADDS FEATHERWEIGHT WARMTH.

★ ★

FOLKLORE CARDIGAN

SIZE

Woman's Small (Medium, Large), bust 30-32 (33-35, 36-38) in. - 76-81.5 (84-89, 91.5-97) cm. Finished bust measurements: 42½ (46¼, 49½) in. - 108 (117, 126) cm, length: 28 in. (71 cm), sleeve seam: 16½ in. (42 cm).

MATERIALS

4 (5, 5) skeins sport weight kid mohair (approx. 110 yds (100 m) per 50 g skein) each colour grey and black and 1 skein each colour light green, green, light lilac, pale yellow, dark pink, light grey, dark lilac and salmon.
Crochet hook U.S. size F/5 (U.K. size 8) (Metric size 4) or size needed to obtain tension. Knitting needles U.S. size 4 (U.K. size 9) (Metric size 3.5). 9 buttons. Stitch holder. **To save time, take time to check tension!**

TENSION

15 htr and 10½ rows = 4 in. (10 cm).

STITCHES

**Chain (ch),
single crochet (sc),
half treble crochet (htr).
Jacquard pattern st:**
Work in htr by foll chart. When changing colours, work the last loop of the last st with the colour of the next st. Use small bobbins of yarn for each section of colour and beg each row with ch 2 = first htr.
1/1 ribbing: Row 1: *K1, p1*. Rep * to * across.
Row 2 and all foll rows: Work sts as established in previous row.

BODY

Worked in 1 piece to armholes. With knitting needles and black, cast on 169 (183, 197) sts and work 2 in. (5 cm) in 1/1 ribbing, beg and end on right side of work with k1. Make 1 buttonhole on right edge by casting off the 3rd and 4th sts from right edge. On foll row, cast on 2 sts over cast off sts. Work until border measures 2½ in. (6 cm), then place 5 sts at each edge on holder. Cast off centre 159 (173, 187) sts.
Foundation row: With crochet hook and black, work 1 htr in each cast off st, inc 1 st at each edge = 161 (175, 189) htr. Work in jacquard st by foll chart. Work jacquard chart from point C (B, A) to point D (E, F). Work for 44 (43, 42) rows = point I (H, G). Piece will measure 19 (18½, 18) in. - 48 (47, 46) cm from beg. Divide work for armholes. Work right front over 40 (44, 47) sts, inc 1 st at left edge (leave rem sts unworked). Work these sts to point J on chart. The armhole now measures 7 (7½, 8) in. -18 (19, 20) cm. Shape neck. At right edge, with right side facing, sc over 4 sts, work to end of row, turn.

Work to last 2 sts, turn, leave last 2 sts unworked. Sc over first st, work to end of row, turn. Work to last st, turn, leave last st unworked. Sc across first st and work to last row of chart. Fasten off.
Work the 40 (44, 47) sts of left front, rev shapings. Fasten off.
Work over the centre 81 (87, 95) sts, inc 1 st at each edge. Work by foll chart. When chart is complete, fasten off.

SLEEVES

With knitting needles and black, cast on 45 (47, 49) sts and work 1½ in. (4 cm) in 1/1 ribbing. Cast off. With crochet hook and black, work 45 (47, 49) htr across the cast off sts of ribbing. Beg jacquard htr st by foll chart with point C (B, A), end at point D (E, F). At each edge every 1¼ in. (3 cm), inc 1 st 12 times total (to inc, work 2 sts in each edge st). Work inc sts in jacquard htr. You now have 69 (71, 73) sts. When last row of chart is complete, fasten off. Piece will measure 16½ in. (42 cm) from beg. Work the 2nd sleeve by rev the order of the chart, beg at left edge of point D (E, F) and ending at point C (B, A).

FINISHING

Block pieces to indicated measurements. Front bands: With knitting needles and black, pick up 5 sts from left front and inc 1 st at body edge for border st. Work in 1/1 ribbing until band reaches neck. Dec the border st, then place rem sts on holder. Work the right band the same, making buttonholes when piece measures 5½, 9, 12½, 16, 19¾ and 23¼ in. (14, 23, 32, 41, 50 and 59 cm) from beg. For each buttonhole, cast off 2 sts. On foll row, cast on 2 sts. Sew bands to fronts. Sew shoulder seams. With knitting needles and black, pick up and knit 75 sts around neck and work in 1/1 ribbing, beg and end with k1 on right side of work row. Work 1/3 in. (1 cm), then make 1 buttonhole above previous ones. When band measures 1¼ in. (3 cm), cast off all sts. Reinforce buttonholes and sew sleeves to armholes, matching centre and sleeve with shoulder seam. Sew side and sleeve seam. Sew on buttons. Make small bobbles in each colour to sew to flower motifs as you desire.

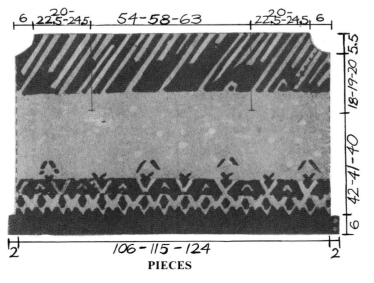

6 | 20-22.5-24.5 | 54-58-63 | 20-22.5-24.5 | 6

5.5
18-19-20
42-41-40
6

2 | 106-115-124 | 2

PIECES

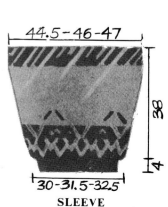

44.5-46-47

38

4

30-31.5-32.5

SLEEVE

AUTUMN JACQUARD CARDIGAN

SIZE

Woman's Medium, bust 33-35 in. (84-89 cm). Finished bust measurements: 45 in. (114 cm), length: 31 in. (79 cm), sleeve seam: 17¾ in. (45 cm).

MATERIALS

7 skeins mohair yarn (approx. 130 yds (119 m) per 50 g skein) colour orange, 2 skeins each colour ecru and blue-green, and 1 skein each colour pink, light gold, green, rust and brown. Crochet hook U.S. size F/5 (U.K. size 8) (Metric size 4) or size needed to obtain tension. Knitting needles U.S. size 4 (U.K. size 9) (Metric size 3.5). 8 buttons. Stitch holder. **To save time, take time to check tension!**

TENSION

14½ htr and 10 rows in jacquard htr = 4 in. (10 cm).

STITCHES

**Chain (ch),
single crochet (sc),
half treble crochet (htr).
Jacquard htr:** Work by foll chart in htr. The border sts are not shown on the chart. When changing colours, work the last loop of the last st in 1 colour with the colour of the next st. Hold the unused yarn against the wrong side of work. When inserting hook, work around the unused yarn so that the new sts hold it against the work. Work the border sts in the same colour as the adjacent st in pat. Beg each row with ch 2 which counts as the first htr. Use a separate ball of yarn for each section of colour.

1/1 ribbing: Row 1: *K1, p1*. Rep * to * across.
Row 2 and all foll rows: Work sts as established in previous row.

POCKET LININGS

With crochet hook and orange, ch 19 + ch 2 to turn. **Foundation Row:** 1 htr in the 4th ch from hook, htr across. Work in htr = 19 htr until piece measures 6¼ in. (16 cm). Fasten off. Make 2.

BODY

Worked in 1 piece beg at lower edge. With knitting needles and orange, cast on 171 sts and work 3/4 in. (2 cm) in 1/1 ribbing. At right edge, work 2 sts, cast off 2 sts, then work to end of row in 1/1 ribbing. On foll row, cast on 2 sts over cast off sts and continue in 1/1 ribbing until piece measures 2½ in. (6 cm). Place 5 sts at each edge on stitch holders. Cast off center 161 sts. Crochet across these sts in htr foll jacquard chart, inc 1 st at each edge for border sts. (Work 2 sts in each edge st = 163 sts). Work for 8½ in. (22 cm) from beg, then work as foll: work first 14 sts, skip 19 sts of body and work 19 htr of 1 pocket lining, work to last 33 sts, skip 19 htr of body and work 19 sts of 2nd pocket lining, work last 14 sts. Work these sts until piece measures 21¼ in. (54 cm) from beg, that is to point C on chart. Now work the first 37 sts, leaving rem sts unworked. Inc 1 st at left edge (work 2 sts in edge st) (= 1 border st). Work these 38 dc, shaping raglans as foll: with right side facing, work to last 2 sts, turn, leave last 2 sts unworked. Sc over first 2 sts, work to end of row, turn. Work to last st of row, leaving last st unworked, turn. Sc over first st and work to end of row. You are now at point D on chart. Fasten off. Work last 37 sts at left edge, inc 1 st at right edge = 38 sts, by rev shapings. Fasten off. 9 sts from the end of the right front, work 71 sts in htr (ending 9 sts from the beg of the left front). Inc 1 st at each edge for border sts. Work these 73 sts in htr foll the chart, working raglan shapings as foll: sc over first 2 sts of row, work to last 2 sts of row, turn, leave last 2 sts unworked. Sc over first 2 sts of row, work to last 2 sts of row, turn. Sc over first st, work to last st on row, turn, leaving last st unworked. Sc over first st, work to last st on row, turn, leaving last st unworked. You are now at point D on chart. Fasten off.

RIGHT SLEEVE

With knitting needles and orange, cast on 40 sts and work 2 in. (5 cm) in 1/1 ribbing. Cast off. With crochet hook work in htr by foll jacquard chart for right sleeve, across the cast off sts of ribbing, inc 5 sts across first row = 43 htr + 1 border st at each edge. *At each edge of every 3rd row, work 2 sts in each edge st, then work 2 sts in each edge st of every 4th row.* = 8 incs every 7 rows. Work inc sts in jacquard pat. Work * to * until you have 65 sts. Continue until sleeve measures 17¾ in. (45 cm) from beg which is point C on chart. Then shape raglan: sc over the first 4 sts, work to last 4 sts, leaving last 4 sts unworked, turn. *Sc over first 2 sts, work to last 2 sts, leave last 2 sts unworked, turn*, work *

to * 3 times total. Sc over first st, work to last st, turn, leaving last st unworked. Leave rem sts unworked (point D on chart). Fasten off.

LEFT SLEEVE

Work same as right sleeve, but rev jacquard chart by beg at point A and working to point B.

YOKE

Work in htr (foll chart from point D) over the sts of the right front, right sleeve, back, left sleeve and left front as foll: *work to 3 sts before raglan edge, 2 htr tog: (yo, inserting hook in first htr, yo and draw up loop, insert hook in 2nd htr and draw through loop, yo and draw through loops on hook), 2 htr, 2 htr tog*, rep * to * 4 times total = 8 dec. Rep these dec every row 18 times. On the last 2 dec rows, eliminate the 2 htr between the dec. **At the same time,** on the same row as the 13th dec row, beg neck shapings. At beg of row, sc over the first 6 sts, then work to last 6 sts, turn, leaving last 6 sts unworked. Sc over first 2 sts, work to last 2 sts, leave last 2 sts unworked, turn. *Sc 1 , work to last st, turn, leaving last st unworked.* Work * to * twice total. Fasten off.

FINISHING

Block pieces to indicated measurements. Sew the armhole seams. With knitting needles and orange, pick up and knit 21 sts along top of each pocket and work 1 in. (2.5 cm) of 1/1 ribbing. Cast off in ribbing. Sew pocket lining and bands in place. Front bands: with knitting needles, pick up and knit 5 sts from left front holder and inc 1 st at inner edge and work in 1/1 ribbing until piece measures to neck. Dec 1 st at inner edge and place 5 sts on holder. Work right band same as left band, making 6 buttonholes as the first, placed 5, 9, 13, 17,21, 25 in. (13, 23, 33, 43, 53, 63 cm) apart. Sew bands to fronts. With knitting needles and orange, pick up and knit 75 sts around neck and work 1/3 in. (1 cm) of 1/1 ribbing, then work 3/4 in. (2 cm) more in 1/1 ribbing, forming buttonhole above previous ones. Cast off loosely. Reinforce buttonholes. Sew on buttons.

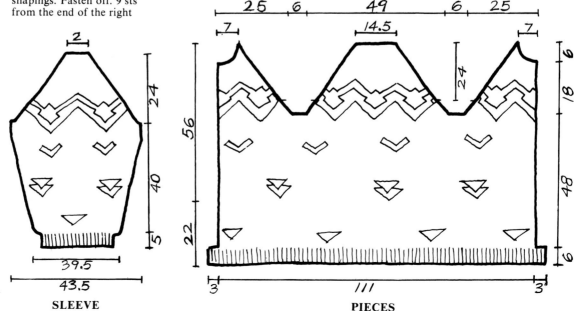

SLEEVE

PIECES

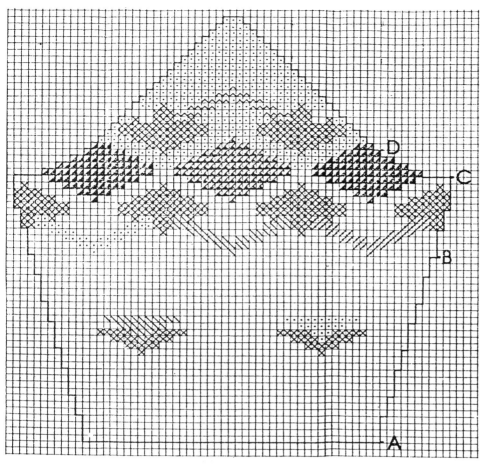

SLEEVE (RIGHT) AUTUMN JACQUARD CARDIGAN

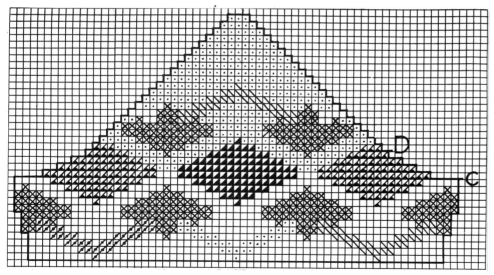

SLEEVE (LEFT) AUTUMN JACQUARD CARDIGAN

KEY TO CHART

☐ = orange
⊡ = ecru
⊠ = blue-green
⬂ = green
◩ = pink
◪ = brown
◤ = rust
⬔ = light gold

74

KEY TO CHART

⊞ = light green
ⓘ = salmon
☒ = grey
◪ = black
◩ = green
◪ = light lilac
⊡ = pale yellow
◉ = dark pink
⊟ = light grey
◙ = dark lilac

black

gray

black

CBA

SLEEVE
FOLKLORE CARDIGAN

KEY TO CHART

- ☐ = orange
- ⊡ = ecru
- ⊠ = blue-green
- ⧄ = green
- ◹ = pink
- ◪ = brown
- ◩ = rust
- ◪ = light gold

KEY TO CHART

- ⊞ = light green
- ⊞ = salmon
- ⊠ = grey
- ◼ = black
- ⌐ = green
- ◪ = pale lilac
- ⊡ = light yellow
- ⊙ = dark pink
- ⊟ = light grey
- ⊡ = dark lilac

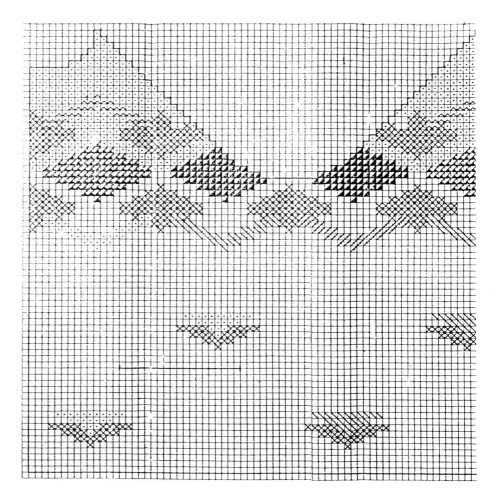

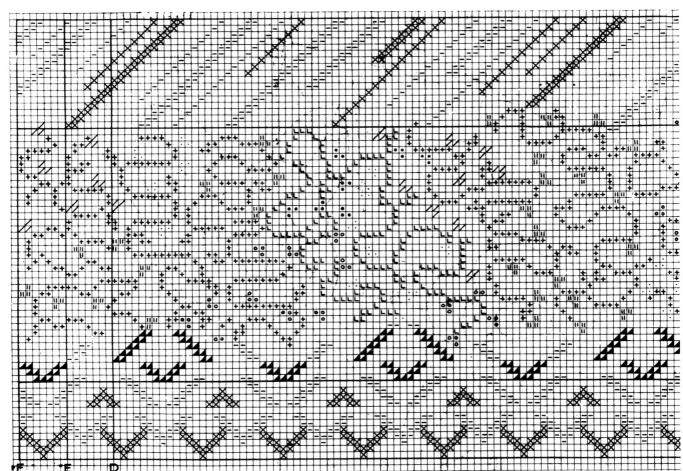

76

BACK AND FRONT (FOLKLORE CARDIGAN)

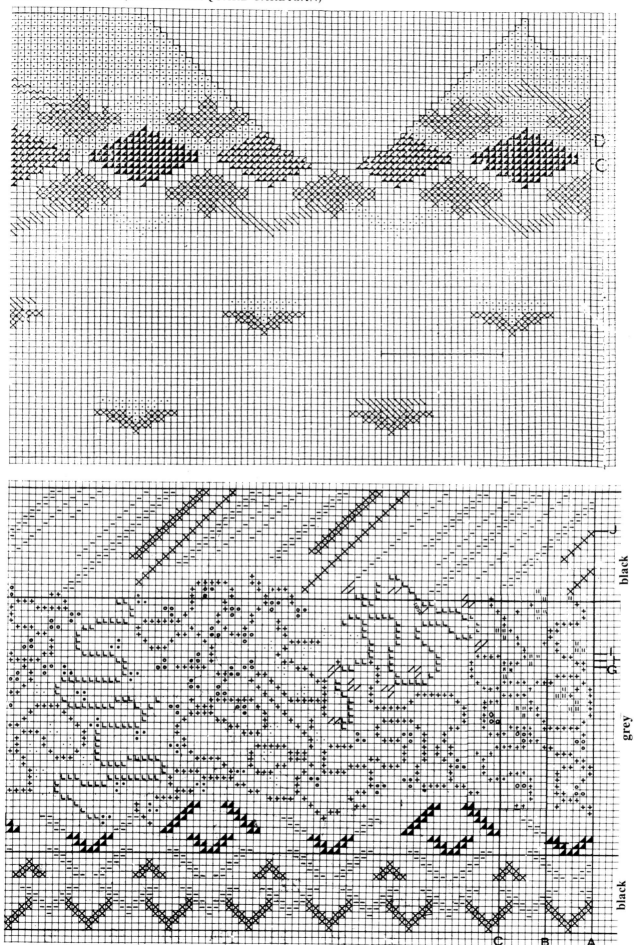

COVETED HANDWOVEN

LOOK IS EASY ONCE YOU MASTER
THIS CROCHET TECHNIQUE USING
TWO STRANDS OF YARN. ALPACA
INTERACTS WITH BULKY WOOL ON
OUR SHAWL COLLAR PULLOVER.

PULLOVER

For the woven look, work
the thin strand around a
thick strand. During the
work, on every row, lay
the thick strands along
the top of the underlying
row and crochet by
inserting hook under the
thick strand. Be sure to
have the turning of the
thick yarn showing on the
wrong side of work.
Check your tension as you
work.

SIZE

Woman's Small
(Medium, Large), bust
30-32 (33-35, 36-38) in. -
76-81.5 (84-89, 91.5-97)
cm. Finished bust
measurements: 41 (44½,
48) in. - 104 (113, 122)
cm, length: 25½ in. (65
cm), sleeve seam 17¼ in.
(44 cm).

MATERIALS

5 (6, 6) skeins fingering
weight alpaca yarn (approx.
206 yds (188 m) per 50 g
skein) colour ecru and 8 (9,
10) skeins bulky yarn
(approx. 110 yds (100 m)
per 50 g skein) colour ecru.
Crochet hook U.S. size B/1
(U.K. size 12) (Metric size
2.5) or size needed to obtain
tension. Circular or double
pointed knitting needles
U.S. size 9 (U.K. size 5)
(Metric size 5.5). **To save
time, take time to check
tension!**

TENSION

9 squares (1 dc + ch 3)
and 11 rows = 4 in.
(10 cm).

STITCHES

**Chain (ch),
single crochet (sc),
double crochet (dc).
1/1 ribbing: Row 1:** *K1,
p1*. Rep * to * across.
Row 2 and all foll rows:
Work sts as established in
previous row.

BACK

With crochet hook and
alpaca, ch 192 (208, 224)
and work in woven
crochet st as foll: lay 2
strands of bulky yarn on
the ch row and crochet
around them with alpaca.
Row 1: 1 dc in the 3rd ch
from hook, *ch 3, skip 3,
1 dc in the foll ch*, rep *
to *, end with 1 dc in the
last ch = 47 (51, 55)
squares and 1 border st at
each edge. **Row 2:** Ch 2
(border st), 1 dc in the
foll dc, *ch 3, 1 dc in the
ch-3 sp,* rep * to *, end
with ch 1, 1 dc in the foll
dc, 1 dc in the turning of
the thick yarn (border st).

Row 3: Ch 2 (border st),
1 dc in the foll dc, ch 3,
1 sc in the ch-3 sp, ch 3,
rep * to *, end with 1 dc
in the foll dc, 1 dc in the
turning of the thick yarn
(border st). Always rep
rows 2 and 3. Work until
piece measures 23½ in.
(60 cm) from beg, then
fasten off.

FRONT

Work same as back until
piece measures 18¾ (18½,
18) in. - 48 (47, 46) cm,
then mark the centre 15
(17, 19) squares. Work
right side, inc 1 st at neck
edge once for 4¾ (5, 5½)
in. - 12 (13, 14) cm from
beg, then fasten off. (To
inc, work 2 sts in edge st.)
Work left side the same,
inc 1 st at neck edge.
Fasten off.

SLEEVES

With alpaca, ch 96 (104,
112) then work in pat st =
23 (25, 27) squares + 1
border st at each edge of
first row. At beg of 2nd
and 3rd rows, inc 1 st 7
times. At beg of 4th and
5th row inc 1 st 6 times.
Work inc as foll: at beg of
2nd row, ch 5, 1 dc in the
3rd ch from hook, ch 1,
skip 1 ch, 1 dc in the foll
ch, ch 3, 1 dc around the
foll ch-sp and continue
across as on row 3 of pat.
Inc at the beg of 3rd row:
ch 5, 1 dc in the 3rd ch
from the hook, ch 3, skip
1 dc, 1 dc, ch 3, 1 dc
around the ch-sp,
continue across as on row
3 of pat. Work inc sts =
49 (51, 53) squares + 1
border st at each edge
until piece measures 15¾
in. (40 cm) from beg.
Fasten off.

FINISHING

Block pieces to indicated
measurements. Sew
shoulder seams. With
double pointed needles
and bulky yarn, along
back and side of front
neck edges, pick up and
knit 92 (96, 100) sts and
work 7 in. (18 cm) in 1/1
ribbing, working back
and forth. Cast off
loosely. Lap right collar
over left and sew in place.
With knitting needles and
bulky yarn, pick up and
knit 112 (114, 116) sts
along back edge and
work 2 in. (5 cm) in 1/1
ribbing. Cast off loosely.
Work same band along
front edge. With knitting
needles and bulky yarn,
pick up and knit 28 (30,
32) sts along each sleeve
edge and work 1½ in. (4
cm) in 1/1 ribbing. Cast
off loosely. Sew sleeves to
side seams, matching
centre of sleeve with
shoulder seam. Sew side
and sleeve seams.

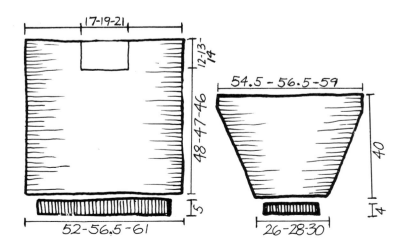

FRONT-BACK **SLEEVE**

COOL OFF IN THIS

DELICIOUS SUMMER COOLER
MADE FROM BUTTERY-SOFT
COTTON. BASKETWEAVE STITCH
LENDS AN AIR OF DISTINCTION.

PULLOVER

SIZE

Woman's Medium
(Large, X Large), bust
33-35 (36-38, 39-42) in. -
84-89 (91.5-97, 99-107)
cm. Finished bust
measurements: 41½ (44½,
47) in. - 106 (113, 120)
cm, length: 23½ in.
(60 cm) sleeve seam 17
in. (43 cm).

MATERIALS

24 (25, 26) skeins
"Mayflower Helarsgarn"
(100% cotton - approx. 88
yds (80 m) per 50 g skein)
colour yellow.
Crochet hooks U.S. sizes
B/1 and E/4 (U.K. sizes
12 and 9) (Metric sizes 2.5
and 3.5) or size needed to
obtain tension. Knitting
needles U.S. size 3 (U.K.
size 10) (Metric size 3).
**To save time, take time to
check tension!**

TENSION

12 relief tr motifs and 13
rows in pat st = 4 in.
(10 cm) using larger size
hook.

STITCHES

**Chain (ch),
double crochet (dc),
half treble crochet (htr),
treble crochet (tr).
Front Relief tr:** Worked
around the post of the st
of the previous row. Yo
over hook insert hook
back to front between
next 2 sts, then back
again between the st
worked and the foll st,
hook is now placed hori-
zontally in front of st,
complete the tr.
Back Relief tr: Worked
around the post of the st
of the previous row. Yo
over hook, insert hook
front to back between
next 2 sts, then back
again between the st
worked and the foll st,
hook is now placed hori-
zontally in back of st,
complete the tr.
Front Relief dc: Worked
around the post of the st
of the previous row.
Insert hook back to front
between next 2 sts, then
back again between the st
worked and the foll st,
hook is now placed hori-
zontally in front of st,
complete the dc.
Back Relief dc: Worked
around the post of the st
of the previous row.
Insert hook front to back
between next 2 sts , then
back again between the st
worked and the foll st,
hook is now placed hori-
zontally in back of st,
complete the dc.
Pattern stitch: Row 1: 1
htr in the 6th ch from
hook, *ch 1, skip 1 ch, 1
htr*. Rep * to *.
Row 2: Ch 3 (= 1 border
st + ch 1), skip 1 ch, *1
front relief tr, ch 1, skip 1
ch, 1 back relief tr, ch 1,
skip 1 ch*, rep * to *, end

1 htr (= 1 border st). **Row
3:** Ch 3 (= 1 border st + ch
1), skip 1 ch, *1 back
relief tr, ch 1, skip 1 ch, 1
front relief tr, ch 1, skip 1
ch*, rep * to *, end 1 htr
(= 1 border st). Rep rows
2 and 3 to stagger the
motif, that is, work 1
front relief over 1 front
relief and vice versa.
1/1 ribbing: Row 1: *K1,
p1*. Rep * to * across.
Row 2 and all foll rows:
Work sts as established in
previous row.

BACK

With larger size hook, ch
131 (139, 147) + ch 2 (= 1
border st) + ch 1.
continue in pat st as foll:
Row 1: Work * to * of
row 1, 64 (68, 72) times.
Row 2: Work * to * of
row 2, 32 (34, 36) times =
64 (64, 72) relief sts + 1
border st at each edge.
Work in pat st until piece
measures 21¼ in. (54 cm)
from beg. Change to
smaller size hook and
work 1 row of pat st as
foll: Ch 2 (= border st), ch
1, skip 1 ch, *1 front
relief dc, ch 1, skip 1 ch, 1
back relief dc, ch 1, skip 1
ch,* rep * to *, end 1 dc
(= border st). Fasten off.

FRONT

Work same as back.

SLEEVES

With larger size hook, ch
75 + ch 2 (= border st) +
ch 1. Work in pat st. On
row 1, rep * to * 36 times.
On row 2: rep * to * 18
times = 36 relief tr + 1
border st at each edge.
*Inc 1 tr and ch 1 at each
edge of every 3rd row
once, inc 1 tr and ch 1 at
each edge of every 4th
row once*, rep * to * 6
times (for each inc, work
1 tr and ch 1) = 60 relief tr
+ 1 border st at each edge.
When piece measures 15
in. (38 cm) from beg,
change to smaller size
hook and work last row
same as back. Fasten off.

FINISHING

Block piece to indicated
measurements. With
knitting needles, pick up
and knit 72 (76, 80) sts
from lower edge of back
and work 2½ in. (6 cm) of
1/1 ribbing. Cast off.
Work same border on
front. With knitting
needles, pick up and knit
38 sts from lower edge of
each sleeve and work 2 in.
(5 cm) of 1/1 ribbing.
Cast off. Sew shoulder
seams over 5 (5½, 6) in. -
13 (14, 15) cm. Sew
sleeves to armholes,
matching centre of sleeve
with shoulder seams. Sew
side and sleeve seams.

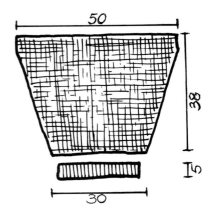

SLEEVE

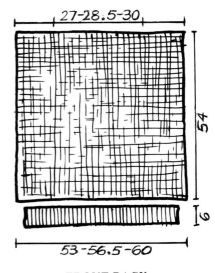

FRONT-BACK

★★

GLOWING APRICOT
PULLOVER IS A SUMPTUOUS
SAMPLER OF BOBBLE AND RELIEF
STITCHES. SCOOP NECK AND
BATWING SLEEVES HEIGHTEN THE
SUMMERY LOOK.

BATWING PULLOVER

SIZE

Woman's size Small
(Medium, Large), bust
30-32 (33-35, 36-38) in. -
76-81.5 (84-89, 91.5-97)
cm. Finished bust
measurements: 41 (44,
47¼) in. - 104 (112, 120)
cm, length: 21½ in. (55
cm), sleeve seam: 15¾
(40 cm).

MATERIALS

10 (11, 12) skeins sport
weight boucle cotton yarn
(approx. 153 yds (140 m)
per 50 g skein) colour
apricot.
Crochet hook U.S. size
H/8 (U.K. size 6) (Metric
size 5) or size needed to
obtain tension. Knitting
needles U.S. size 3 (U.K.
size 10) (Metric size 3).
**To save time, take time to
check tension!**

TENSION

14 tr and 10 rounds = 4
in. (10 cm).

STITCHES

**Chain (ch),
single crochet (sc),
double crochet (dc),
half treble crochet (htr),
treble crochet (tr).
Front Relief stitch:**
Worked in tr by working
around the post of the st
below. For front relief sts,
yo, and insert hook from
right to left around the
post of the indicated st at
front of work. Yo, and
draw through loop, then
continue as you would for
a tr.
Back Relief stitch:
Worked in tr by working
around the post of the st
below. For back relief sts,
yo, and insert hook from
right to left around the
post of the indicated st in
back of work. Yo, and
draw through loop, then
continue as you would for
a tr.

**Relief pattern stitch:
Row 1:** wrong side of
work: Ch 3 (counts as
first tr), 1 tr in the 5th ch
from the hook, 1 tr in
each of the foll ch sts.
Row 2: Ch 2, front relief
tr across, end with 1 htr
as last st.
Row 3: Ch 2, back relief
tr across, end with 1 htr
as last st.
Always rep rows 2 and 3.
1/1 ribbing: Row 1: *K1,
p1*. Rep * to * across.
Row 2 and all foll rows:
Work sts as established in
previous row.

BODY

Worked from side to side.
The front V neck is
deeper than the back. Beg
with the lower edge of the
right sleeve. Ch 40 (42,
44) + ch 3. Work in relief
pat st. At each edge of
4th row, inc 1 st at each
edge (work 2 relief sts in
each edge st). At each
edge of every 2nd row,
inc 1 st 5 times, inc 2 sts 4
times, inc 3 sts twice, inc
4 sts 3 times, inc 6 (6, 5)
sts twice, inc 8 (7, 8) sts
once. (Inc by extending a
chain from the side edge,
then work back along the
chain on the next row.)
After inc, the piece will
have 38 rows and will
measure 15 in. (38 cm) =
144 sts. Work straight for
9 (11, 13) rows. Divide
work in half. Work the
first 71 sts for front. At
neck edge of every 2nd
row, dec 1 st once, dec 2
sts once, dec 1 st once,
dec 2 sts once, dec 1 st
once, dec 2 sts 3 times.
(For each dec, sc over
required number of sts.)
Work rem 58 sts until 26
(28, 30) rows from beg of
front. You are now at
centre of work. Work 2nd
half by rev shapings:
work 10 (12, 14) rows
even, then at neck edge of
every 2nd row, inc 2 sts 3
times, inc 1 st once, inc 2
sts once, inc 1 st once, inc
2 sts once, inc 1 st once.
Piece will have 43 (45, 47)
rows. Now, beg 2 sts after
neck edge of front, work
back sts. At neck edge of
every 2nd row, dec 2 sts
once, dec 3 sts once, dec 2
sts once, dec 3 sts once,
dec 2 sts once, dec 3 sts
once, dec 2 sts twice.
Work rem 52 sts until you
have 26 (28, 30) rows
from beg of back. You
are now at centre of back
neck. Work 2nd half to
correspond by rev
shapings: work 10 (12, 14)

rows straight, then at
neck edge of every 2nd
row, inc 2 sts twice, inc 3
sts once, inc 2 sts once,
inc 3 sts once, inc 2 sts
once, inc 3 sts once.
Work these 71 sts for a
total of 43 (45, 47) rows.
Work across all sts, ch 2
at centre = 144 sts. Work
9 (11, 13) rows, then
shape 2nd sleeve by rev
shapings of first sleeve: at
each edge of every 2nd
row, dec 8 (7, 8) sts once,
6 (6, 5) sts twice, dec 4 sts
3 times, dec 3 sts twice,
dec 2 sts 4 times, dec 1 st
5 times. (For each st dec
at beg of row, sc over
specified number of sts.
At end of row, leave the
specified number of sts
unworked and turn.) You
now have 40 (42, 44) sts
and 38 rows on sleeve.
Fasten off.

FINISHING

Block pieces to indicated
measurements. With
knitting needles, pick up
and knit 28 (30, 32) sts
from each sleeve end and
work 3/4 in. (2 cm) of
1/1 ribbing. Cast off.
With knitting needles,
pick up and knit 60 (64,
68) sts from front and
back and work 1½ in. (4
cm) of 1/1 ribbing. Cast
off. With knitting needles,
pick up and knit 61 sts
from each side of neck,
beg at centre front and
end at back neck and
work 3/4 in. (2 cm) of
1/1 ribbing. Cast off
loosely. Lap right end
over left end and sew in
place. Sew side and sleeve
seams.

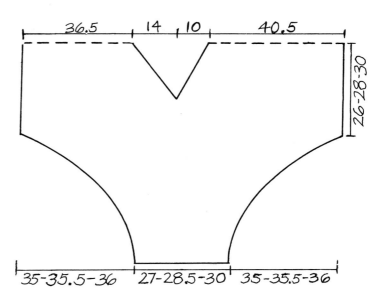

BACK, FRONT AND SLEEVES

CORAL PULLOVER

SIZE

Woman's Small (Medium, Large), bust 30-32 (33-35, 36-38) in. - 76-81.5 (84-89, 91.5-97) cm. Finished bust measurements: 41 (44, 47) in. - 104 (112, 120) cm, length: 23¼ in. (59 cm), sleeve seam 17 in. (43 cm).

MATERIALS

13 (14, 15) skeins "Scheepjeswol Voluma" (85% acrylic, 15% kid mohair - approx. 209 yds (191 m) per 50 g skein) colour coral. Crochet hooks U.S. sizes C/2 and E/4 (U.K. sizes 11 and 9) (Metric sizes 3 and 3.5) or size needed to obtain tension. **To save time, take time to check tension!**

TENSION

20 tr and 13 rows = 4 in. (10 cm) using larger size hook.

STITCHES

Chain (ch),
single crochet (sc),
double crochet (dc),
half treble crochet (htr),
treble crochet (tr).
Front Relief stitch:
Worked in tr by inserting hook from right to left around the post of the st below. For front relief sts, yo, and insert hook from right to left around the post of the indicated st at front of work. Yo, and draw through loop, then continue as you would for a tr.
Back Relief stitch:
Worked in tr by inserting hook from right to left around the post of the st below. For back relief sts, yo, and insert hook from right to left around the post of the indicated st in back of work. Yo, and draw through loop, then continue as you would for à tr.
Post stitch: Row 1: Ch 3 (counts as first st) 1 tr in each st.

KEY TO CHART

◨ = 1 front relief st on right side of work, 1 back relief st on wrong side of work.

☐ = 1 back relief st on right side of work, 1 front relief st on wrong side of work.

Row 2: *1 front relief tr, 1 back relief tr*, rep * to * across row.
Row 3: Work opposite st of the previous row, that is, work 1 relief tr in the front of the st above a back relief st so that the border alternates front and back relief sts on both sides of the work.
Zigzag stitch: Worked by foll chart in front and back relief st. Chart shows sts as they appear on the right side of work. Beg each row with ch 2 and end with 1 htr.

BACK

With larger size hook, ch 106 (114, 122). **Row 1:** Ch 3 (counts as first st), 1 tr in the 5th ch from hook, 1 tr in each ch = 106 (114, 122) tr. Work by foll chart, beg sizes Small (Medium, Large) as indicated on chart by S (M, L) as foll: right side of work: ch 2, 104 (112, 120) relief tr, 1 htr. Continue by foll chart until piece measures 20 in. (50 cm) from beg, then work 1¼ in. (3 cm) in post st, beg with 1 front relief st, 1 back relief st (omit Row 1). Fasten off.

FRONT

Work same as back.

SLEEVES

With larger crochet hook, ch 64 (66, 68). **Row 1:** Ch 3 (counts as first st), 1 tr in 5th ch from hook, 1 tr in each ch = 64 (66, 68) tr. Work by foll chart, beg with point 1 (2, 3) on chart. Work 1 row without inc, then work 2 sts in each edge st of next 2 rows = 4 incs every 3 rows 8 times. Work until you have 96 (98, 100) sts + 1 border st at each edge. Work inc sts in zigzag pattern. When piece measures 15¾ in. (40 cm) from beg, fasten off.

FINISHING

Block pieces to indicated measurements. Hold the back and front pieces with right sides tog and join with 1 row of dc, using smaller crochet hook. (Insert hook through corresponding sts of back and front and work across 5¼ (6, 6½) in. - 13.5 (15, 16.5) cm at armhole edge for each shoulder, leaving centre open for neck. Crochet sleeves to side seams, matching centre of sleeves with shoulder seam. (With right sides tog, work 2 dc every row, working through both thicknesses.) Crochet side and sleeve seams in the same way. With smaller crochet hook, work 32 (34, 36) dc around lower edge of each sleeve, joining round with a sc. Work 1¼ in. (3 cm) in rounds of post st, joining each round with a sc. With smaller size crochet hook, work 170 (184, 198) dc around lower edge of back and front, joining round with a sc. Work 2 in. (5 cm) in post st, joining rounds with a sc. Fasten off.

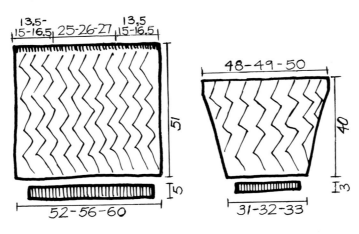

FRONT-BACK   **SLEEVE**

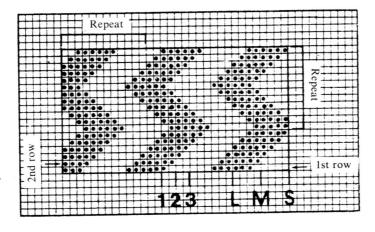

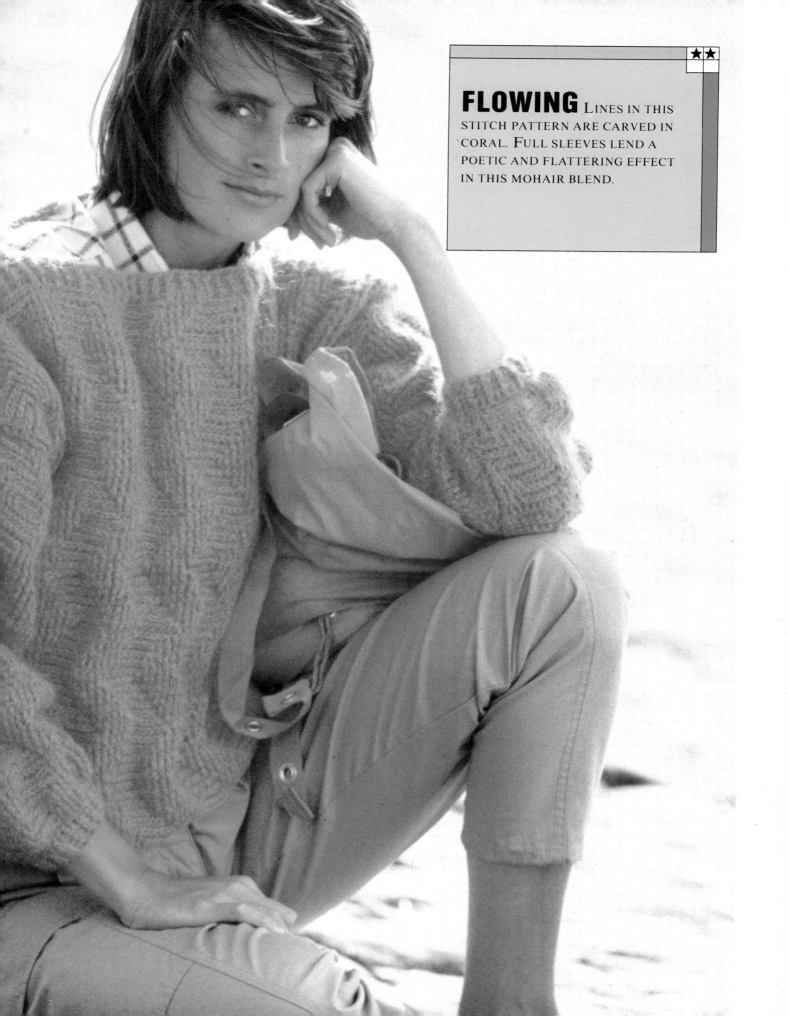

FLOWING LINES IN THIS
STITCH PATTERN ARE CARVED IN
CORAL. FULL SLEEVES LEND A
POETIC AND FLATTERING EFFECT
IN THIS MOHAIR BLEND.

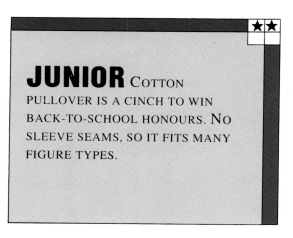

★ ★

JUNIOR COTTON

PULLOVER IS A CINCH TO WIN
BACK-TO-SCHOOL HONOURS. NO
SLEEVE SEAMS, SO IT FITS MANY
FIGURE TYPES.

TEEN PULLOVER

SIZE

Woman's X Small (Small, Medium), bust 30-32 (33-35, 36-38) in. - 76-82.5 (84-89, 91.5-97) cm. Finished bust measurements: 41½ (43, 45) in. - 106 (110, 114) cm, length: 23¾ in. (58 cm), sleeve seam 15¾ in. (40 cm).

MATERIALS

21 (22, 22) skeins "Mayflower Helarsgarn" (100% cotton - approx. 88 yds (80 m) per 50 g skein) colour gold. Crochet hook U.S. size E/4 (U.K. size 9) (Metric size 3.5) or size needed to obtain tension. Knitting needles U.S. size 3 (U.K. size 11) (Metric size 3). **To save time, take time to check tension!**

TENSION

12 groups (1 tr + ch 1) and 11½ rows = 4 in. (10 cm).

STITCHES

**Chain (ch),
single crochet (sc),
double crochet (dc),
half treble crochet (htr),
treble crochet (tr).
Relief tr:** Worked around the post of the st of the previous row. Yo over hook, insert hook back to front between next 2 sts, then back again between the st worked and the foll st, hook is now placed horizontally in front of st, complete the tr.
Relief pattern stitch:
Multiple of 2 + 1.
Row 1: Ch 3 (counts as 1 htr + ch 1), 1 htr in the 6th ch from the hook, *ch 1, skip 1 ch, 1 htr*.
Row 2: Ch 2 (= 1 border st), ch 1, sk 1 ch, *1 relief tr, ch 1, skip 1 ch*, rep * to *, end with 1 htr (= 1

border st). Always rep row 2.
1/1 ribbing: Row 1: *K1, p1*. Rep * to * across.
Row 2: Work sts as established in previous row.

BODY

Worked from lower end of left sleeve to lower end of right sleeve. With crochet hook ch 75 and work in relief pat st = 36 groups + 1 border st at each edge. At each edge of every 4th row, inc 1 group (1 htr, ch 1 in the st next to the border sts) 4 times. At each edge of every 3rd row, inc 1

group 4 times. At each edge of every row, inc 1 group 10 times = 72 groups + 1 border st at each edge. Work until piece measures 14 in. (36 cm) from first row of relief pat st (diagram shows 1½ in. (4 cm) of knitted ribbing added later). At right edge, ch 58. Fasten off.
Working separately, ch 58 and join to left edge. Work as foll: 1 border st, *ch 1, skip 1 ch, 1 htr*, rep * to * 28 times, work 74 groups of sleeve, *ch 1, skip 1 ch, 1 htr*, 1 border st. On the foll row, work 130 groups + 1 border st at each edge for 5 (5½, 6) in. - 13 (14, 15) cm. **Back:** Work the first 65 groups only for 11¾ (12¼, 12½) in. - 30 (31, 32) cm, end on wrong side of work. Working separately, work the last 65 groups for the front for 11¾ (12¼, 12½) in. -30 (31, 32) cm, leaving 5 groups at the centre unworked. End on wrong side of work. Now work across all sts, ch 11 across centre for neck. On the foll row, work in relief pat st to centre 11 chains as foll: skip 1 ch,

1 htr, ch 1, skip 1 ch, rep * to * 4 times, then work across rem sts in relief pat st, end with 1 border st. Work until piece measures 20¾ (21½, 22½) in. - 53 (55, 57) cm from beg. Break yarn. Work over the centre 72 groups in relief pat st with 1 border st at each edge. Dec 1 group every row 10 times, dec 1 group every 3rd row 4 times, dec 1 group every 4th row 4 times = 36 groups + 1 border st at each edge. Fasten off.

FINISHING

Block piece to indicated measurements. With knitting needles, pick up and knit 38 sts from lower edge of each sleeve and work 1½ in. (4 cm) of 1/1 ribbing. Cast off. With knitting needles, pick up and knit 72 (74, 76) sts from lower edge of back and work 1½ in. (4 cm) of 1/1 ribbing. Cast off. Work same border on lower front. Sew side and sleeve seams. Work 1 round of dc around neck; sc to join. Fasten off.

Sweaters which are worked from sleeve to sleeve have a tendency to stretch, especially at the shoulders and sleeves. Take extra care to measure the sleeve length, allowing for the natural give of the stitch. You may want to use knitting elastic in the sleeve cuffs as well to ensure a comfortable fit.

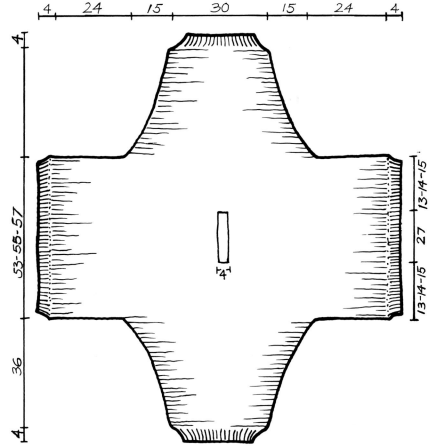

IMPECCABLE

Styling is assisted by a tweed texture and a shawl collar. This flexible mohair jacket works on the job or after hours.

MOHAIR JACKET

SIZE
Woman's Large (X Large), bust 36-38 (39-42) in. - 91.5-97 (99-107) cm. Finished bust measurements: 49¼ (51½) in. - 125 (131) cm, length: 27½ (28¾) in. 70 (73) cm, sleeve seam: 18¾ (19¼) in. - 48 (49) cm.

MATERIALS
34 (36) skeins bulky weight fancy mohair yarn (approx. 71 yds (65 m) per 50 g skein) colour green tweed. Crochet hook U.S. size I/9 (U.K. size 5) (Metric size 5.5) or size needed to obtain tension. **To save time, take time to check tension!**

TENSION
15 tr and 9 rows in relief pat = 4 in. (10 cm).

STITCHES
**Chain (ch),
single crochet (sc),
double crochet (dc),
half treble crochet (htr),
treble crochet (tr).
Front Relief stitch:**
Worked in tr by working around the post of the st below. For front relief sts, yo, and insert hook from right to left around the post of the indicated st at front of work. Yo, and draw through loop, then continue as you would for a tr.
Back Relief stitch:
Worked in tr by working around the post of the st below. For back relief sts, yo, and insert hook from right to left around the post of the indicated st in back of work. Yo, and draw through loop, then continue as you would for a tr.
Post stitch: Row 1: 1 tr in each st.

Row 2: Ch 2 (= 1 border st) *1 front relief tr, 1 back relief tr*, rep * to * across row, end with 1 front relief tr, 1 htr (= 1 border st).
Row 3: Ch 2, *1 back relief tr, 1 front relief tr*, rep * to * across row, end with 1 back relief tr, 1 htr.
Always rep rows 2 and 3.

BACK
Ch 95 (99), then work in post st = 91 (95) sts with 1 border st at each edge (the border sts are not included in the final measurements on the chart). When piece measures 6 (6¼) in. - 15 (16) cm from beg, dec 1 st at each edge of work as foll: work border st, work 2 sts tog in relief, work to last 3 sts, work 2 sts tog in relief, work border st. (To work 2 sts tog, insert hook in first st, draw through loop, insert hook in 2nd st, draw through loop, yo, draw through 2 loops, yo, draw through 2 loops. On foll row work in relief tr as established.) Work these dec every 2½ in. (6 cm) 4 times = 83 (87) tr. Work until piece measures 18½ (19¼) in. - 47 (49) cm from beg. Shape armholes: Sc over first 8 sts, ch 2, work 1 htr, work to last 9 sts, 1 htr, leave last 8 sts unworked = 67 (71) tr. Turn. Continue in relief st until piece measures 9 (9¼) in. - 23 (24) cm from armhole. Fasten off.

RIGHT FRONT
Ch 57 (59) and work in relief st = 53 (55) tr + 1 border st at each edge. When piece measures 6 (6¼) in. - 15 (16) cm from beg, dec 1 st at left edge every 2½ in. (6 cm) 4 times. Work until piece measures 18½ (19¼) in. - 47 (49) cm from beg. Shape armhole: Work to

last 9 sts, 1 htr, turn, leaving last 8 sts unworked. Ch 2, work the rem 41 (43) tr in relief until piece measures 9 (9¼) in. - 23 (24) cm from armhole.
Shape shoulder: Work to last 22 (23) tr, then turn and work on rem 19 (20) tr for 3 (3¼) in. - 7.5 (8) cm, end on right side of work. Work 14 (15) sts, turn, work 5 htr, 9 (10) relief tr, turn, work 4 (5) relief tr. Fasten off.

LEFT FRONT
Work same as right front, rev shapings.

SLEEVES
Ch 33 (35), Work in relief st until piece measures 3¼ in. (8 cm) from beg = 29 (31) tr + 1 border st at each edge. In 8 front relief tr, evenly spaced across row, work 1 back relief tr, 1 front relief tr, 1 back relief tr = 45 (47) tr. 1 st in from each edge every 1¼ in. (3 cm), inc 1 st 11 (12) times = 67 (71) tr. Piece will measure 19¾ (20¼) in. - 50 (51) cm from beg. Fasten off.

POCKETS
Ch 25. Work in relief st for 6¼ in. (16 cm). Fasten off. Make 2.

FINISHING
Block pieces to indicated measurements. Sew the seam of the shawl collar and sew to centre of back. Sew shoulder and side seams. Sew sleeves to armhole, matching upper 2 in. (5 cm) of each sleeve edge to body underarm edges. Sew sleeve seams. Sew pockets to front 2¾ in. (7 cm) from lower edge and 3¼ in. (8 cm) from side seams.

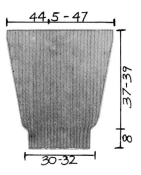

44,5 - 47
37-39
8
30-32

SLEEVE

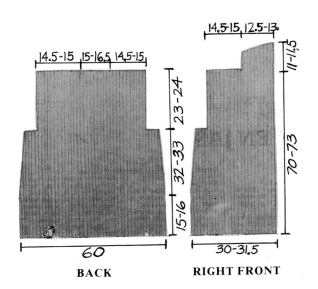

14.5-15   15-16,5   14.5-15
14.5-15, 12.5-13
23-24
32-33
15-16
11-11,5
70-73
60
30-31.5

BACK   **RIGHT FRONT**

LATTICE PULLOVER

SIZE

Woman's Small (Medium, Large), bust 30-32 (33-35, 36-38) in. - 76-81.5 (84-89, 91.5-97) cm. Finished bust measurements: 44 (48, 52) in. - 112 (122, 132) cm, length: 24¾ in. (63 cm), sleeve seam 17¼ in. (44 cm).

MATERIALS

22 (24, 26) skeins worsted weight yarn (approx. 99 yds (90 m) per 50 g skein) colour grey.
Crochet hooks U.S. sizes E/4 and F/5 (U.K. sizes 9 and 8) (Metric sizes 3.5 and 4) or size needed to obtain tension. **To save time, take time to check tension!**

TENSION

16 sts and 8½ rows = 4 in. (10 cm) in lattice st using larger size hook.

STITCHES

**Chain (ch),
single crochet (sc),
double crochet (dc),
half treble crochet (htr),
treble crochet (tr),
double treble crochet (dtr).**
Front Relief tr: Worked in tr by working around the post of the st below. For front relief sts, yo, and insert hook from right to left around the post of the indicated st at front of work. Yo, and draw through loop, then continue as you would for a tr.
Back Relief tr: Worked in tr by working around the post of the st below. For back relief sts, yo, and insert hook from right to left around the post of the indicated st in back of work. Yo, and draw through loop, then continue as you would for a tr.

RUGGED PULLOVER SET WITH INTERLACED DIAMONDS IS A *TOUR DE FORCE* IN CROCHET. GENEROUS SIZING AND EASY CONSTRUCTION MAKE IT SUITABLE FOR ACTIVE SPORTS AS WELL AS WINTER EVENINGS BY THE FIRESIDE.

Front Relief dtr: Worked in dtr by working around the post of the st below. For front relief sts, yo twice, and insert hook from right to left around the post of the indicated st at front of work. Yo, and draw through loop, then continue as you would for a dtr.

Back Relief dtr: Worked in dtr by working around the post of the st below. For back relief sts, yo twice, and insert hook from right to left around the post of the indicated st in back of work. Yo, and draw through loop, then continue as you would for a dtr.

Lattice stitch: Multiple of 8 + 10.

Row 1: Right side of work: ch 3 (counts as first tr), 1 tr in the 5th ch and the 6th ch from hook, *skip 2 sts, 2 tr, 2 front relief tr in the skipped sts, 4 tr*, rep * to *, end with 3 tr instead of 4 tr.

Row 2: Ch 3 (counts as first tr), *skip 2 sts, 2 back relief dtr, 2 tr in skipped sts (pass hook in front of the back relief dtr), skip 2 sts, 2 tr, 1 back relief dtr in the skipped sts*, rep * to *, end 1 tr.

Row 3: Ch 3 (counts as first tr), skip 1 st, 1 front relief dtr, 1 front relief dtr in the skipped st, 2 tr, *2 tr, 1 front relief dtr in the 3rd and 4th skipped sts, 2 tr*, rep * to *, skip 1 st, 1 front relief dtr in the first skipped st, 1 tr.

Row 4: Ch 3 (counts as first tr), *2 back relief tr, 4 tr, 2 back relief tr*, rep * to *, end 1 tr.

Row 5: Work same as row 3.

Row 6: Ch 3 (counts as first tr), *skip 2 sts, 1 tr in the 3rd and 4th st, 1 back relief dtr in the first and 2nd skipped, sts, then skip 2 sts, 1 back relief dtr in the 7th and 8th sts, 1 tr in the skipped sts by passing the hook in front of the 7th and 8th sts, 2 tr*, rep * to *, end 1 tr.

Row 7: Ch 3 (counts as first tr), *2 tr, skip 2 sts, 1 front relief dtr in the 3rd and 4th sts, 1 front relief dtr in the first and 2nd sts (around the skipped sts), 2 tr*, rep * to *, end 1 tr.

Row 8: Ch 3 (counts as first tr), *2 tr, 4 back relief tr, 2 tr* rep * to *, end 1 tr.

Row 9: Work same as row 7.

Always rep rows 2 to 9.

Post stitch: Row 1: Tr.

Row 2: *1 front relief tr, 1 back relief tr*, rep * to * across row.

Row 3: Work opposite st of the previous row, that is, work 1 front relief tr in the front of the st above a back relief st so that the border alternates front and back relief sts on both sides of the work.

BACK

With larger hook, ch 90 (98, 106) + ch 3 (counts as first tr). Work in lattice st by foll chart. Beg first row with 1 tr in the 5th ch from hook, *1 tr in the foll ch, skip 2 sts, 2 tr, 1 front relief tr in skipped sts, 3 tr*, rep * to * 10 (11,12) times = 11 (12, 13) lattice motifs. Continue in lattice st until piece measures 23½ in. (60 cm) from beg. Fasten off.

FRONT

Work same as back for 46 rows. Mark centre 28 (30, 32) sts and work each side separately. At neck edge of first 3 rows, work 2 tr tog (insert hook in first tr to be worked tog, draw through loop and insert hook in 2nd tr, yo and draw through loop, yo and draw through 4 loops on hook). You now have 28 (31, 34) sts. Continue in lattice st until piece measures 23½ in. (60 cm) from beg. Fasten off.

SLEEVES

With larger hook ch 58 + ch 3 (counts as first tr). Work in lattice st across = 7 lattice motifs. Inc 1 tr at each edge of every 2nd row 12 (14, 16) times (work 2 tr in each edge st). Work new sts in lattice st. You now have 82 (86, 90) sts. When sleeve measures 16 in. (41 cm) from beg, fasten off.

FINISHING

Block pieces to indicated measurements. Sew shoulder seams. Sew sleeves to side seams, matching centre of sleeve with shoulder seams. Sew side and sleeve seams. With smaller hook work 34 (36, 38) dc along edge of each sleeve, skipping 1 st in each group of crossed sts. Join round with a sl st, then work in rounds of post st, joining each round with a sl st and beg each round with ch 3. Work post st for 1¼ in. (3 cm). Fasten off. Work 1 round of dc around lower edge of body, skipping 1 st in each group of crossed sts. Join round with a sl st, then work in rounds of post st, joining each round with a sl st and beg each round with ch 3. Work post st for 1¼ in. (3 cm). Fasten off. Work 34 (36, 38) dc around neck, skipping 1 st in each group of crossed sts. Join round with a sl st, then work 2 rounds of post st, joining each round with a sc and beg each round with ch 3. Then work 1 round of tr and 1 round of post st. Fasten off.

9th row
8th row
7th row
6th row
5th row
4th row
3rd row
2nd row
Repeat
← 1st row

KEY TO CHART

- • = ch 1
- | = 1 tr
- ↓ = 1 relief tr
- ⇓ = 1 relief dtr

The chart shows sts as they appear on right side of work.
Repeat
toer = row

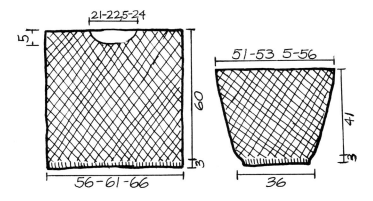

21-22.5-24

5

60

3

56-61-66

FRONT-BACK

51-53 5-56

41

3

36

SLEEVE

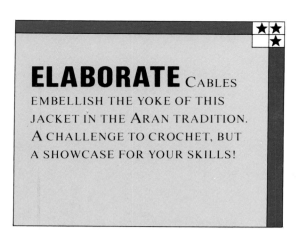

ELABORATE CABLES

EMBELLISH THE YOKE OF THIS JACKET IN THE ARAN TRADITION. A CHALLENGE TO CROCHET, BUT A SHOWCASE FOR YOUR SKILLS!

ARAN-STYLE CABLE CARDIGAN

SIZE

Woman's Small/Medium (Large/X Large), bust 30-35 (36-42) in. - 76-89 (91.5-107) cm. Finished bust measurements: 44½ (52) in. - 113 (132) cm, length: 25¼ (26) in. - 64 (66) cm, sleeve seam: 17 in. (43 cm).

MATERIALS

21 (23) skeins worsted weight yarn (approx. 99 yds (90 m) per 50 g skein) colour ecru.
Crochet hooks U.S. sizes E/4 and F/5 (U.K. sizes 9 and 8) (Metric sizes 3.5 and 4) or size needed to obtain tension. 7 buttons.
To save time, take time to check tension!

TENSION

16 tr and 8 rows = 4 in. (10 cm) in cable lattice using larger size hook.

STITCHES

Chain (ch),
single crochet (sc),
double crochet (dc),
half treble crochet (htr),
treble crochet (tr),
double treble (dtr).
Relief stitches: Worked in tr or dtr by working around the post of the st below. For front relief sts, yo, and insert hook from right to left around the post of the indicated st at front of work. Yo, and draw through loop, then continue as you would for a tr or dtr. For back relief sts, yo, and insert hook from right to left under the post of the indicated st at back of work. Yo, and draw through loop, then continue as you would for a tr or dtr.

Right Cable: Row 1: 1 tr in 5th ch from hook, *1 tr in foll ch; skip 2 ch; 1 dtr in foll 2 ch; passing hook in front of 2 dtr, work 1 dtr in each of 2 skipped sts; 1 tr in each of foll 3 ch*, rep * to * across, 1 tr = 1 border st.
Row 2: Ch 3 = 1 border st, *1 tr in each of foll 3 tr, 1 back relief tr around each of foll 4 dtr, 1 tr*, rep * to * across, 2 tr (last tr = border st).
Row 3: Ch 3 = border st, 1 tr, *1 tr, skip 2 sts, work 1 relief dtr in front and around next 2 sts (= 2 front relief dtr), 1 front relief dtr in each of 2 skipped sts, 1 tr in each of next 3 tr*, rep * to * across, 1 tr (= border st). Always rep rows 2 and 3.
Lattice Cable: Worked 3 times at top of sweater. Rep top 8 rows of chart twice for lattice cable, end with last 4 rows of chart.

KEY TO CHART

‖ = tr
⇊ = relief tr
↓ = relief dc
· = ch
| = dc

Post stitch: Row 1: 1 tr in each st.
Row 2: *1 relief tr in the front of the st, 1 relief tr in the back of the st*, rep * to * across.
Row 3: Work opposite st of the previous row, that is, work 1 relief tr in the front of the st above a back relief st so that the border alternates front and back relief sts on both sides of the work.

BACK

With larger size crochet hook, ch 90 (106) + ch 3 to turn. Work in right cable st foll chart. You will have 11 (13) cables across + 1 border st at each edge. Work 27 (29) rows of cable, ending with 3rd row of pat repeat. Then work in lattice cable pat: rep rows 1 to 8 for a total of 20 rows, ending with the 4th row of lattice cable. Fasten off.

RIGHT FRONT

With larger size crochet hook, ch 42 (50) + ch 3 to turn. Work in right cable st foll chart. You will have 5 (6) cables across + 1 border st at each edge. Work for 27 (29) rows of cable, ending with the 3rd row of pat repeat.

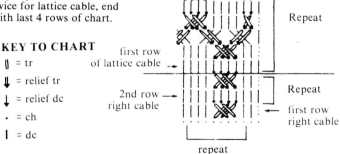

first row of lattice cable →

2nd row right cable →

Repeat

Repeat

first row right cable

← first row right cable

repeat

Continue in lattice cable pat. On the 16th row of lattice pat rep, sc over the first 11 (14) sts, work to end of row. On foll row, work to last 2 sts, yo, insert hook in next st, yo and draw through loop, yo, draw through 2 loops, yo, insert hook in next st, yo and draw through loop, yo and draw through 2 loops, yo, draw through 3 loops on hook (= 1 dec). Turn and work 1 dec over the first 2 sts. Work to end of row. Fasten off.

LEFT FRONT

Work same as right front, rev neck shapings.

SLEEVES

With larger size crochet hook, ch 58 + ch 3 to turn (counts as first tr). Work in right cable st foll chart. You will have 7 cables + 1 border st at each edge. At each edge of every 2nd row, work 2 tr in each edge st 12 (15) times. Work inc sts in right cable sts as you inc. You now have 82 (88) sts. After the 31st row of right cable st, fasten off.

FINISHING

Block pieces to indicated measurements. Sew shoulder seams. Sew sleeves to side seams, matching centre of sleeve with shoulder seam. Work top 2 rows of sleeve and edge st of body armhole in seam allowance. Sew sleeve and side seams. With smaller size crochet hook, work 30 (32) dc along lower edge of sleeve and join with sc. Then work 1 round alternating back relief tr and front relief tr. Join with sc. Work 1½ in. (4 cm) in post st. Fasten off. With smaller size crochet hook, work 1 row of dc along lower edge of body as foll: work 1 dc in each st, but skip 1 st on each cable. Be sure to work an odd number of sts. Work 2 in. (5 cm) in post st. Fasten off. With smaller size crochet hook, work 1 row of dc along neck edge, skipping 1 st every cable. (Be sure to work an odd number of sts.) Work 1 row of tr, 1 row of post st. With larger size crochet hook, work 1 row of dc along left front border, working 3 dc every 2 rows. Work 3 (2) rows of dc, then change to smaller size crochet hook and work 1 row of dc. Work same border on right front, but on the 2nd row, mark positions for 7 evenly spaced buttonholes. For each buttonhole, ch 2 and skip 2 sts. On foll row, work 2 dc over ch-2 space. Fasten off. Reinforce buttonholes. Sew on buttons.

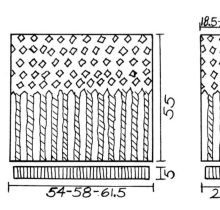

BACK
54-58-61.5
55
5

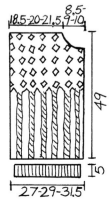

RIGHT FRONT
18.5-20-21.5
8.5-9-10
49
5
27-29-31.5

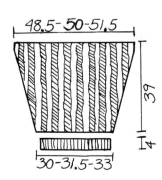

SLEEVE
48.5-50-51.5
39
4
30-31.5-33

BOBBLE CABLES MADE FROM A WORSTED YARN IN WINTER WEIGHT MAKES THIS CARDIGAN A FAVOURITE SWEATER IN COLD WEATHER.

BOBBLE CARDIGAN

SIZE

Woman's Small (Medium, Large), bust 30-32 (33-35, 36-38) in. - 76-81.5 (84-89, 91.5-97) cm. Finished bust measurements: 43 (46, 49) in. - 109 (117, 125) cm, length: 23½ in. (60 cm), sleeve seam 17 in. (43 cm).

MATERIALS

18 (19, 20) skeins worsted weight yarn (approx. 91 yds (183 m) per 50 g skein) colour ecru. Crochet hooks U.S. sizes E/4 and F/5 (U.K. sizes 9 and 8) (Metric sizes 3.5 and 4) or size needed to obtain tension. 7 buttons.
To save time, take time to check tension!

TENSION

14 sts and 7 rows = 4 in. (10 cm) in pat sts using larger size hook.

STITCHES

Chain (ch),
single crochet (sc),
double crochet (dc),
half treble crochet (htr),
treble crochet (tr),
double treble (dtr).
Relief stitches: Worked in tr or dtr by working around the post of the st below. For front relief sts, yo, and insert hook from right to left around the post of the indicated st. Yo, and draw through loop, then continue as you would for a tr or dtr.
Bobble: All in 1 st: *yo, insert hook in st, yo, draw through loop*, rep * to * 5 times total so that you have 11 loops. Yo and draw through 10 loops, yo and draw through last 2 loops.
Cable motif: worked over 8 sts. Foll the chart and work as foll:
Row 1: Right side of work: 1 tr in the first and 2nd st, skip 2 sts, 1 dtr relief st in the 5th and 6th sts, skip 2 sts, 1 front dtr relief st in the 3rd and 4th sts, 1 tr in the 7th and 8th sts.
Row 2: Wrong side of work: skip the next 2 tr, 1 back dtr in the 3rd and 4th sts, 1 front dtr in the 2nd st, 1 front dtr in the 7th and 8th tr, skip 2 sts, 1 back dtr relief st in the 5th and 6th sts.

Row 3: 1 bobble in the first st, 1 tr in the foll st, skip 2 sts, front dtr relief st in the 3rd and 4th sts, 2 front dtr relief sts in the 2 skipped sts, 1 tr in the 7th st, 1 bobble in the 8th st. Rep the 2nd and 3rd row.
Post stitch: Row 1: Tr.
Row 2: *1 front relief tr, 1 back relief tr*, rep * to * across row.
Row 3: Work opposite st of the previous row, that is work 1 front relief tr in the st above a back relief st so that the border alternates front and back relief sts on both sides of the work.

BACK

With larger size crochet hook, ch 76 (81, 86) + ch 2 to turn (counts as the first htr). **Row 1:** 1 htr in the 4th ch from the hook = 76 (81, 86) htr, ch 3.
Row 2: 4 tr, *8 sts in cable motif, 4 (5, 6) tr*, work * to * 5 times total, 8 sts in cable motif, 4 tr.
Row 3: Ch 3 = first st, 5 tr, *skip 2 sts, 1 front dtr relief st in the foll 2 htr, 1 front dtr relief st in each of the foll 2 skipped htr, 8 (9, 10) tr*, rep * to * 6 times, end with 6 tr. You have 6 repeats of the cable motif horizontally with 4 (5, 6) tr between them and 4 tr at each edge. Work Rows 2 and 3 until piece measures about 21½ in. (55 cm) from beg, ending with the 3rd row (with bobbles) of the cable motif. Fasten off.

RIGHT FRONT

Ch 38 (41, 44) + ch 2 to turn (= first htr). **Row 1:** 1 htr in the 4th ch from the hook = 38 (41, 44) htr.
Row 2: 2 (3, 4) tr, then *8 sts of cable motif, 4 (5, 6) tr*, work * to * twice, end with 8 sts of cable motif, 4 tr. Work until piece measures about 19¼ in. (49 cm) from beg (4 rows less than back). Shape Neck: At right edge, right side facing, sc over first 10 (11, 12) sts. Work to end of row, turn and continue to last st of foll row. Turn, leaving last st unworked. Sc over first st, work to end of row. Work 1 row over 26 (28, 30) sts. Fasten off.

LEFT FRONT

Work same as right front, but rev order of pat st as foll: 4 tr, *8 sts of cable motif, 4 (5, 6) tr*, work * to * twice, end with 8 sts of cable motif, 2 (3, 4) tr. Complete same as right front, working neck shaping as foll: work to last 10 (11, 12) sts, turn. Work to last st, turn. Sc over first st, work to end of row. Work 1 row over rem 26 (28, 30) sts. Fasten off.

SLEEVES

Ch 42 (44, 46) + ch 2 to turn (= first htr). **Row 1:** 1 htr in the 4th ch from the hook = 42 (44, 46) htr.
Row 2: 5 tr, *8 sts of cable motif, 4 (5, 6) tr*, work * to * twice, end with 8 sts of cable motif, 5 tr. At each edge of every 2nd row, work 2 tr in each edge st 13 times. Work inc sts in pat = 68 (70, 72) sts. When piece measures about 15¼ in. (39 cm) from beg, ending with row 3 of pat. Fasten off.

FINISHING

Block pieces to indicated measurements. Sew shoulder seams. Sew sleeves to side seams, matching centre of sleeve with shoulder seam. Sew side and sleeve seams. With smaller size hook, work 28 (30, 32) dc along lower edge of each sleeve, join the end of round to first st of round with 1 sc. Work in post stitch joining each round with a sc and beg each round with a ch 3. Work for 1½ in. (4 cm), then fasten off. With smaller size crochet hook, work 1 row of dc along lower edge of body, skipping every 5th st. (Be sure to work odd number of sts.) Work in post st for 2 in. (5 cm). Fasten off. With smaller size crochet hook, work 1 dc in each st and 2 dc at each corner of neck edges. (Be sure to work an odd number of sts.) Work 2 rows of post st. Fasten off. With smaller size crochet hook, work 3 dc every 2 rows along the left front edge. Work 3 rows of post st. Fasten off. Work same band along the right front edge, but on the 2nd row, make 7 buttonholes. Mark positions for buttonholes evenly spaced along edge. For each buttonhole, ch 2, skip 2 dc. On foll row, work 2 dc over each ch-2 space. Fasten off. Reinforce buttonholes. Sew on buttons.

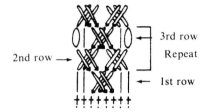

3rd row
2nd row →
Repeat
1st row

KEY TO CHART

- • = ch
- 0 = bobble
- ↓ = relief tr
- 0 = relief quad
- + = htr
- | = tr

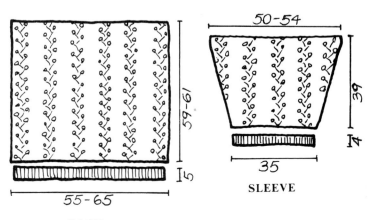

18-21 8-10

54-56

25-30

5

FRONT

59-61

55-65

5

BACK

50-54

39

35

4

SLEEVE

MOTIFS ARE EASY WHEN YOU FOLLOW A CHART. THE THUNDERBOLT MOTIF ON THIS BOATNECK SWEATER ADDS REAL DISTINCTION. A GOLD PULLOVER IS SHOWN, BUT TRY IT ALSO IN BLUE.

★ ★

BOATNECK PULLOVERS

SIZE
Woman's Small (Medium, Large), bust 30-32 (33-35, 36-38) in. - 76-81.5 (84-89, 91.5-97) cm. Finished bust measurements: 41 (44, 47) in. - 104 (112, 120) cm, length: 23¼ in. (59 cm), sleeve seam 17 in. (43 cm).

MATERIALS
14 (15, 16) skeins "Scheepjeswol Voluma" (85% acrylic, 15% kid mohair - approx. 209 yds (191 m) per 50 g skein) colour blue or gold. Crochet hooks U.S. sizes C/2 and E/4 (U.K. sizes 11 and 9) (Metric sizes 3 and 3.5) or size needed to obtain tension. **To save time, take time to check tension!**

TENSION
20 tr and 13 rows = 4 in. (10 cm) in relief stitch using larger size hook.

STITCHES
Chain (ch),
single crochet (sc),
double crochet (dc),
half treble crochet (htr),
treble crochet (tr).
Front Relief stitch:
Worked in tr by working around the post of the st below. For front relief sts, yo, and insert hook from right to left around the post of the indicated st at front of work. Yo, and draw through loop, then continue as you would for a tr.
Back Relief stitch:
Worked in tr by working around the post of the st below. For back relief sts, yo, and insert hook from right to left around the post of the indicated st in

back of work. Yo, and draw through loop, then continue as you would for a tr.
Pattern stitch: Foll the chart. The chart shows sts as they appear on right side of work. At each edge of every row, work 1 border st at each edge: ch 2 at beg of each row and 1 htr at end of each row. The border sts are not shown on chart.
BLUE PULLOVER: Foll chart for blue pullover. Beg back and front at point A (B, C). Beg sleeve at points D (B, E). Beg wrong side rows with point Z.
GOLD PULLOVER: Foll chart for gold pullover. Beg back and front with points A (B, C). Beg sleeve at points D (B, E). Beg wrong side of work rows with point Z. Repeat lower part of chart until piece measures 11½ in. (29 cm) from beg, then work 6 rows reversing direction of diagonals as shown on chart. Work top part of chart until piece measures 20 in. (50 cm) from beg, end with the last row of chart. Beg sleeve with points D (B, E). Work the lower part of chart (left to right diagonals) for about 13¾ in. (35 cm), then work centre 6 rows of chart (right to left diagonals).
Post stitch: Row 1: Tr.
Row 2: *1 front relief tr, 1 back relief tr*, rep * to * across row.
Row 3: Work opposite st of the previous row, that is, work 1 front relief tr above a back relief st so that the border alternates front and back relief sts on both sides of the work.

BACK
With larger size crochet hook, ch 106 (114, 122). **Foundation row:** Ch 3 (counts as first st), 1 tr in the 5th ch from hook, tr across = 106 (114, 122) tr, continue by foll chart for blue or gold pullover. With right side facing, ch 2 (first st), 104 (112, 120) relief sts, 1 htr. Continue by foll chart until piece measures 20 in. (51 cm) from beg. Work 1¼ in. (3 cm) in post st. Fasten off.

FRONT
Work same as back.

SLEEVES
With larger size crochet hook, ch 64 (66, 68). **Foundation Row:** Ch 3 (counts as first st), 1 tr in 5th ch from hook, tr across = 64 (66, 68) tr. Work by foll chart, beg on right side of work: ch 2, 62 (64, 66) relief, 1 htr. Continue by foll chart. **At the same time,** at each edge of 2nd row and each edge of every 3rd row, inc 1 st 17 times (4 incs every 3 rows) = 96 (98, 100) relief tr + 1 border st at each edge. For each inc work 2 sts in edge sts. Work inc sts in relief st by foll chart. When piece measures 15¾ in. (40 cm) from beg, fasten off.

FINISHING
Block pieces to indicated measurements. With smaller size crochet hook, dc the shoulders tog: hold the back and front with right sides tog. Insert hook through both thicknesses in corresponding sts and dc across for 5¼ (6, 6½) in. - 13.5 (15, 16.5) cm at each armhole edge. Fasten off. With smaller size crochet hook, dc the sleeves to the side seams, matching centre of sleeve with shoulder seam and dc sleeve and side seams: hold the piece with right sides tog. Insert hook through both thicknesses in corresponding sts and work across in dc, working 2 sts every row. Fasten off. With smaller size hook, crochet 32 (34, 36) dc along lower edge of each sleeve and sc into round. Work 1¼ in. (3 cm) of post st. Join each round with a sc and begin each round with ch 3. Fasten off. With smaller size hook, work 170 (184, 198) dc along lower edge of body and sc into round. Work 2 in. (5 cm) of post st. Fasten off.

Your choice of colour can make the same sweater look strikingly different. For another look, try changing the colour when the direction of the diagonals change to further emphasize the relief pattern.

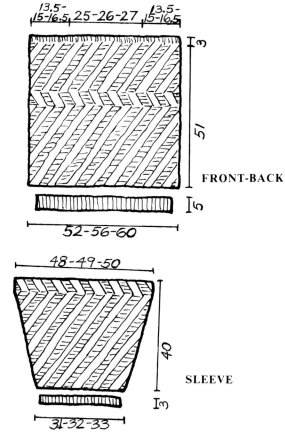

13.5-15-16.5 / 25-26-27 / 13.5-15-16.5

3

51

5

52-56-60

FRONT-BACK

48-49-50

40

3

31-32-33

SLEEVE

repeat

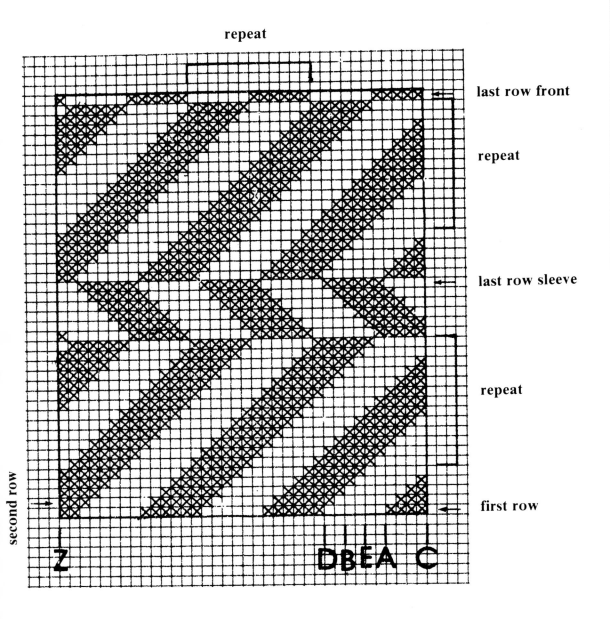

last row front

repeat

last row sleeve

repeat

first row

second row

Z

DBEA C

KEY TO CHART

☐ = 1 front relief st on right
side of work, 1 back relief st
on wrong side of work row.
⊠ = 1 back relief st on right
side of work, 1 front relief st
on wrong side of work row.

BASKET-WEAVE PULLOVER

SIZE

Woman's Small (Medium, Large), bust 30-32 (33-35, 36-38) in. - 76-81.5 (84-89, 91.5-97) cm. Finished bust measurements: 41 (44, 47) in. - 104 (112, 120) cm, length: 23½ in. (60 cm), sleeve seam 17 in. (43 cm).

MATERIALS

18 (18, 20) skeins sport weight cotton yarn (approx. 120 yds (110 m) per 50 g skein) colour blue.
Crochet hook U.S. size C/2 (U.K. size 11) (Metric size 3) or size needed to obtain tension. Knitting needles U.S. size 2 (U.K. size 12) (Metric size 2.5). **To save time, take time to check tension!**

TENSION

5 groups of 3 relief tr and 13 rows = 4 in. (10 cm).

STITCHES

Chain (ch),
single crochet (sc),
double crochet (dc),
half treble crochet (htr),
treble crochet (tr).
Relief stitches: Worked in tr by working around the post of the st below. For front relief tr, yo, and insert hook from right to left around the post of the indicated st. Yo, and draw through loop, then continue as you would for a tr. For back relief tr, work the same as above, but work under the post of the st of the previous row, but work in back of st.

Pattern stitch: Worked over 8 + 1.
Row 1: Ch 3 (counts as first tr), 1 tr in the 5th ch from hook, 2 tr, *ch 1, skip ch-1 sp, 3 tr*, rep * to * across, end with 1 tr in the last ch.
Row 2: Ch 2 (= border st), *3 front relief tr, skip ch-1 sp, ch 1, 3 back relief tr, ch 1, skip ch-1 sp*, rep * to * across, end the last rep with 1 htr instead of ch 1, skip ch-1 sp = 1 border st.
Row 3: Work same sts as established in previous row, with 1 border st at each edge.
Row 4: Ch 2 (= border st), *3 back relief tr, skip ch-1 sp, ch 1, 3 front relief tr, ch 1, skip ch-1 sp*, rep * to * across, end the last rep with 1 htr instead of ch 1, skip ch-1 sp = 1 border st.
Row 5: Work same sts as established in previous row, with 1 border st at each edge.
Rep rows 2 to 5.
1/1 ribbing: Row 1: *K1, p1*. Rep * to * across.
Row 2 and all foll rows: Work sts as established in previous row.

BACK

With crochet hook, ch 105 (113, 121), then continue in pat st, beg row 1 with ch 3. After the first row, you will have 26 (28, 30) groups of 3 tr + 1 border st at each edge. Continue until piece measures 20¾ in. (53 cm) from beg, ending with the 3rd or 5th row of pat st. Mark the centre 14 groups for the neck. Shape shoulders: Work the first 6 (7, 8) groups in pat st. After the last group of 3, ch 1, then 1 htr in the first st of the foll group (= border st). Work 1 row in pat st, then fasten off. Work 2nd shoulder to correspond.

FRONT

Work same as back.

SLEEVES

Ch 53 (57, 61). Work in pat st, beg row 1 with ch 3. You will have 13 (14, 15) groups of 3 tr + 1 border st at each edge. At each edge of every 2nd row, work 2 sts in each edge st until you have 23 (24, 25) groups of 3 tr. Work the edge sts in pat as you inc. When sleeve measures 15 in. (38 cm) from beg, fasten off.

FINISHING

Block pieces to indicated measurements. With knitting needles, pick up and knit 30 (34, 38) sts along lower edge of sleeves and work 2 in. (5 cm) of 1/1 ribbing. Cast off loosely. With knitting needles, pick up and knit 70 (78, 86) sts along lower edge of back and front and work 2 in. (5 cm) of 1/1 ribbing. Cast off loosely. Crochet shoulder seams tog: with right sides facing, hold the pieces tog and work 1 row of dc along each shoulder, working 1 dc in each st, skipping the ch sts between the groups of tr. Fasten off. Sew sleeves to side seams, matching centre of sleeve with shoulder seam. Sew side and sleeve seams using mattress st: lay the pieces tog, right sides facing. Insert needle around the strand after the border st, then insert needle around the strand after the border st on the next piece, but 1 row above. Continue to work from piece to piece, joining the 2 edges. With crochet hook, work 1 row of dc around neck, working 1 dc in each st, skipping the ch sts between the groups. Fasten off.

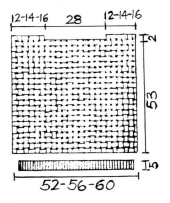

FRONT-BACK

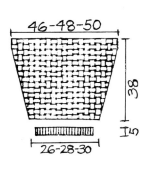

SLEEVE

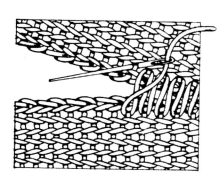

INTENSE
INDIGO COTTON IS A BOLT FROM THE BLUE. THE BASKETWEAVE STITCH, EASILY MASTERED, ADDS IMPACT TO THIS SIMPLE SILHOUETTE.

CABLE CARDIGAN

SIZE

Woman's Small (Medium, Large), bust 30-32 (33-35, 36-38) in. - 76-81.5 (84-89, 91.5-97) cm. Finished bust measurements: 42½ (45½, 49) in. - 108 (116, 124) cm, length: 23½ in. (60 cm), sleeve seam: 17¾ in. (45 cm).

MATERIALS

9 (9, 10) skeins worsted weight yarn (approx. 100 yds (90 m) per 50 g skein) colour ecru.
Crochet hook U.S. size F/5 (U.K. size 8) (Metric size 4) or size needed to obtain tension. 7 leather buttons. **To save time, take time to check tension!**

TENSION

14 tr and 10 rows = 4 in. (10 cm).

STITCHES

**Chain (ch),
single crochet (sc),
double crochet (dc),
half treble crochet (htr),
treble crochet (tr).
Front Relief stitches:**
Worked in tr by working around the post of the st below. For front relief sts, yo, and insert hook from right to left around the post of the indicated st at front of work. Yo, and draw through loop, then continue as you would for a tr.

Back Relief stitch:
Worked in tr by working around the post of the st below. For back relief sts, yo, and insert hook from right to left around the post of the indicated st at back of work. Yo, and draw through loop, then continue as you would for a tr.

Pattern stitch:
Row 1: Ch 2 (counts as first htr), 1 htr in the 4th ch from the hook, htr across, ch 2 to turn.
Row 2: wrong side of work: *2 htr, 2 back relief tr, 2 htr*, rep * to * across, ch 2 to turn.
Row 3: right side of work: *2 htr, 1 front relief tr around the 2nd relief tr, 1 front relief tr around the first tr, 2 htr*, rep * to * across row, ch 2 to turn.
Row 4: *2 htr, 1 back relief tr in each of the crossed relief tr of the previous row, 2 htr*, rep * to * across, ch 2 to turn.
Always rep rows 3 and 4.
Post stitch: Row 1: 1 tr in each st.
Row 2: *1 front relief tr, 1 back relief tr*, rep * to * across row.
Row 3: Work opposite st of the previous row, that is, work 1 front relief tr above a back relief st so that the border alternates front and back relief sts on both sides of the work.

BACK

Ch 78 (84, 90). Work in pat st as foll: **Row 1:** Ch 2, 1 htr in the 4th ch from the hook, 76 (82, 88) htr = 78 (84, 90) htr. **Row 2:** *2 htr, 2 back relief tr, 2 htr*, rep * to * 13 (14, 15) times = 13 (14, 15) cables + 2 htr at each edge and 4 htr between each cable. When piece measures 21½ in. (55 cm) from beg, fasten off.

RIGHT FRONT

Ch 38 (41, 44). Work in pat st as foll: **Row 1:** Ch 2, 1 htr in the 4th ch from hook, 36 (39, 42) htr across row = 38 (41, 44) htr. **Row 2:** *2 htr, 2 back relief tr, 2 htr*, rep * to * 6 (6, 7) times, end 2 htr, 0 (2, 0) back relief tr, 0 (1, 0) htr = 6 (7, 7) cables + 4 (1, 4) htr at right edge and 2 htr after last cable at left edge. Work until piece measures 19¼ in. (49 cm) = 6 rows less than back.
Shape neck: at right edge, sc over 7 (8, 9) sts, work to end of row. Work foll row to last 3 sts, turn. Sc over first 2 sts, ch 2, work to end of row. Work 3 more rows over rem 26 (28, 30) sts. Fasten off.

LEFT FRONT

Ch 38 (41, 44). Work in pat as foll: **Row 1:** Ch 2, 1 htr in the 4th ch from hook, 36 (39, 42) htr across row = 38 (41, 44) htr. **Row 2:** Ch 2, 0 (1, 0) htr, 0 (2, 0) back relief tr, *2 htr, 2 back relief tr, 2 htr*, rep * to * 6 (6, 7) times, end with 0 (1, 0) htr = 6 (7, 7) cables + 4 (1, 4) htr at left edge and 2 htr after last cable at right edge. Work until piece measures 19¼ in. (49 cm) = 6 rows less than back.
Shape neck: work to last 7 (8, 9) sts, turn. Sc over first 3 sts, work to end of row, turn, ch 2. Work to last 2 sts, turn. Work 3 more rows over rem 26 (28, 30) sts. Fasten off.

SLEEVES

Ch 44 (46, 48). Work in pat st as foll: **Row 1:** Ch 2, 1 htr in the 4th ch from hook, 42 (44, 46) htr = 44 (46, 48) htr. **Row 2:** Ch 2, *2 htr, 2 back relief tr, 2 htr*, rep * to * 7 (7, 8) times = 7 (7, 8) cables with 4 htr between each cable. At beg edge you will have 2 htr and at end you will have 4 (0, 2) htr. Continue in pat st. At each edge of every 3rd row, inc 1 st 12 times. (For each inc, work 2 sts in each edge st) = 68 (70, 72) sts = 11 (12, 12) cables and 2 htr at 1 edge and 4 (0, 2) htr. Work until piece measures 15¾ in. (40 cm) from beg. Fasten off.

FINISHING

Block pieces to indicated measurements. Sew shoulder seams. Work 32 (34, 36) dc along lower edge of each sleeve, then 1 row of tr, then work 4 rows of post st. Join each round with a sc and begin each round with ch 3. Fasten off. Sew sleeves to side seams, matching centre of sleeve with shoulder seam. Sew side and sleeve seams. Along lower edge of body, work 1 dc in every st, skipping every 4th st, being sure to have an uneven number. Work 1 row of tr, then 4 rows of post st. Fasten off. Work 63 (65, 67) dc around neck and then work 1 row of tr, then 1 row of post st. Fasten off. Along the left front edge, work in dc, working 3 dc every 2 rows. Work 2 more rows in dc. Fasten off.
Along right front edge work as foll: **Row 1:** Work 3 dc every 2 rows. **Row 2:** Mark positions for 7 buttonholes. Work in dc and for each buttonhole, ch 2 and skip 2 dc. **Row 3:** Dc across, working dc in the ch sts of previous row. Fasten off. Reinforce buttonholes. Sew on buttons.

BACK

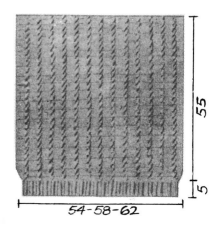

55

5

54-58-62

RIGHT FRONT

17,5- 8,5-
18,5-20 9,5-10

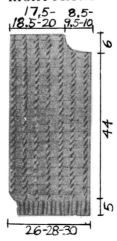

6

44

5

26-28-30

SLEEVE

47-48,5-50

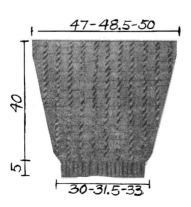

40

5

30-31,5-33

104

CREAMY CABLES CLIMB THE LADDER OF SUCCESS. LEATHER BUTTONS COMPLETE THE SPORTSWEAR LOOK OF OUR CROCHETED CARDIGAN.

STREAKS OF
LIGHTNING-LIKE PASTEL COLOURS
ELECTRIFY THIS WHITE BOATNECK
PULLOVER. THE COOL, COTTON
YARN MAKES IT COMFORTABLE
ALL SUMMER LONG.

ZIGZAG PULLOVER

SIZE
Woman's Small (Medium, Large, X Large), bust 30-32 (33-35, 36-38, 39-42) in. - 76-81.5 (84-89, 91.5-97, 99-107) cm. Finished bust measurements: 43 (47, 51, 54) in. - 110 (120, 129, 138) cm, length: 25½ in. (65 cm), sleeve seam 17¾ in. (45 cm).

MATERIALS
13 (14, 15, 16) skeins double strand "Mayflower Cotton 8" (100% cotton yarn - approx. 187 yds (170 m) per 50 g skein) or "Mayflower Helarsgarn" (100% cotton yarn - approx. 88 yds (80 m) per 50 g skein) colour white, 1 skein each colour gold, green, pink and blue. Crochet hook U.S. size F / 5 (U.K. size 8) (Metric size 4) or size needed to obtain gauge. Knitting needles U.S. size 3 (U.K. size 10) (Metric size 3).
To save time, take time to check tension!

TENSION
13 dc and 11 rows = 4 in. (10 cm).

STITCHES
Chain (ch), single crochet (sc), double crochet (dc).
Relief dc: work in dc by working around the post of the st below. Insert hook from right to left around the post of the indicated st at front of work. Yo, and draw through loop.
Relief pattern: Worked over 6 sts + 1 border st at each edge.
Row 1: Dc across.
Row 2: Ch 1 (= border st), *1 dc in each of the foll 3 dc, 1 relief dc in each of the foll 3 dc*, rep * to * across, end with 1 dc (= border st).
Row 3 and all foll rows: Ch 1, *1 dc in each of the foll 3 relief dc, 1 relief dc in each of the foll 3 dc*, rep * to *, end with 1 dc.

Stripes: 4 rows white, *2 rows green, 8 rows white, 2 rows gold, 8 rows white, 2 rows blue, 8 rows white, 2 rows pink. 8 rows white*, rep * to *. When changing colours, work the last loop of the last st of 1 colour with the colour of the next st. Hold the unused yarn against the wrong side of work. When inserting hook, work around the unused yarn so that the new sts hold it against the work. Work the border sts in the same colour as the adjacent st in pat. Ch 3 at the beg of each row (= 1 border st).
2/2 ribbing: Row 1: *K2, p2*. Rep * to * across.
Row 2 and all foll rows: Work sts as established in previous row.

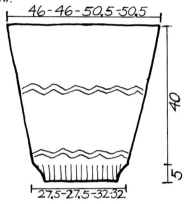

SLEEVE

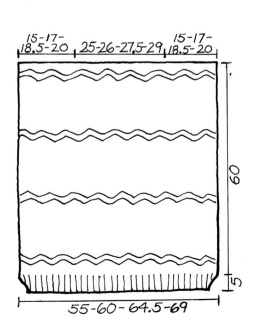

FRONT-BACK

108

ICE CREAM COLOURS MAKE AN APPEALING TOP TO COORDINATE WITH MUM'S PULLOVER. THE WOVEN STITCHES PROVIDE A PLEASING CONTRAST IN TEXTURE.

BACK

With knitting needles and white, cast on 86 (90, 94, 98) sts and work 2 in. (5 cm) in 2/2 ribbing. Cast off. With crochet hook, work 72 (78, 84, 90) dc along cast off edge of ribbing and work in relief pat in stripes with 1 border st at each edge. When piece measures 25½ in. (65 cm) from beg, fasten off.

FRONT

Work same as back.

SLEEVES

With knitting needles and white, cast on 34 (34, 38, 38) sts and work 2 in. (5 cm) in 2/2 ribbing. Cast off loosely.
With crochet hook, work 36 (36, 42, 42) sc + 1 border st at each edge along top edge of ribbing and work in relief pat in stripes as foll: 4 rows white, 2 rows blue, 8 rows white, 2 rows pink, 8 rows white, 2 rows green, 2 rows gold, then complete sleeve in white. **At the same time**, at each edge of every 3rd row, inc 1 st by working 2 dc in each edge st. Work incs 12 times. Work inc sts in pat st. You now have 60 (60, 66, 66) sts + 1 border st at each edge. When sleeve measures 17¾ in. (45 cm) from beg, fasten off.

FINISHING

Block pieces to indicated measurements. Sew shoulder seams along 6 (6½, 7¼, 8) in. - 15 (17, 18.5, 20) cm from each armhole edge. Sew sleeves to side seams, matching centre of sleeve with shoulder seam. Sew side and sleeve seams.

CHILD'S STRIPED PULLOVER

SIZE

Child's size 4 (6, 8, 10) years, chest 23 (25, 27, 28½) in. - 58.5 (63.5, 69, 72.5) cm. Finished chest measurements: 26½ (28, 29½, 31½) in. - 67 (71, 75, 80) cm, length: 13¼ (15, 16½, 18) in. - 34 (38, 42, 46) cm.

MATERIALS

1 (2, 2, 2) skeins "Mayflower Cotton 8" (100% cotton -approx. 187 yds (170 m) per 50 g skein) colour white, 1 skein each colour blue, pink, gold and green. Crochet hook U.S. size C/2 (U.K. size 11) (Metric size 3) or size needed to obtain tension. Knitting needles U.S. size 2 (U.K. size 10) (Metric size 2.5). **To save time, take time to check tension!**

TENSION

18 sts (= 9 motifs) and 16 rows = 4 in. (10 cm).

STITCHES

Chain (ch), single crochet (sc), double crochet (dc), treble crochet (tr).
Pattern stitch: When changing colours, work the last loop of the last st of 1 colour with the colour of the next st. Hold the unused yarn against the wrong side of work. When inserting hook, work around the unused yarn so that the new sts hold it against the work. Work the border sts in the same colour as the adjacent st in pat. Ch 3 at the beg of each row (= 1 border st).

Row 1: with white, right side of work: ch 3 (= 1 border st), *2 tr in the foll dc, skip 1 dc*, rep * to * across, end 1 tr in the last tr (= 1 border st). Do not turn, leave the white strand dangling.
Row 2: with blue, right side of work: 1 dc in the ch 3 at beg of row, *1 dc between the 2 tr, ch 1*, rep * to * across, end with 1 dc between the 2 tr, 1 dc in the last st using the dangling strand of white. Cut the blue thread. Turn.
Row 3: with white, wrong side of work, ch 3, *2 tr in ch-1 sp*, rep * to *, end 1 tr in the last dc. Turn and leave the white strand dangling.
Row 4: with pink, right side of work, 1 dc in the tr and the white loop, *ch 1, 1 dc between the 2 tr of the group*, rep * to * across, end with 1 dc in the 3rd ch of the turning ch. Do not turn. Cut the pink strand and draw through the loop on hook.
Row 5: with white, right side of work, ch 3, *2 tr in the ch-1 sp*, rep * to * across, end with 1 tr in the last dc. Do not turn, leave the white strand dangling.
Row 6: with gold, right side of work, 1 dc in the 3rd ch, *1 dc between the 2 tr of the group, ch 1*, rep * to *, end 1 dc in the last tr using the loose strand of white, turn and cut gold yarn.
Row 7: with white, wrong side of work, ch 3, *2 tr in the ch-1 sp*, rep * to *, end 1 tr in the last dc. Turn and leave the white strand dangling.

Row 8: with green, right side of work, 1 dc in the tr at end of previous row, *ch 1, 1 dc between the group of 2 tr*, rep * to *, end 1 dc in the 3rd ch. Do not turn. Cut the yarn and draw through loop on hook.
Row 9: with white, right side facing, ch 3, *2 tr in the ch-1 sp*, rep * to *, end 1 tr in the last dc, leave the white strand dangling and do not turn. Always rep rows 2 to 9.
2/2 ribbing: Row 1: *K2, p2*. Rep * to * across. **Row 2 and all foll rows:** Work sts as established in previous row.

BACK

With knitting needles and gold, cast on 70 (74, 78, 82) sts and work in 2/2 ribbing for 5 rows, then work 6 rows in green. Cast off. With green and crochet hook, work 60 (64, 68, 72) dc along cast off edge of ribbing. Continue in pat st beg row 1 working 1 border st at each edge (= 30 (32, 34, 36) motifs) until piece measures 13 (14½, 15¼, 17¾) in. - 33 (37, 41, 46) cm from beg. Fasten off. With knitting needles and pink, pick up and knit 92 (96, 100, 104) sts and work 3/4 in. (2 cm) in 2/2 ribbing as foll: k1, *k2, p2*, end with k3. Cast off loosely.

FRONT

Work same as back, but work top ribbing in blue.

FINISHING

Block pieces to indicated measurements. Lap the back top border over the front top border for 2 (2¼, 2½, 2¾) in. - 5 (5.5, 6.7) cm and sew in place. With knitting needles and green, cast on 74 (78, 82, 86) sts and work in 2/2 ribbing as foll: 12 rows of green and 6 rows of gold. Cast off loosely. Sew to centre 11 (12, 12½, 13) in. - 28 (30, 32, 34) cm side seams with seam showing on right side of work, the cast off edge on right side of body. Fold borders in half to inside and sc in place. Sew side seams.

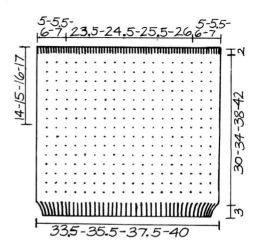

FRONT-BACK

EXUBERANT
PATTERNED PULLOVERS ADD
SPICE TO COLLEGE LIFE. THE
TRIANGLE STITCH IS A
FASCINATING GEOMETRY LESSON.

RELIEF STITCH PULLOVER

SIZE

Woman's Small (Medium/Large, X Large), bust 30-32 (33-38, 39-42) in. - 76-81.5 (84-97, 99-107) cm. Finished bust measurements: 41½ (47¼, 53) in. - 105 (120, 135) cm, length: 27½ in. (70 cm), sleeve seam 18½ (19¼, 20) in. - 47 (49, 51) cm.

MATERIALS

11 (13, 15) skeins sport weight mohair blend yarn (approx. 190 yds (173 m) per 50 g skein) colour red. Crochet hooks U.S. sizes C/2 and E/4 (U.K. sizes 11 and 9) (Metric sizes 3 and 3.5) or size needed to obtain tension. **To save time, take time to check tension!**

TENSION

14 sts and 8 rows = 3 in. (7.5 cm) wide x 2½ in. (6 cm) high using larger size hook.

STITCHES

Chain (ch), single crochet (sc), double crochet (dc), half treble crochet (htr), treble crochet (tr).
Front Relief tr: Worked in tr by working around the post of the st below. For front relief sts, yo, and insert hook from right to left around the post of the indicated st at front of work. Yo, and draw through loop, then continue as you would for a tr.
Back Relief tr: Worked in tr by working around the post of the st below. For back relief sts, yo, and insert hook from right to left around the post of the indicated st in back of work. Yo, and draw through loop, then continue as you would for a tr.
Post stitch: Row 1: 1 tr in each st.
Row 2: *1 front relief tr, 1 back relief tr*, rep * to * across row.
Row 3: Work opposite st of the previous row, that is, work 1 relief tr in the front of the st above a back relief st so that the border alternates front and back relief sts on both sides of the work.

Triangle stitch: Worked in rounds by foll the chart in relief st. Each square equals 1 relief st. Ch 2 at the beg of each round instead of 1 relief st. Join rounds with sc. When working 1 back relief st at beg of round, work in back of ch 2 of previous round. When working 1 front relief st at beg of round, work in front of ch 2 of previous round.

BODY

With larger size crochet hook, ch 196 (224, 253) and join in ring with sc. Work 1 round of tr, begin with ch 3 = 195 (223, 251) tr. Join with sc in the 3rd ch. **Round 2:** Work by foll chart, beg as indicated on chart: ch 2 (counts as the first back relief tr), *13 front relief tr, 1 back relief tr*, work * to * 13 (15, 17) times, end with 13 front relief tr. Join round with sc. Work 1 back relief tr in the ch st at beg of round. **Round 3:** Ch 3 for the first back relief tr, 1 back relief tr, *11 front relief tr, 3 back relief tr*, rep * to *, end with 11 front relief tr, 1 back relief st. Join rounds by foll chart, creating 6 rounds of triangle motifs until piece measures 14 in. (36 cm) from beg.
Divide for armholes: Work 7 (8, 9) triangles and work back and forth by foll chart. Beg each row with ch 2 for border st (above the first st of the previous row) = first st of chart. End each row with 1 htr = 1 border st (work in triangle st). Work these 99 (113, 127) sts for 4 rows of triangle motifs and piece measures 23½ in. (60 cm) from beg. Now work 2 rows of post st, working 1 st in each st of last row. Work 2nd half the same.
With wrong side facing, join the back and front shoulders tog by working through 2 thicknesses in sc over 6 (6¾, 8) in. - 15 (17.5, 20) cm.

Sleeves: With larger size crochet hook, work 98 sts along armholes edges, beg between the 49th and 50th sts from the shoulder seam and work 1 round of tr, then continue in rounds of triangle st. You will have 7 triangles. On every round, dec 1 st at underarm until you have 5 complete triangles. When 7 triangle motifs have been worked vertically and sleeve measures about 16½ in. (42 cm) from beg, fasten off. Work 2nd sleeve.

FINISHING

Block pieces to indicae measurements. With smaller size crochet hook, work 160 (180, 200) dc along lower edges of body and work 3¼ in. (8 cm) of post st. Join each round with a sc and begin each round with ch 3. Fasten off. With smaller size crochet hook, work 38 (42, 46) dc along lower edges of each sleeve and work 2 (2¾, 3½) in. - 5 (7, 9) cm of post st. Join round with sc. Fasten off.

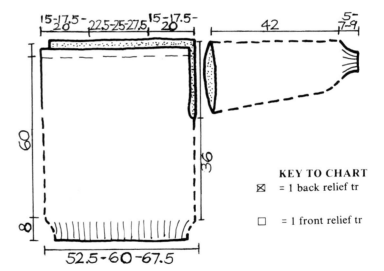

KEY TO CHART
⊠ = 1 back relief tr

☐ = 1 front relief tr

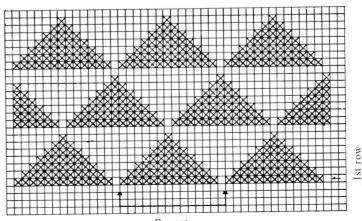

Repeat

ANGELIC

TRIO OF GIRL'S SHIRT COLLAR PULLOVERS IS HEAVEN SENT FOR CROCHETERS. THREE STITCH PATTERNS OFFER VARIATIONS ON A THEME: EYELET IN LILAC, YELLOW CABLED LACE; OR GREEN FILET CROCHET.

★ ★

KEY TO CHART

- ● = Ch 1
- V = 1 dc
- † = 1 tr

CHILD'S LILAC POLO TOP

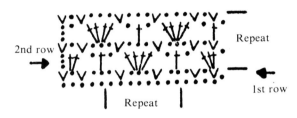

2nd row → / Repeat / 1st row ← / Repeat

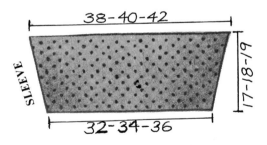

38-40-42

SLEEVE

32-34-36

17-18-19

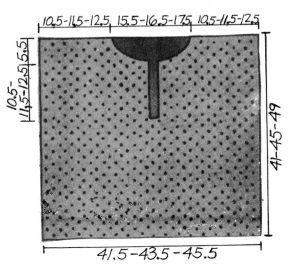

10.5-11.5-12.5 15.5-16.5-17.5 10.5-11.5-12.5

10.5-11.5-12.5

41-45-49

41.5-43.5-45.5

SIZE

Child's size 8 (10, 12) years, chest 27 (28½, 30) in. - 69 (72.5, 76) cm. Finished chest measurements: 32½ (34½, 36) in. - 83 (87, 91) cm, length: 17¼ (19, 20½) in. - 44 (48, 52) cm, sleeve seam: 7¼ (7¾, 8¼) in. - 19 (20, 21) cm.

MATERIALS

6 (7, 7) skeins fingering weight yarn (approx. 220 yds (201 m) per 50 g skein) colour lilac. Crochet hook U.S. size B/1 (U.K. size 12) (Metric size 2.5) or size needed to obtain tension. Knitting needles U.S. size 2 (U.K. size 13) (Metric size 2). 3 buttons. **To save time, take time to check tension!**

TENSION

42 sts and 18 rows in pat st = 4 in. (10 cm).

STITCHES

**Chain (ch),
single crochet (sc),
double crochet (dc),
treble crochet (tr).
1/1 ribbing: Row 1:** *K1, p1*. Rep * to * across.
Row 2 and all foll rows: Work sts as established in previous row.

BACK

With crochet hook ch 177 (185, 193) + ch 1 to turn.
Row 1: right side of work: 1 dc in the 2nd ch from the hook, ch 1, skip 1, 1 dc, *ch 3, skip 3, 1 dc*, rep * to *, end with ch 1, skip 1, 1 dc in the last ch. **Row 2:** Ch 3, 2 tr in the ch-1 sp, *ch 1, 1 tr in the ch-3 sp, ch 1, 4 tr in the ch-3 sp*, rep * to *, end with ch 1, 1 tr in the ch-3 sp, ch 1, 2 tr in the last ch-1 space, 1 tr in the dc. Continue in pat st by foll chart, rep rows 2 to 5 until piece measures 16 (17¾, 19¼) in. - 41 (45, 49) cm from beg. Fasten off.

FRONT

Work same as back until piece measures 9¾ (11, 12¼) in. - 25 (28, 31) cm from beg. Divide work for front opening. Work the first 85 (89, 93) sts and work straight for 4¼ (4¾, 5) in. - 11 (12, 13) cm from beg, then shape neck. *With right side facing, work to last 6 (6, 7) sts, leave these sts unworked, turn, work to end of row*, rep * to * 4 times total. With right side facing, work to last 5 (7, 5) sts, turn, work to end of row. Continue on

rem 56 (58, 60) sts until piece measures 16 (17¾, 19¼) in. - 41 (45, 49) cm. Fasten off. Work over last 85 (89, 93) sts and work by rev shapings. (For neck dec, sc over specified number of sts on right side of work.) Leave the 7 sts between the 2 halves unworked.

SLEEVES

Ch 137 (145, 153) + ch 1 to turn. Work by foll chart. At each edge of every 4th (5th, 5th) row, inc 2 sts 6 times. (For each inc, work 3 sts in each edge st.) Work inc sts in pat. You now have 161 (169, 177) sts. When piece measures 6½ (7, 7½) in. - 17 (18, 19) cm from beg, fasten off.

FINISHING

Block pieces to indicated measurements. With knitting needles, pick up and knit 110 (118, 126) sts along lower edge of back and work 1¼ in. (3 cm) in 1/1 ribbing. Cast off loosely. Work same ribbing on front. With knitting needles, pick up and knit 94 (100, 106) sts along lower edge of each sleeve and work 1¼ in. (3 cm) in 1/1 ribbing. Cast off loosely. With knitting needles, pick up and knit 33 (36, 39) sts along left front opening and work ¾ in. (2 cm) in ss (knit right side of work rows, purl wrong side of work rows.) Cast off loosely. Work same band on right front, making 3 buttonholes evenly spaced when band measures 1/3 in. (1 cm). Place the first and 3rd buttonholes 1/3 in. (1 cm) from each edge of band, space second buttonhole evenly between them. For each buttonhole, cast off 2 sts. On foll row, cast on 2 sts over cast off sts. Sew shoulder seams. With knitting needles, pick up and knit 115 (121, 127) sts around neck, not including front bands and work 1¼ in. (3 cm) in 1/1 ribbing. Cast off. With crochet hook work 1 row of dc around front bands and collar, working 1 dc, ch 1, 1 dc in each corner. Fasten off. Lap right border over left and sew end in place. Sew on buttons. Sew sleeves to armholes, matching centre of sleeve with shoulder seams. Sew side and sleeve seams.

CHILD'S YELLOW POLO PULLOVER

SIZE

Child's size 3 (5, 7) years, chest 22 (24, 26) in. - 56 (61, 66) cm. Finished chest measurements: 26½ (28½, 31½) in. - 67 (73, 80) cm, length: 11¾ (13¼, 14¾) in. - 30 (34, 38) cm, sleeve seam: 4½ (4¾, 5¼) in. - 11 (12, 13) cm.

MATERIALS

3 (4, 5) skeins fingering weight yarn (approx. 220 yds (201 m) per 50 g skein) colour yellow. Crochet hook U.S. size B/1 (U.K. size 12) (Metric size 2.5) or size needed to obtain tension. Knitting needles U.S. size 2 (U.K. size 13) (Metric size 2). 3 buttons. **To save time, take time to check tension!**

TENSION

31 sts and 18 rows in pat st = 4 in. (10 cm).

STITCHES

**Chain (ch),
single crochet (sc),
double crochet (dc),
treble crochet (tr).
Cross 4 on right side:** Skip 1, 3 tr, 1 tr in the skipped st by passing hook behind the 3 tr.
Cross 4 on wrong side: Skip 1, 3 tr, 1 tr in the skipped st by passing hook in front of the 3 tr.
Pattern stitch: Row 1: right side of work: 1 tr in the 7th ch from hook, *ch 1, skip 1, 1 tr*, rep * to *, end with 1 tr in the last st.
Row 2: Ch 1, 1 dc in each st.
Row 3: right side of work: ch 3, *4 sts crossed on right side*, rep * to *, end with 1 tr.
Row 4: wrong side of work: ch 3, *4 sts crossed on wrong side*, rep * to *, end with 1 tr.
Row 5: Same as row 2.
Row 6: Same as row 1.
Rep rows 1 to 6.
1/1 ribbing: Row 1: *K1, p1*. Rep * to * across.
Row 2 and all foll rows: Work sts as established in previous row.

BACK

Worked side to side. With crochet hook ch 90 (102, 114) + ch 4. Work in pat st for 60 (66, 72) rows.

116

Piece will measure 13¼ (14¼. 15¾) in. - 33.5 (36.5, 40) cm from beg. Fasten off.

FRONT

Work same as back until piece measures 4¼ (4½, 5) in. - 10.5 (11.5, 13) cm - 19 (21, 23) rows. *At the end of the next row (neck edge), leave 4 sts unworked. Work 1 row straight.* Work * to * 4 times total = 74 (86, 98) sts and a total of 28 (31, 34) rows. On foll row, leave 28 (28, 32) sts unworked at neck edge. Work rem 46 (58, 66) sts for 3 rows, then ch 28 (28, 32) sts at neck edge and work in pat st = 74 (86, 98) sts. Rev neck shapings on 2nd half by ch 4 at neck edge every 2nd row 4 times and work these sts in pat st = 90 (102, 114) sts for a total of 60 (66, 72) rows from beg, fasten off.

SLEEVES

Worked side to side. Ch 10 (14, 18) + ch 4 to turn. Work by foll chart. At beg of 4th and 6th row, ch 8 sts and work these 26 (30, 34) sts until piece measures 9¾ (10½, 11½) in. - 25 (27, 29) cm at left edge of right side of work row. With wrong side facing, sc over 8 sts on first and 3rd row. Work 3 rows straight, then fasten off.

FINISHING

Block pieces to indicated measurements. With knitting needles, pick up and knit 68 (74, 80) sts along lower edge of each sleeve and work 3/4 in. (2 cm) in 1/1 ribbing. Cast off loosely. With knitting needles, pick up and knit 100 (108, 116) sts along lower edge of back and work 1¼ in. (3 cm) in 1/1 ribbing. Cast off loosely. Work same ribbing on front. With knitting needles, pick up and knit 28 (28, 32) sts along left front opening and work 3/4 in. (2 cm) in ss (knit right side of work rows, purl wrong side of work rows.) Cast off loosely. Work same band on right front, making 3 buttonholes evenly spaced when border measures 1/3 in. (1 cm). Place the first and 3rd buttonholes 1/3 in. (1 cm) from each edge of band. Space 2nd buttonhole between these 2. For each buttonhole, cast off 2 sts. On foll row, cast on 2 sts over cast off sts. Sew shoulder seams. With knitting needles, pick up and knit 77 (83, 89) sts around neck, not including front bands and work 1¼ (3 cm) in 1/1 ribbing. Cast off. With crochet hook work 1 row of dc around front bands and collar, working 1 dc, ch 1, 1 dc in each corner. Fasten off. Lap right band over left and sew end in place. Sew on buttons. Sew sleeves to armholes, matching centre of sleeve with shoulder seams. Sew side and sleeve seams.

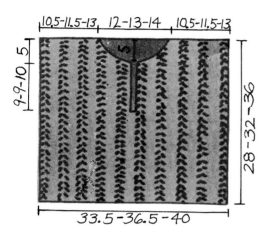

10.5-11.5-13   12-13-14   10.5-11.5-13

9-9-10   5

28-32-36

33.5-36.5-40

FRONT-BACK

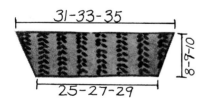

31-33-35

8-9-10

25-27-29

SLEEVE

KEY TO CHART

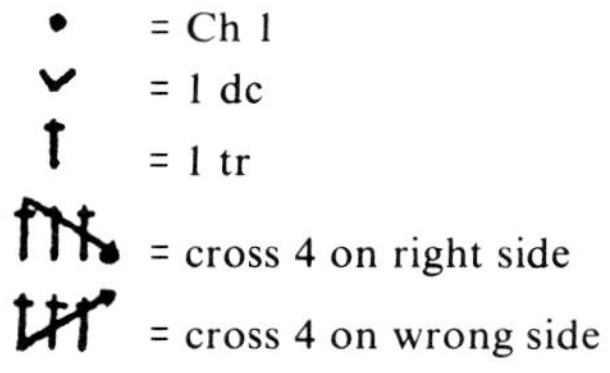

- • = Ch 1
- ⌄ = 1 dc
- ↑ = 1 tr
- ⋀⋀ = cross 4 on right side
- ⋁⋁ = cross 4 on wrong side

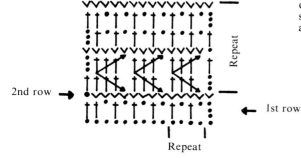

2nd row →

← 1st row

Repeat

Repeat

CHILD'S GREEN POLO TOP

SIZE

Child's size 6 (8, 10) years, chest 25 (27, 28½) in. - 63.5 (69, 72.5) cm. Finished chest measurements: 30 (32, 34½) in. - 76 (82, 88) cm, length: 15¼ (16¾, 18) in. - 40 (44, 47) cm, sleeve seam: 5½ (6, 6¼) in. - 14.5 (15.5, 16.5) cm.

MATERIALS

5 (5, 6) skeins fingering weight yarn (approx. 220 yds (201 m) per 50 g skein) colour green. Crochet hook U.S. size B/1 (U.K. size 12) (Metric size 2.5) or size needed to obtain tension. Knitting needles U.S. size 2 (U.K. size 13) (Metric size 2). 3 buttons. **To save time, take time to check tension!**

TENSION

33 sts and 22 rows in pat st = 4 in. (10 cm).

STITCHES

Chain (ch), single crochet (sc), double crochet (dc), treble crochet (tr).
1/1 ribbing: Row 1: *K1, p1*. Rep * to * across.
Row 2 and all foll rows: Work sts as established in previous row.

BACK

Worked side to side. With crochet hook ch 124 (136, 148) + ch 3 to turn. **Row 1:** right side of work: 1 tr in the 5th ch from the hook, 1 tr, *ch 1, skip 1, 2 tr*, rep * to *, end with 1 tr in the last ch. **Row 2:** Ch 1, dc across, inserting hook in the back loop of each st. Continue in pat st by foll the chart, always working in the back loop of the sts of the previous row until piece measures 15 (16, 17¼) in. - 38 (41, 44) cm from beg. End with 1 row of tr. Fasten off.

FRONT

Work same as back until piece measures 4¾ (5, 5½) in. - 12 (13, 14) cm from beg. Shape neck. With wrong side facing, sc over first 6 sts, work to end of row, turn, work 1 row straight. *Sc over first 3 sts, work to end of row, turn, work 1 row even*, rep * to * 3 times total. Work rem 109 (121, 133) sts until piece measures about 2½ (2½, 2¾) in. - 6 (6.5, 7) cm from beg of neck. Leave 33 (36, 39) sts unworked at neck edge. Work rem 76 (85, 94) sts for 4 rows. At neck edge, ch 33 (36, 39) sts and work over 109 (121, 133) sts in pat st. **At the same time,** work 2nd half of neck shapings by inc at neck edge to correspond to dec. Work straight on 124 (136, 148) sts for 4¾ (5, 5½) in. - 12 (13, 14) cm, ending with 1 row of tr. Fasten off.

SLEEVES

Worked side to side. Ch 16 (19, 22) + ch 3 to turn. Work these sts in pat st by foll chart. At end of 2nd, 4th and 6th row, ch 9 and work over these sts in pat st = 43 (46, 49) sts. Continue in pat st until piece measures 11¾ (12½, 13¼) in. - 30 (32, 34) cm, measured after edge inc. At right edge of every 2nd row, sc over 9 sts 3 times. Work 1 row over rem 16 (19, 22) sts. Fasten off.

FINISHING

Block pieces to indicated measurements. With knitting needles, pick up and knit 118 (126, 134) sts along lower edge of back and work 1¼ in. (3 cm) in 1/1 ribbing. Cast off loosely. Work same ribbing on front. With knitting needles, pick up and knit 88 (94, 100) sts along lower edge of each sleeve and work 1¼ in. (3 cm) in 1/1 ribbing. Cast off loosely. With knitting needles, pick up and knit 30 (33, 36) sts along left front opening and work 3/4 in. (2 cm) in ss (knit right side of work rows, purl wrong side of work rows.) Cast off loosely. Work same band on right front, making 3 buttonholes evenly spaced when band measures 1/3 in. (1 cm). Place the first and 3rd buttonholes evenly spaced when band measures 1/3 in. (1 cm). Place the first and 3rd buttonholes 1/3 in. (1 cm) from each edge of ends of band, evenly spacing 2nd buttonhole. For each buttonhole, cast off 2 sts. On foll row, cast on 2 sts over cast off sts. Sew shoulder seams. With knitting needles, pick up and knit 109 (115, 121) sts around neck, not including front bands and work 1¼ in. (3 cm) in 1/1 ribbing. Cast off. With crochet hook work 1 row of dc around front bands and collar, working 1 dc,

ch 1, 1 dc in each corner. Fasten off. Lap right band over left and sew ends in place. Sew on buttons. Sew sleeves to armholes, matching centre of sleeve with shoulder seams. Sew side and sleeve seams.

KEY TO CHART

- • = Ch 1
- V = 1 dc
- † = 1 tr

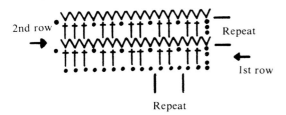

2nd row

Repeat

1st row

Repeat

FRONT-BACK

10-11-12 21-25.5-27 10-11-12

12-13-14

38-41-44

37-41-44

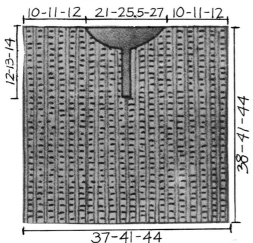

SLEEVE

36-38-40

12.5-13.5-14.5

30-32-34

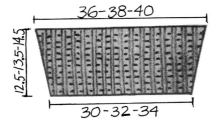

★★

SEASIDE SENSATION OF KHAKI COTTON WITH CAP SLEEVES. THE INDIAN BASKET PATTERN STITCH MAKES THIS PULLOVER A BEACHCOMBER'S TREASURE.

WOMAN'S TOP

SIZE
Woman's Small (Medium, Large), bust 30-32 (33-35, 36-38) in. 76-81.5 (84-89, 91.5-97) cm. Finished bust measurements: 37 (41½, 45½) in. - 94 (106, 116) cm, length: 22½ (22½, 23½) in. - 57 (57, 60) cm.

MATERIALS
10 (12, 14) skeins sport weight cotton yarn (50 g skein) colour khaki. Crochet hook U.S. size C/2 (U.K. size 11) (Metric size 3) or size needed to obtain tensiongauge. Knitting needles U.S. size 2 (U.K. size 12) (Metric size 2.5).
To save time, take time to check tension !

TENSION
22 dc and 16 rows = 4 in. (10 cm).

STITCHES
**Chain (ch), single crochet (sc), double crochet (dc), half treble crochet (htr), double treble crochet (dtr), treble treble crochet (tr tr).
Triangle stitch:** Worked in dtr, but wrap yarn around hook 3 times, yo and draw through 2 loops 4 times = tr tr.

Pattern stitch: Worked on a multiple of 6 + 2.
Rows 1, 2 and 3: 1 dc in each st, ch 1, turn.
Row 4: Ch 4 instead of ch 1 (counts as first dtr), *skip 3 dc, then work 3 triangle sts in the foll 3 dc, work 3 triangle sts in the 3 skipped dc by working behind the first 3 sts*, rep * to *, end with 1 dtr in the last dc, ch 1, turn.
Always rep these 4 rows.
1/1 ribbing: Row 1: *K1, p1*. Rep * to * across.
Row 2 and all foll rows: Work sts as established in previous row.

BACK
Ch 12 for the sleeve. Fasten off and save this piece.
With knitting needles, cast on 100 (112, 145) sts and work 2 in. (5 cm) in 1/1 ribbing. Cast off. With crochet hook, work 1 dc in each st of cast off edge, inc 4 sts by working 2 dc in 4 sts evenly spaced across. You now have 104 (116, 128) dc. Work in pat st. You will have 17 (19, 21) motifs across.

Work 44 (44, 48) rows. When piece measures about 12½ (12½, 13¾) in. - 32 (32, 35) cm, ch 12 at end of row. On foll row, work across in pat st, place the ch 12 piece previously made at left edge and work across in pat st = 128 (140, 152) dc on the first row of pat st, 21 (23, 25) pat motifs on 4th row of pat st. Work a total of 84 (84, 88) rows. Work 1 row of dc across all sts and fasten off.

FRONT
Work same as back for 80 (80, 84) rows. Mark the centre 34 sts and work right shoulder separately for 6 rows. Leave rem sts unworked. On the first row, you will have 47 (53, 59) dc on shoulder. On each of the next 5 rows, dec 2 sts at neck edge of every row. (At end of row at neck edge, leave 2 sts unworked. At beg of row at neck edge, sc over 2 sts.) You now have 37 (43, 49) dc on shoulder. Fasten off. Work 2nd shoulder, rev shapings.

FINISHING
Block pieces to indicated measurements. Sew 1 shoulder seam. With knitting needles, pick up and knit 112 sts around neck and work 1¼ in. (3 cm) in 1/1 ribbing. Cast off loosely. Sew 2nd shoulder and neckband seam. Along each sleeve end, pick up and knit 100 (108, 116) sts and work 1¼ in. (3 cm) in 1/1 ribbing. Cast off loosely. Sew side and sleeve seams.

FRONT-BACK

17-20-22.5 24 17-20-22.5

25

5.5

27-27-30

5

47-53-58

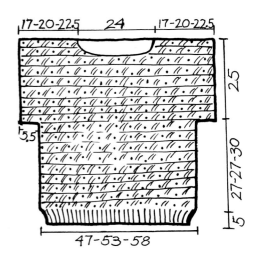

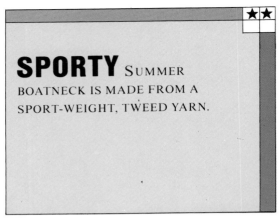

SPORTY SUMMER

BOATNECK IS MADE FROM A SPORT-WEIGHT, TWEED YARN.

WHITE BOAT NECK PULLOVER

SIZE

Woman's Small (Medium, Large), bust 30-32 (33-35, 36-38) in. 76-81.5 (84-89, 91.5-97) cm. Finished bust measûrements: 41½ (44, 47¼). in. - 105 (112, 120) cm, length: 23¼ in. (59 cm), sleeve seam: 18½ in. (47 cm).

MATERIALS

12 (13, 14) skeins sport weight yarn (50 g skeins) colour white tweed. Crochet hook U.S. size B / 1 (U.K. size 12) (Metric size 2.5) or size needed to obtain tension. Knitting needles U.S. size 2 (U.K. size 12) (Metric size 2.5). **To save time, take time to check tension!**

TENSION

5½ fan sts and 10 rounds = 4 in. (10 cm).

STITCHES

Chain (ch),

single crochet (sc), double crochet (dc), treble crochet (tr).
Fan stitch: Multiple of 4 + 5 worked on a ch base.
Row 1: Work 5 tr in the 7th ch from the hook, *skip 4 ch, 5 tr in foll ch (fan st)*, rep * to * 28 (30, 32) = 29 (31, 33) fans, skip 2 ch, 1 tr in the last 2 ch. Turn.
Row 2: Ch 3 (counts as first tr), 5 tr in the middle tr of the fan st*, rep * to * across, end with 1 tr in 3rd ch from end.
Row 3 and all foll rows: Work same as 2nd row, end with 1 tr in top of turning ch of previous row.
1/1 ribbing: Row 1: *K1, p1*. Rep * to * across.
Row 2 and all foll rows: Work sts as established in previous row.

BACK

With crochet hook ch 147 (157, 167) + ch 3 (counts as first st). Work in fan st until piece measures 21¼ in. (54 cm) from beg. Fasten off. With knitting needles, pick up and knit 147 (157, 167) sts from last row of crochet and work 3/4 in. (2 cm) in 1/1 ribbing. Cast off loosely.

FRONT

Work same as back.

SLEEVES

With crochet hook ch 82 + ch 3 (counts as first st). Continue in fan st = 16 fan sts with 1 border st at each edge. At each edge of every 6th row, inc 1 fan st at each edge as foll: at beg of 6th row, ch 3 to turn, work 1 fan st in the first st, *1 fan st in the center of the foll fan st*, rep * to * across 15 times, work 6 tr in the last st (= 1 fan st in 1 tr), turn. Continue in fan st, inc 1 fan st at each edge of every 6th row until you have 28 fan sts across and sleeve measures 15¾ in. (40 cm). Fasten off. With knitting needles, pick up and knit 142 sts across last crochet row and work 3/4 in. (2 cm) in 1/1 ribbing. Cast off loosely.

FINISHING

Block pieces to indicated measurements. With crochet hook work 88 (94, 100) dc along lower edge of front and back pieces. With knitting needles, pick up and knit 1 st from each dc and work 1¼ in. (3 cm) in 1/1 ribbing. Cast off loosely. Work 40 dc along lower edge of sleeves. With knitting needles, pick up and knit 1 st from each dc and work 2 in. (5 cm) in 1/1 ribbing. Bind off loosely. Sew shoulder seams over 5 (5¾, 6¼) in. - 13 (14.5, 16) cm from armhole edge. Sew sleeves to side seams, matching centre of sleeve with shoulder seam. Sew side and sleeve seams.

GILDED LACE SETS A NEW GOLD STANDARD. LIGHTWEIGHT COTTON PULLOVER HAS THREE-QUARTER LENGTH SLEEVES FOR ALL-SEASON COMFORT.

GOLD LACE PULLOVER

SIZE

Woman's Small (Medium, Large, X Large), bust 30-32 (33-35, 36-38, 39-42) in. - 76-81.5 (84-89, 91.5-97, 99-107) cm. Finished bust measurements: 42 (45, 47, 50) in. - 108 (114, 120, 126) cm, length: 23¼ in. (59 cm), sleeve seam: 17 in. (43 cm).

MATERIALS

4 skeins cotton yarn (100% cotton - approx. 175 yds (160 m) per 50 g skein) colour gold. Crochet hook U.S. size B / 1 (U.K. size 12) (Metric size 2.5) or size needed to obtain tension. Knitting needles U.S. size 2 (U.K. size 11) (Metric size 2.5). **To save time, take time to check tension!**

TENSION

1 pattern repeat = 1¼ in. (3 cm)
10 rows = 4 in. (10 cm).

SLEEVE

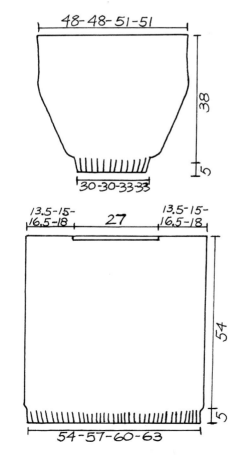

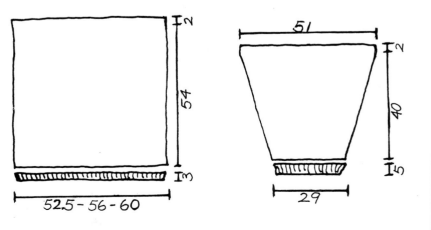

STITCHES

Chain (ch),
single crochet (sc),
double crochet (dc),
treble crochet (tr),
double triple crochet (dtr).
3 Tr sts tog: work 1 tr in each of the foll 3 sts, but leave the last loop of each tr on the hook: after the first tr, there will be 2 loops on the hook, after the 2nd tr, there will be 3 loops on the hook, after the 3rd tr, there will be 4 loops on the hook. Yo and draw through the 4 loops on hook.
Pattern stitch: Worked on a base of dc.
Row 1: Ch 3 (counts as first st), *3 dc, work 3 dtr, ch 1, 1 tr in next st; ch 3, 3 tr tog over next 3 sts, ch 1*. Rep * to *, end with 1 tr in the last st after the last 3 tr tog instead of ch 1.
Row 2: Ch 3, *insert hook in ch-1 space between tr and the 3 dtr of the previous row and work 3 dtr, ch 1, 1 tr in next st; ch 3, 3 tr tog over next 3 dtr, ch 1*. Rep * to *, end with 1 tr in the 3rd turning ch of the previous row.
Always rep row 2.
2/2 ribbing: Row 1: *K2, p2*. Rep * to * across.
Row 2 and all foll rows: Work as established in previous row.

BACK

With knitting needles, cast on 118 (126, 130, 138) sts and work 2 in. (5 cm) in 2/2 ribbing, beg and end with k2. Cast off. With crochet hook, work 119 (126, 132, 139) dc in the cast off row of ribbing. Continue in pat st, having 18 (19, 20, 21) motifs and 1 border tr at each edge. (On first row, alternately skip 3 sts, then 2 sts between *'s of pat rep.) Work until piece measures 23¼ in. (59 cm) from beg. Fasten off.

FRONT

Work same as back, until you have 1 less row than the back. **Last row:** Work 4½ (5, 5½, 6) motifs, end with 1 tr. Fasten off. Skip the foll 9 motifs and join yarn. Work the last 4½ (5, 5½, 6) motifs, fasten off.

SLEEVES

With knitting needles, cast on 50 (50, 54, 54) sts and work 2 in. (5 cm) in 2/2 ribbing. Cast off. With crochet hook, work 52 (52, 57, 57) dc in the cast off row of ribbing. Work in pat st as foll: On row 1 instead of skipping 3 dc for each pat rep, skip 1 dc. Beg with row 2, inc 1 st at each edge by working 1 additional tr in the first and last sts of row. When you have 4 extra sts at each edge, beg a new motif (every 9th row). Work inc every 2nd row until you have 16 (16, 17, 17) motifs. Work straight until piece measures 17 in. (43 cm). Fasten off.

FINISHING

Block pieces to indicated measurements. Sew shoulder seams. Work 1 round of dc around neck. Fasten off. Sew sleeves into armholes, matching centre of sleeve with shoulder seams. Sew side and sleeve seams.

PULLOVER

SIZE

Woman's Small (Medium, Large, X Large), bust 30-32 (33-35, 36-38, 39-42) in. - 76-81.5 (84-89, 91.5-97, 99-107) cm. Finished bust measurements: 41 (44, 47) in. - 104 (112, 120) cm, length: 23½ in. (60 cm), sleeve seam: 17¾ in. (45 cm).

MATERIALS

11 (12, 13) skeins cotton linen blend (approx. 150 yds (137 m) per 50 g skein) colour camel. Crochet hook U.S. size E/4 (U.K. size 9) (Metric size 3.5) or size needed to obtain tension. Knitting needles U.S. size 3 (U.K. size 10) (Metric size 3).
To save time, take time to check tension!

TENSION

5 motifs x 12 rows = 4 in. (10 cm).

STITCHES

Chain (ch),
single crochet (sc),
double crochet (dc),
treble crochet (tr).
Judith stitch: Multiple of 4 + ch 2.
Row 1: Ch 1 (= 1 border st), 1 dc in the 3rd ch from the hook, dc across. The last dc counts as the border st.

Row 2: Ch 3 (= 1 border st), *skip 1 dc, 1 tr in each of the foll 3 dc, then pass the hook in front of the 3 previous sts, insert hook in back loop of st, yo and draw through 1 loop, yo and draw through 2 loops on hook = 1 group*, rep * to *, end with 1 tr in the last ch (= 1 border st).
Row 3: Ch 1 (= 1 border st), 1 dc in each of the foll sts, end 1 dc in the 3rd ch of the border st. Rep rows 2 and 3.
1/1 ribbing: Row 1: *K1, p1*. Rep * to * across.
Row 2 and all foll rows: Work sts as established in previous row.

BACK

Ch 106 (114, 122) and work in Judith st = 26 (28, 30) groups = 1 border st at each edge. Work until piece measures 20½ in. (52 cm), work 1 row of dc. Fasten off.

FRONT

Work same as back.

SLEEVES

Ch 54 (62, 70) and work in Judith st = 13 (15, 17) groups + 1 border st at each edge. At each edge of every 2nd row (Dc row), work 2 dc in each edge st, 12 times. At each edge of every 4th row dc row), work 2 dc in each edge st 4 times. Work inc sts in Judith st = 21 (23, 25) groups + 1 border st at each edge. Work until piece measures 15¼ in. (39 cm) from beg with 2½ in. (6 cm) straight at top of sleeve. Fasten off.

FINISHING

Block pieces to indicated measurements. With knitting needles, pick up and knit 108 (116, 124) sts from lower edge of back and work 3¼ in. (8 cm) in 1/1 ribbing. Cast off loosely. Work same ribbing on front. With knitting needles, pick up and knit 54 (58, 62) sts from lower edge of each sleeve and work 2½ in. (6 cm) in 1/1 ribbing. Cast off loosely. Sew shoulder seams over 6½ (7, 7½) in. - 17 (18, 19) cm. Sew sleeves to armholes, matching centre of sleeve with shoulder seams. Sew side and sleeve seams.

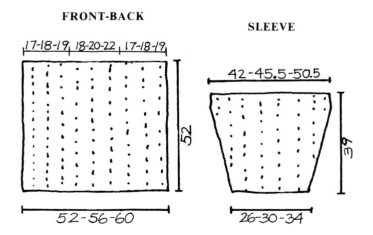

FRONT-BACK | 17-18-19 | 18-20-22 | 17-18-19 | 52 | 52-56-60

SLEEVE | 42-45.5-50.5 | 39 | 26-30-34

REFINED LINEN-COTTON
BLEND SPANS THE SEASONS IN
CAFE AU LAIT. THE PATTERN
STITCH MAKES IT ONE OF A KIND.

REFINED STYLING LENDS THESE JACKETS EXTRA CHIC. THE CROCHETED FABRIC GIVES THEM AN APPEALING, BODY-SKIMMING LOOK.

WHITE JACKET

SIZE

Woman's Small (Medium, Large), bust 33-35 (36-38, 39-42) in. - 84-89 (91.5-97, 99-107) cm. Finished bust measurements: 38½ (42½, 45¾) in. - 98 (108, 116) cm, length: 23¼ (24, 24¾) in. - 59 (61, 63) cm, sleeve seam: 16½ in. (42 cm).

MATERIALS

13 skeins sport weight cotton yarn (approx. 110 yds (100 m) per 50 g skein) colour white. Crochet hook U.S. size E/4 (U.K. size 9) (Metric size 3.5) or size needed to obtain tension. **To save time, take time to check tension!**

TENSION

19 tr and 16 rows = 4 in. (10 cm).

STITCHES

**Chain (ch),
single crochet (sc),
double crochet (dc),
half treble crochet (htr),
treble crochet (tr).**
Pattern stitch: Ch an even number of sts + ch 2.
Row 1: wrong side of work row: 1 tr in the 4th ch from the hook, *1 tr in the foll ch*, rep * to *.
Row 2: right side of work row: ch 1, 1 dc in the first tr, *1 dc by inserting hook around the vertical post of the foll tr from right to left, 1 dc in the foll tr*, rep * to *, end with 1 dc in the last tr.
Row 3: Ch 2, *1 tr in the foll dc*, rep * to *.
Rep rows 2 and 3.
Shrimp stitch: Work like dc, but work from left to right instead of right to left.

BACK

Ch 92 (100, 108) + ch 2 to turn. Work in pat st. Work straight until piece measures 3½ (4, 4¼) in. - 9 (10, 11) cm from beg, dec 1 st at each edge (sc over first st, work to last st, turn, leaving last st unworked). Then at each edge of every 3rd row 4 times total = 84 (92, 100) sts and piece measures 7 (7½, 8) in. - 18 (19, 20) cm from beg. Now inc 1 st at each edge of every 4th row 4 times (work 2 st in each edge st on each inc row) = 92 (100, 108) sts and piece measures 15 (15¼, 15¾) in. - 38 (39,

40) cm from beg. Shape armholes: *Sc over first 3 sts and work to last 3 sts, turn, leaving last 3 sts unworked. Work 1 row straight.* Work * to * 3 (4, 4) times. *Sc over first st, work to last st, turn, leaving last st unworked. Work 1 row straight.* Work * to * 1 (1, 2) times = 72 (74, 80) sts until armhole measures 8¼ (8½, 9) in. -21 (22, 23) cm. Work over the first 28 (29, 31) sts to first marker. Turn. Sc over first 4 sts, work to end of row, turn. Work to end of row. Turn, sc over first 3 sts, work to end of row. Work 1 more row and fasten off. Work 2nd shoulder by rev shapings.

RIGHT FRONT

Ch 34 (40, 44) + ch 2 and work in pat st. At right edge of every row, inc 2 sts by working 3 sts in right edge st 3 times, inc 1 st by working 2 sts in right edge st 5 (5, 6) times = 45 (51, 56) sts. Work until piece measures 3½ (4, 4¼) in. - 9 (10, 11) cm.

At left edge, dec 1 st by working to 1 st before end of row, turn, leaving last st unworked. Then at left edge of every 3rd row dec 1 st 4 times total = 41 (47, 52) sts. Work straight until piece measures 7 (7½, 8) in. - 18 (19, 20) cm from beg. At left edge inc 1 st, then inc 1 st at left edge of every 4th row 4 times = 45 (51, 56) sts. Work until piece measures 15 (15¼, 15¾) in. - 38 (39, 40) cm, shape armhole. With right side facing, at left edge, work to last 3 sts, turn, sc over first 3 sts. Work to end of row. Turn and work to last 0 (3, 3) sts, turn. Sc over first 1 (3, 3) sts, work to end of row. Turn. *With right side facing, work to last st, turn, leaving last st unworked. Work 1 row straight.* Rep * to * 2 (0, 1) time total = 35 (39, 42) sts. Work until armhole measures 8¼ (8½, 9) in. - 21 (22, 23) cm from beg. Place marker after 14 (17, 18) sts at right edge, then fasten off all sts.

LEFT FRONT

Work same as right front, rev shapings.

SLEEVES

Ch 46 (50, 52) + ch 2 and work in pat st. Work straight for 3¼ in. (8 cm). Then at each edge of every 2nd row, inc 1 st 15 (15, 16) times. (For each inc, work 2 sts in each edge st.) You now have 76 (80, 84) sts. Work until piece measures 18½ in. (47 cm) from beg, then shape sleeve cap. Sc over 4 sts and work to last 4 sts, turn, leave last 4 sts unworked. Sc over first 3 sts once, work to last 3 sts, leave last 3 sts unworked, turn. *Sc over first st, work to last st, turn, leaving last st unworked.* Rep * to * 26 (27, 28) times. Work 1 row over rem 10 (12, 14) sts. Fasten off.

FINISHING

Block pieces to indicated measurements. Sew shoulder seams. Along the right front neck edge, work 16 (19, 22) tr, work 37 (41, 43) tr along back neck and 16 (19, 22) tr along left front neck edge. Continue in pat st. On the first, 3rd, 5th, 6th and 7th row, dec 1 st at each edge and on the 8th row, dec 2 sts at each edge. Fasten off. Gather top of sleeve and set in sleeves. Sew side and sleeve seams. With double strand of yarn, work around edge of jacket as foll: **Round 1:** Beg at side seam, sc around piece, join round with sc. **Round 2:** Ch 2, 1 dc in each sc, join round with sc in the 2nd ch at beg. **Round 3:** Work in shrimp st, working the first st in the first ch. Join round with sc in the first ch at the beg. Work same border along the lower edge of the sleeves.

BLACK JACKET

SIZE

Woman's Small (Medium, Large), bust 33-35 (36-38, 39-42) in. - 84-89 (91.5-97, 99-107) cm. Finished bust measurements: 39 (43, 46) in. - 100 (110, 118) cm, length: 23¼ (24, 24¾) in. - 59 (61, 63) cm, sleeve seam: 16½ in. (42 cm).

MATERIALS

13 (14, 16) skeins fingering weight yarn (approx. 247 yds (225 m) per 50 g skein) colour black. Crochet hooks U.S. sizes B/1 and D/3 (U.K. sizes 12 and 10) (Metric sizes 2.5 and 3.5) or size needed to obtain tension. **To save time, take time to check tension!**

TENSION

22 sts and 18 rows = 4 in. (10 cm) with larger hook.

STITCHES

**Chain (ch),
single crochet (sc),
double crochet (dc),
treble crochet (tr).**
Pattern stitch: Worked on an even number + 2 ch sts.
Row 1: Wrong side of work: 1 tr in the 4th ch from the hook, *1 tr in the foll ch*, rep * to * across.
Row 2: Ch 1, 1 dc in the first tr, *1 dc inserting hook from right to left around the post of the foll tr, 1 dc in the foll tr*, rep * to *, end with 1 dc in the last tr.
Row 3: Ch 2, *1 tr in the foll dc*, rep * to * across.
Rep rows 2 and 3.
Shrimp stitch: Worked same as dc, but work from left to right instead of right to left.

BACK

With larger hook ch 109 (117, 125) and work in pat st = 107 (115, 123) sts. Work straight until piece measures 3½ (4, 4¼) in. - 9 (10, 11) cm from beg, dec 1 st at each edge (sc over first st, work to last st, turn, leaving last st unworked). Then at each edge of every 4th row, dec 1 st 3 times = 99 (107, 115) sts. When piece measures 7 (7½, 8) in. - 18 (19, 20) cm from beg, inc 1 st at each edge of every 6th row 4 times total (work 2 sts in each edge st on each inc row) = 107 (115, 123) sts. When

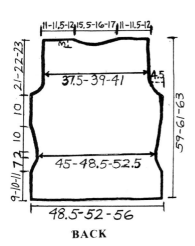

BACK

11-11.5-12 5.5-16-17 11-11.5-12

37.5-39-41

4.5

21-22-23

10

10

72

45-48.5-52.5

59-61-63

9-10-11

48.5-52-56

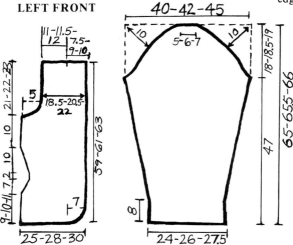

LEFT FRONT

11-11.5-12

7.5-9-10

5

18.5-20.5

22

21-22-23

10

10

72

59-61-63

9-10-14

7

25-28-30

SLEEVE

40-42-45

10

5-6-7

10

18-18.5-19

65-65.5-66

47

8

24-26-27.5

126

piece measures 15 (15¼, 15¾) in. - 38 (39, 40) cm from beg, shape armholes: *Sc over first 2 sts and work to last 2 sts, turn, leaving last 2 sts unworked. Work 1 row straight.* Work * to * 3 (4, 5) times. *Sc over first st, work to last st, turn, leaving last st unworked. Work 1 row straight.* Work * to * 6 times = 83 (87, 91) sts until armhole measures 7 (7½, 8) in. -18 (19, 20) cm. Work over the first 35 (36, 37) sts. Turn and work straight in pat st to end of row, turn. Work to last 4 sts, turn. Work 1 row straight, turn. Work to last 4 sts, turn. Work 1 row straight. Then work to last 2 sts, turn, leaving last 2 sts unworked. Fasten off rem 25 (26, 27) sts. Leave the centre 13 (15, 17) sts unworked, then work the last 35 (36, 37) sts by rev shapings.

RIGHT FRONT

With larger hook ch 43 (49, 57) and work in pat st = 41 (47, 55) tr. At right edge of every row, inc 2 sts by working 3 sts in right edge st 3 times. Inc 1 st by working 2 sts in right edge st 8 times. Then at right edge of every 2nd row, inc 1 st by working 2 sts at right edge twice = 57 (63, 71) sts. Work until piece measures 3½ (4, 4¼) in. - 9 (10, 11) cm. At left edge, dec 1 st by working 1 st before end of row, turn. Then at left edge of every 6th row dec 1 st 3 times = 53 (59, 67) sts. Work straight until piece measures 7 (7½, 8) in. - 18 (19, 20) cm from beg. At left edge inc 1 st, then inc 1 st at left edge of every 6th row 4 times total = 57 (63, 71) sts.

Work until piece measures 15 (15¼, 15¾) in. - 38 (39, 40) cm, shape armholes. With right side facing, *at left edge, work to last 4 sts, turn, work 1 row straight*, work * to * 1 (2, 3) times, **work to last 2 sts, turn, work 1 row straight**, work ** to ** 4 (3, 3) times, ***work to last st, turn, leaving last st unworked, work 1 row straight***, work *** to *** 4 times = 41 (45, 49) sts. Work until armhole measures 8¼ (8½, 9) in. -21 (22, 23) cm from beg, fasten off.

LEFT FRONT

Work same as right front, rev shapings.

SLEEVES

With larger hook ch 55 (59, 63) and work in pat st = 53 (57, 61) sts. Work straight for 3¼ in. (8 cm). Then at each edge of every 3rd row, inc 1 st 18 (18, 19) times. (For each inc, work 2 sts in each edge st.) You now have 89 (93, 99) sts. Work until piece measures 18½ in. (47 cm) from beg, then shape sleeve cap. *Sc over 2 sts and work to last 2 sts, turn*, work * to * 3 times. Then work the foll 25 (26, 28) rows as foll: sc at beg of work, work to last st, turn, leaving last st unworked. *Sc over 2 sts, work to last 2 sts, turn, leaving last 2 sts unworked*. Work * to * 4 times total. Work 1 row over rem 11 (13, 15) sts. Fasten off.

FINISHING

Block pieces to indicated measurements. Sew shoulder seams. With larger hook, along the right front neck edge, work 16 (19, 22) tr, work

37 (41, 43) tr along back neck and 16 (19, 22) tr along left front neck edge. Continue in pat st. On the first, 3rd, 5th, 6th and 7th row, dec 1 st at each edge and on the 8th row, dec 2 sts at each edge. Fasten off. Gather top of sleeve and set in sleeves. Sew side and sleeve seams. With smaller hook and double strand of yarn, work around edge of jacket as foll: **Round 1:** Beg at side seam, sc around piece, join round with sc. **Round 2:** Ch 2, 1 dc in each sc, join round with sc in the 2nd ch at beg. **Round 3:** Work in shrimp st, working the first st in the first ch. Join round with sc in the first ch at the beg. Fasten off. Work same border along the lower edge of each sleeve. Fasten off. sleeve. Fasten off.

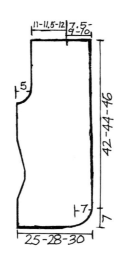

RIGHT FRONT

SLEEVE

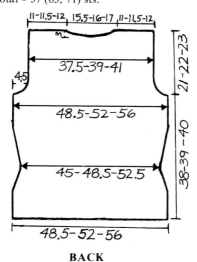

BACK

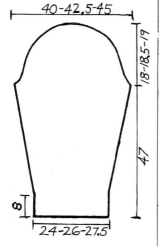

PULLOVER

SIZE

Woman's Medium (Large, X Large), bust 33-35 (36-38, 39-42) in. - 84-89 (91.5-97, 99-107) cm. Finished bust measurements: 40 (44, 48) in. - 102 (112, 122) cm, length: 27½ in. (70 cm), sleeve seam: 17¾ in. (45 cm).

MATERIALS

22 (23, 24) skeins "Mayflower Helarsgarn" (100% cotton - approx. 88 yds (80 m) per 50 g skein) colour red or white. Crochet hook U.S. size F/5 (U.K. size 8) (Metric size 4) or size needed to obtain tension. Knitting needles U.S. size 3 (U.K. size 10) (Metric size 3). **To save time, take time to check tension!**

TENSION

Approx. 4 fan sts = 4¼ in. (11 cm) and 7 rows = 4 in. (10 cm).

STITCHES

**Chain (ch),
single crochet (sc),
double crochet (dc),
half treble crochet (htr).
Fan stitch:** Multiple of 4 + 3. Worked on a ch base. **Row 1:** Ch 3 (counts as first tr), 1 tr in the 4th ch from hook, *skip 3 ch, 1 fan st = 1 dc, ch 3, 3 tr in the foll ch*, rep * to *, end by skipping 1 ch, 1 dc in last ch. **Row 2:** Ch 3, 1 tr in the last dc of the previous row, 1 fan st in the ch-3 space of the previous fan st, 1 fan st in the last ch-3 space of each fan st across row, end with 1 dc in the last st of the row. Always rep row 2. **1/1 ribbing: Row 1:** *K1, p1*. Rep * to * across. **Row 2 and all foll rows:** Work sts as established in previous row.

BACK

With smaller size needles,

cast on 84 (93, 102) sts and work 2¾ in. (7 cm) in 1/1 ribbing. Cast off. With crochet hook, continue into cast off sts as foll: 2 tr in the first st, *skip 3 sts, 1 fan st in the foll st, skip 4 sts, 1 fan st in the foll st*, rep * to * 8 (9, 10) times = 18 (20, 22) fan sts, ending by skip 1 st, 1 dc in the last st. Rep 2nd row of fan st until piece measures 27 in. (69 cm), ending with wrong side of work row. **Last row:** Ch 3, 2 tr in the last dc of the previous row, *1 dc in the ch-3 sp of the fan st, 3 tr in the foll dc*, rep * to *, end with 1 dc in the last st. Fasten off.

FRONT

Work same as back.

SLEEVES

With smaller size needles, cast on 47 sts and work 2¾ in. (7 cm) in 1/1 ribbing. Cast off. With crochet hook, crochet into cast off sts as foll: 2 tr in the first st, *skip 3 sts, 1 fan st in the foll st, *, rep * to * 10 times = 11 fan sts, ending by skip 1 st, 1 dc in the last st. Rep 2nd row of fan st until piece measures 7 in. (18 cm). At beg of foll 2 rows, inc 1 fan st as foll: ch 3, 1 tr in the last dc of the previous row, 1 fan st in the middle tr of the first fan st, 1 fan st in the last ch-3 sp of the first fan st, 1 fan st in the last ch-3 sp of each of the fan sts across. Work these 2 inc rows when sleeve measures 11 in. (28 cm) and 15 in. (38 cm). Work these 17 fan sts until sleeve measures 19¾ in. (45 cm), ending with last row as on back. Fasten off.

FINISHING

Block pieces to indicated measurements. Sew shoulder seams over 5 (6, 6½) in. - 13 (15, 17) cm from armhole edge. Sew sleeves to side seams, matching centre of sleeve with shoulder seam. Sew side and sleeve seams.

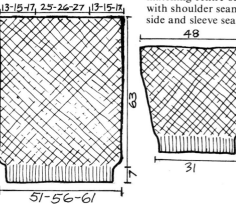

WINTER WHITE OR FIERY RED? THE CHOICE IS YOURS. WHY NOT MAKE ONE OF EACH IN THIS CLASSIC FAN STITCH?

PEERLESS PULLOVER USES THE SAME STITCH FOR A DAMASK EFFECT. THE COWL NECK AND CUFFS ARE KNITTED IN RIBBING FOR A SUPPLE, ELASTIC FINISH.

SHOWCASE YOUR
TECHNIQUE WITH THIS TRIUMPH
OF EXCELLENCE. THE CROCHETED
DAMASK JACKET IS A REAL
DESIGN TREASURE.

ZIGZAG PULLOVER

SIZE

Woman's Small (Medium, Large), bust 30-32 (33-35, 36-38) in. 76-81.5 (84-89, 91.5-97) cm. Finished bust measurements: 43½ (46½, 49) in. - 111 (118, 125) cm, length: 23¼ (24½, 25¾) in. — 59 (62, 65.5) cm, sleeve seam: 16½ in. (42 cm).

MATERIALS

16 (18, 20) skeins Shetland worsted weight yarn (approx. 140 yds (128 m) per 50 g skein) colour ecru.
Crochet hook U.S. size G/6 (U.K. size 7) (Metric size 4.5) or size needed to obtain tension. Knitting needles U.S. size 4 (U.K. size 9) (Metric size 3.5). Circular or double pointed needles U.S. size 4 (U.K. size 9) (Metric size 3.5) **To save time, take time to check tension!**

TENSION

15 sts and 23 rows = 4 in. (10 cm).

STITCHES

Chain (ch), single crochet (sc), double crochet (dc).
1/1 ribbing: Row 1: *K1, p1*. Rep * to * across.
Row 2 and all foll rows: Work sts as established in previous row.

BACK

Working from side to side, beg at left edge. With crochet hook ch 83 (88, 92) = ch 1 (counts as first st). **Row 1:** 1 dc in the 2nd ch from the hook, 1 dc in each ch = 83 (88, 93) dc. **Row 2 and all foll wrong side of rows:** Ch 1, 1 dc in each dc across. **Row 3:** Ch 1, 1 dc in each dc. **Row 5:** Ch 1, 5 dc, *1 long st in the 3rd row

below: insert hook in the st in the 3rd row below foll dc, yo and draw up loop, yo, insert hook from front to back of the same st of the 3rd row, yo, draw through long loop, yo, insert hook in same st, yo, draw through long loop, yo and draw through 5 loops on hook, yo and draw through last 2 loops, 1 dc, 1 long st in 3rd row below, 7 dc*, rep * to *, end with point 1 (2, 1) on chart, 1 dc in the last dc. **Row 7:** Ch 1, 6 dc, *1 long st in first row, 9 dc*, rep * to *, end with point 1 (2, 1) on chart, 1 dc in last dc. **Row 9:** Ch 1, 1 dc in each of the first 2 dc, *1 long st in the 7th row below, 7 dc, 1 long st in the 7th row below, 1 dc*, rep * to *, end with point 1 (2, 1) on chart, 1 dc in the last dc. **Row 11:**

SLEEVE

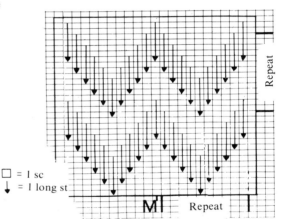

□ = 1 sc
↓ = 1 long st

M

Repeat
Repeat

FRONT-BACK

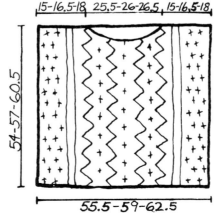

15-16.5-18   25,5-26-26,5   15-16,5-18
54-57-60.5
55.5-59-62.5

SLEEVE

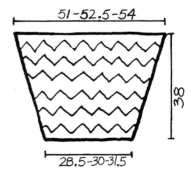

51-52.5-54
38
28.5-30-31.5

Ch 1, 1 dc in the first dc, 1 long st in the 5th row below, 9 dc*, rep * to *, end with point 1 (2, 1) on chart, 1 dc in the last dc. Continue **Row 12** by foll the chart to point 4 (5,6). Then work point 6 to point 7, then from point 9 (8, 7) to point 10. Piece will measure 21¾ (23¼, 24½) in. - 55.5 (59, 62.5) cm from beg, fasten off.

FRONT

Work same as back until piece measures 6 (6½, 7) in. - 15 (16.5, 18) cm from beg, then shape neck. With right side facing, at left edge of every 2nd row, leave 3 sts unworked once, leave 2 sts unworked twice, leave 1 st unworked 3 times. Work wrong side of work rows without decreases. Work over rem 73 (78, 83) sts to centre of work (= M on chart). Work the 2nd half by rev shapings (ch the specified number of sts at neck edge and work these sts in pat st). Work to end of chart. Fasten off.

SLEEVES

Ch 45 (47, 49) + ch 1 to turn. Work in pat st by centring chart (= M on chart). Continue in pat st by foll chart. At each edge of every 4th row, inc 1 st 12 times. At each edge of every 6th row, inc 1 st 5 times. (To inc, work 2 sts in each edge st.) Work inc sts in pat st = 79 (81, 83) sts. Work for a total of 6 zigzag motifs, then work the last 4 rows of chart. The sleeve will measure 15 in. (38 cm) from beg. Fasten off.

FINISHING

Block pieces to indicated measurements. Sew shoulder seams. With double pointed knitting needles, pick up and knit 176 (180, 184) sts around neck and work 4 rows in 1/1 ribbing. Cast off loosely. With knitting needles, pick up and knit 140 (148, 156) sts along lower edge of back and work 2 in. (5 cm) in 1/1 ribbing. Bind off loosely. With knitting needles, pick up and knit 40 (42, 44) sts along each sleeve edge and work 1½ in. (4 cm) in 1/1 ribbing. Cast off. Work same ribbing on front. Sew sleeves to side seams, matching centre of sleeve with shoulder seam. Sew side and sleeve seams.

ZIGZAG CARDIGAN

SIZE

Woman's Small (Medium, Large), bust 30-35 (36-38) in. - 76-89 (91.5-97) cm. Finished bust measurements: 49½ (51¾) in. - 126 (131.5) cm, length: 25½ in. (65 cm), sleeve seam: 18¼ in. (46.5 cm).

MATERIALS

18 (20) skeins worsted weight Shetland yarn (approx. 140 yds (128 m) per 50 g skein) colour ecru.
Crochet hook U.S. size G/6 (U.K. size 7) (Metric size 4.5) or size needed to obtain tension. Knitting needles U.S. size 4 (U.K. size 9) (Metric size 3.5). 7 buttons. **To save time, take time to check tension!**

TENSION

15 sts and 24 rows in pat st = 4 in. (10 cm).

STITCHES

Chain (ch), single crochet (sc), double crochet (dc).
Stocking stitch: *Knit 1 row on right side of work, purl 1 row on wrong side of work*.
1/1 ribbing: Row 1: *K1, p1*. Rep * to * across.
Row 2 and all foll rows: Work sts as established in previous row.

BACK

Working from side to side, beg at left edge. With crochet hook ch 93 + ch 1 to turn. Work in pat st as foll: **Row 1:** 1 Dc in the 2nd ch from the hook, 1 dc in each ch = 93 dc. **Row 2 and all foll wrong side of work rows:** Ch 1, dc across. **Row 3 and 5:** Ch 1, dc across. **Row 7:** Ch 1, 6 dc, *1 long st: insert hook in the st found in the first row below next st, yo and draw up loop, yo, insert hook from front to back of the same st of the first row, yo, draw through long loop, yo, insert hook in same st, yo, draw through long loop, yo and draw through 5 loops on hook, yo and draw through last 2 loops, 9 dc*, rep * to * across, end with 6 dc instead of 9 dc. **Row 9:** Ch 1, 5 dc, *1 long st worked 3 rows below next st, 1 dc, 1 long st worked 3 rows below next st, 7 dc*, rep * to *

across, end with 5 dc instead of 7 dc. **Row 11:** Ch 1, 4 dc, *1 long st worked in the 5th row below next st, ch over the next 3 dc, 1 long st worked in the 5th row below next st, 5 dc*, rep * to * across, end with 4 dc instead of 5 dc. Continue by foll chart. Always rep rows 21 to 34 of chart, making 10 (11) zigzags total. After the last rep work the last 4 rows of chart. Piece will measure 23½ (25¾) in. - 60 (65.5) cm from beg, fasten off.

LEFT FRONT

Ch 93 + ch 1 to turn. Work in pat st by foll chart. After 8 rows, work the first 70 sts, then work the rem 23 sts for 32 rows (pocket front). Ch 23. Fasten off. Work the 70 sts at right edge, join the 23 st ch and work across in pat for 32 rows. Then work 70 sts at right edge and 23 sts from pocket front and work in pat st until piece measures 9 (9¼) in. - 23 (26) cm from beg. With right side facing, sc over first 3 sts, work to end of row, turn. Work to end of wrong side of work row. On right side of work rows, sc over 2 sts 3 times, and sc over 1 st once. Always work wrong side of work rows without dec. Work rem 83 sts until 5 zigzag motifs are complete, then work last 4 rows of chart. Fasten off.

RIGHT FRONT

Work same as left front, but beg at centre edge. Ch 83 + ch 1 to turn. Work in pat st by foll chart. At right edge of every right side of work row, inc 1 st once, inc 2 sts 3 times, inc 3 sts once = 93 sts. (For 2 and 3 st incs, ch the specified number of sts at end of wrong side of work row and work in pat over them on right side of work row.) Beg the pocket after row 34, rev placement of left front. When pocket is complete, work 8 rows, then fasten off.

RIGHT SLEEVE

Ch 45 (47) + ch 1 to turn. Work in pat st by centring chart at point M. Inc 1 st at each edge of every 5th row 18 times. (For inc, work 2 sts in each edge st.) Work inc sts in pat st. You now have 81 (83) sts and 7 complete zigzag motifs.

After the 7th rep, work last 4 rows of chart. Sleeve will measure 16¾ in. (42½ cm) from beg. Fasten off.

LEFT SLEEVE

Work same as right sleeve, centring chart at point M1.

FINISHING

Block pieces to indicated measurements. With knitting needles, pick up and knit about 29 sts along top of each pocket and work 3/4 in. (2 cm) in 1/1 ribbing. Cast off. Sew pocket lining and borders in place. Sew shoulder seams. With knitting needles, pick up and knit about 40 (42) sts along edge of each sleeve and work 1½ in. (4 cm) in 1/1 ribbing, cast off loosely. Sew sleeves to side seams, matching centre of sleeve with shoulder seam. Sew side and sleeve seams. With knitting needles, pick up and knit 287 (299) sts along lower edge of body and work in 1/1 ribbing for 1¾ in. (4.5 cm). Cast off loosely. With smaller size needles, cast on 22 sts and work as foll: **Row 1:** (wrong side facing) P10, p1 in back of st, 11 sts in 1/1 ribbing, beg with k1.

Row 2: 11 sts in 1/1 ribbing, k1 in back of st, k10 (st st). Work until piece fits along left front edge to neck, Cast off first st of wrong side of work, place rem 21 sts on holder. Sew to left front. Work same band for right front, beg with 11 sts in 1/1 ribbing, p1 in back of st, p10 (st st). When piece measures 3/4 in. (2 cm) from beg, make first buttonhole: right side facing: k1, work 2 sts, cast off 3 sts, work 10 sts, cast off 3 sts, work 4 sts. On foll row, cast on 3 sts over cast off sts. Mark positions for 5 more buttons on left band and work buttonholes on right front band to correspond, allowing for last buttonhole on neckband. Cast off last st of wrong side of work row (on sc section). Place rem 21 sts on holder and sew to right front. With knitting needles, pick up 21 sts from right front holder, pick up and knit 97 (101) sts around neck and 21 sts from left front holder and work 3/4 in. (2 cm) in 1/1 ribbing. Then make 1 buttonhole above previous ones. Continue ribbing until band measures 1¼ in. (4 cm), then cast off loosely. Fold the front bands to inside and sc in place. Reinforce buttonholes and sew on buttons.

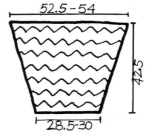

SLEEVE

52.5-54

42.5

28.5-30

FRONT

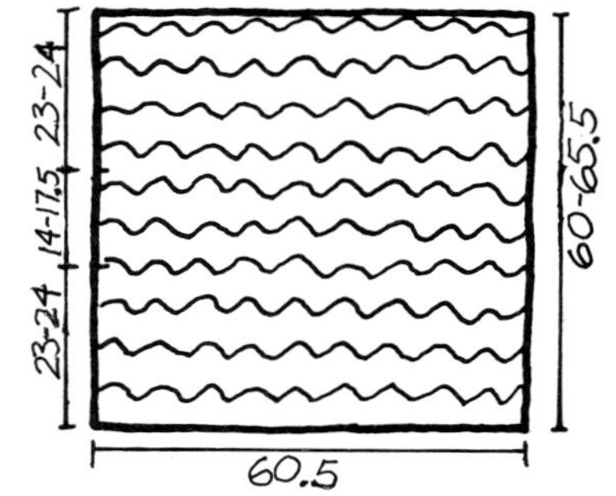

23-24 · 14-17.5 · 23-24

60-65.5

60.5

BACK

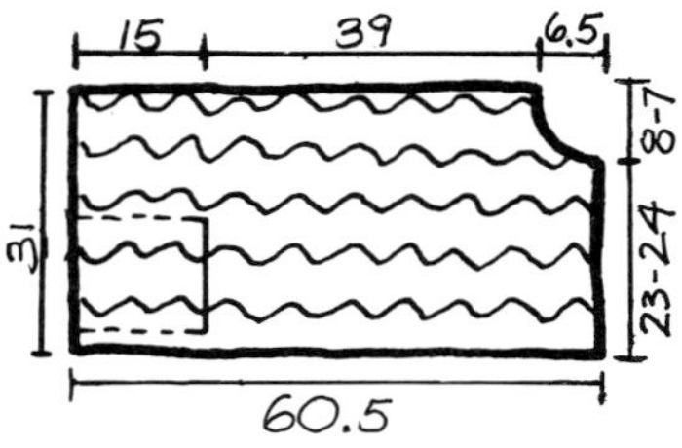

15 · 39 · 6.5

8-7

31

23-24

60.5

134

□ = 1 sc
↓ = 1 long st

**FRONT-BACK
CARDIGAN**

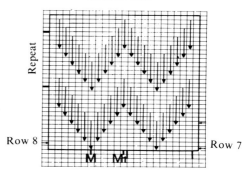

Repeat

Row 8   Row 7

M M

GOLD PULLOVER

SIZE

Woman's Small (Medium, Large), bust 30-32 (33-35, 36-38) in. - 76-81.5 (84-89, 91.5-97) cm. Finished bust measurements: 41½ (45, 48) in. - 106 (114, 122) cm, length: 23¾ in. (60 cm), sleeve seam: 17 in. (43 cm).

MATERIALS

16 (16, 17) skeins "Mayflower Cotton 8" (100% cotton -approx. 186 yds (170 m) per 50 g skein) colour gold. Crochet hook U.S. size B/1 (U.K. size 12) (Metric size 2.5) or size needed to obtain tension. Knitting needles U.S. size 2 (U.K. size 12) (Metric size 2.5). **To save time, take time to check tension!**

TENSION

30 sts and 24 rows in pat st = 4 in. (10 cm).

STITCHES

Chain (ch), single crochet (sc), double crochet (dc), treble crochet (tr), double treble crochet (dtr).
Pattern stitch: Multiple of 4 + 2. At beg of row, ch 1 counts as first dc, ch 3 counts as first tr.
Row 1: Dc across by inserting hook under both loops of previous row.
Rows 2 to 6: Dc in the back loop of the sts of the previous row.
Row 7: Wrong side of work: Ch 3 (= border st), working under both loops of previous row: skip 1, *1 tr in the 2nd, 3rd and 4th sts, 1 dtr in the first st by working behind the 3 tr*, rep * to * across. End with 1 tr (= 1 border st).
Row 8: Right side of row: Ch 3 (= 1 border st), work under both loops of previous row, skip 1, *1 tr in the 2nd, 3rd and 4th sts, 1 dtr in the first st by working in front of the 3 sts*, rep * to * across, end with 1 tr (= 1 border st).
Row 9: Like row 1.
Rows 10 to 14: Like rows 2 to 6.
Row 15: Wrong side of work: Ch 3 (= 1 border st), working under both loops, *skip 3 sts, 1 dtr in the 4th st, 1 tr in front of the dtr in the skipped first, 2nd and 3rd sts*,

rep * to * across, end with 1 tr (= 1 border st). Rep rows 1 to 16.
1/1 ribbing: Row 1: *K1, p1*. Rep * to * across.
Row 2 and all foll rows: Work sts as established in previous row.

BACK

With crochet hook ch 162 (174, 186) + ch 1. Foundation row: Dc across, beg with 2nd ch from hook = 162 (174, 186) dc. Continue in pat st, beg with 2nd row. Work until piece measures 12¾ in. (55.5 cm), ending with 6 rows of dc. Fasten off.

FRONT

Work same as back until you have 5 rows less than back. Mark centre 76 (80, 84) for neck. Work 1 row of dc to last 2 dc before neck marker, sc first st of next row. Work 1 more row to last dc, turn and work 1 row = 39 (43, 47) dc. Fasten off. Work 2nd half by rev shapings.

SLEEVES

Ch 86 (90, 94) + ch 1 (counts as first dc). Dc

across, beg with the 2nd ch from hook = 86 (90, 94) dc. Continue by working in pat st, beg row 2. At each edge of every 3rd row, inc 1 st 8 times. At each edge of every 4th row, inc 1 st 16 times = 134 (138, 142) sts. Work until piece measures 13¾ in. (35.5 cm), then work 6 rows of dc. Fasten off.

FINISHING

Block pieces to indicated measurements. With knitting needles, pick up and knit 110 (118, 126) sts along lower edge of front and back and work 2 in. (5 cm) in 1/1 ribbing. Cast off loosely. With knitting needles, pick up and knit 48 (50, 52) sts along lower edge of each sleeve and work 1¼ in. (4 cm) in 1/1 ribbing. Cast off loosely. Sew shoulder seams. With crochet hook work 1 row of dc around neck, join with sc, fasten off. Sew sleeves to side seams, matching centre of sleeve with shoulder seams. Sew side and sleeve seams.

FRONT-BACK

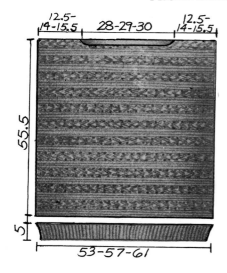

12.5-14-15.5   28-29-30   12.5-14-15.5

55.5

5

53-57-61

44-45-46.5

39.5

4

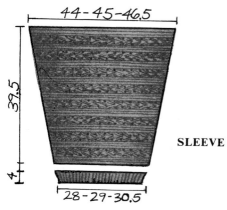

28-29-30.5

SLEEVE

135

HIGHLIGHT YOUR SUMMER TAN WITH THESE COTTON PULLOVERS. THE BATWING SILHOUETTE IS A BREEZE TO WEAR AND SIMPLE TO MAKE.

BATWING PULLOVER

SIZE

Woman's Small (Medium, Large), bust 30-32 (33-35, 36-38) in. 76-81.5 (84-89, 91.5-97) cm. Finished bust measurements: 41½ (44, 46½) in. - 105 (111, 118) cm, length: 21¼ (21½, 22) in. 54 (55, 56) cm, sleeve seam: 15¾ (40.5 cm).

MATERIALS

13 (14, 14) skeins "Mayflower Cotton 8" (100% cotton -approx. 188 yds (171 m) per 50 g skein) colour teal. Crochet hook U.S. size B/1 (U.K. size 12) (Metric size 2.5) or size needed to obtain tension. Knitting needles U.S. size 2 (U.K. size 12) (Metric size 2.5). **To save time, take time to check tension!**

TENSION

30 sts and 24 rows = 4 in. (10 cm).

STITCHES

**Chain (ch),
single crochet (sc),
double crochet (dc),
treble crochet (tr),
double treble crochet (dtr).
Pattern stitch:** Multiple of 8 + 1 border st at each edge. **Row 1:** Ch 1, dc across, working under the 2 strands of the previous row. Turn.
Rows 2 to 6: Ch 1, dc across, working in the back loop of the st of the previous row. Turn.
Row 7: Wrong side of work: Mark centre st, ch 3 (= border st), working under both loops of each st, *skip 3 sts, 1 dtr in the 4th st, 1 tr in the first, 2nd and 3rd skipped sts by passing hook in front of the 4th st*, rep * to * to the center of the row, then **skip 1 st, 3 tr in

2nd, 3rd, and 4th sts, 1 dtr in skipped st by passing the hook behind the 3 tr**, rep ** to ** across, end 1 tr (= border st).
Row 8: right side of work: Mark centre st, ch 3 (= border st), working under both loops of each st, *skip 1 st, 3 tr in the 2nd, 3rd and 4th sts, 1 dtr in skipped st by passing hook in front of the 3 tr (insert hook from back to front of st)*, rep * to * to centre of work, then *skip 3 sts, 1 dtr in the 4th st, 1 tr in the first, 2nd and 3rd skipped sts by working behind the dtr*, rep * to * across, end 1 tr (= border st). Rep rows 1 to 8.
1/1 ribbing: Row 1: *K1, p1*. Rep * to * across.
Row 2 and all foll rows: Work sts as established in previous row.
WORKED IN 1 PIECE, BEG AT LOWER EDGE OF LEFT SLEEVE with crochet hook ch 86 (90, 94) + ch 1 (counts as first dc). **Row 1:** Work 85 (89, 92) dc, beg in 2nd ch from hook = 86 (90, 94) dc. Continue with the 2nd row of pat st. Inc 1 st at each edge of every 3rd row 28 times. (Work 2 sts in each edge st for each inc.) Work inc sts in pat st. On the 7th row, over the 90 (94, 98) sts as foll: ch 3 (= 1 border st), 0 (2, 0) tr, *skip 3 sts, 1 dtr in the 4th st, 1 tr in the first, 2nd, 3rd skipped sts by passing the hook in front of the dtr*, rep * to * 10 (10, 11) times, then *skip 1 st, 3 tr in the first,

2nd, 3rd and 4th sts, 1 dtr in skipped st by passing hook behind the 3 tr*, rep * to * 10 (10, 11) times. End with 0 (2, 0) tr in 1 tr (= border st). Continue on the 142 (146, 150) sts work until piece measures 14¼ in. (36.5 cm), ending with the 8th row of pat st. Ch 74 (76, 78) + ch 1 and join to right edge, work across 142 (146, 150) sts, then ch 74 (76, 78). Continue in pat st over 290 (298, 306) sts for 5¼ (5½, 6) in. -13.5 (14, 15) cm, mark centre 6 sts. Work first 35 (36, 37) motifs + 1 border st. Work straight for 10 (10¾, 11½) in. -25.5 (27.5, 29) cm, then leave sts unworked. Work 2nd half the same, then ch 6 across both halves and work 290 (298, 306) sts in pat st for 5¼ (5½, 6) in. -13.5 (14, 15) cm, ending with 6th row of pat st. Leave 74 (76, 78) sts unworked at each edge and work 2nd sleeve by rev shapings. (For each dec, sc over first st on row and leave last st unworked.)

FINISHING

Block pieces to indicated measurements. With knitting needles, pick up and knit 50 (52, 54) sts along lower edge of each sleeve and work 1½ in. (4 cm) in 1/1 ribbing. Cast off loosely. With knitting needles, pick up and knit 118 (126, 134) sts along lower edge of back and work 2½ in. (6 cm) in 1/1 ribbing. Cast off loosely. Work same ribbing on front. Join the side and sleeve seams by holding right sides tog and using crochet hook join with 1 row of dc, working through both thicknesses. Work 1 round of dc around neck by working 1 dc in each row of dc and 2 dc in each row of tr. Join with sc. Fasten off.

TODDLER'S FLOWER BUD PULLOVER

SIZE

Child's size 1 (2, 3) years, chest 21 (22, 23) in. - 53.5 (56, 58.5) cm. Finished chest measurements: 22½ (24½, 27) in. - 57 (63, 69) cm, length: 11 (13½, 15) in. - 28.5 (34, 38) cm, sleeve seam: 8½ (9½, 10¾) in. - 21.5 (24.5, 27.5) cm.

MATERIALS

4 (5, 6) skeins fingering weight yarn (50 g skein) colour ecru. Crochet hook U.S. size C/2 (U.K. size 11) (Metric size 3) or size needed to obtain tension. Knitting needles U.S. size 2 (U.K. size 12) (Metric size 2.5). 3 buttons. **To save time, take time to check tension!**

TENSION

27 dc and 32 rows = 4 in. (10 cm).

STITCHES

**Chain (ch),
single crochet (sc),
double crochet (dc),
treble crochet (tr).
Cross stitch:** Worked over 2 sts.
Rows 1 and 2: 1 dc in each dc.
Row 3: Insert hook in the first dc (working under

both loops), yo and draw through 1 loop, insert hook in the dc of the previous row under same st, yo and draw through a long loop, yo and draw through 2 loops, yo, draw through 2 loops (= 1 long st), 1 long st in the next dc.
Row 4: 1 dc in each dc.
Row 5: 1 long st in each dc, but insert hook in the long st of the previous row instead of the dc. Always rep rows 4 and 5.
Flower stitch: Worked over 15 (17, 19) st.
Rows 1 to 4: 1 dc in each st = 15 (17, 19) dc.
Row 5: 7 (8, 9) dc, ch 8, 1 dc, ch 8 and 1 dc all in the foll dc, ch 8, 7 (8, 9) dc.
Row 6: 7 (8, 9) dc, ch 1, skip ch 8 of previous row, 1 dc, ch 8, 1 dc, ch 8 of the previous row, 7 (8, 9) dc.
Rows 7 and 8: 1 dc in each st.
Row 9: 4 (5, 6) dc, insert hook through the ch-8 sp and in the foll dc, work 1 dc, 5 dc, insert hook through the 3rd ch-8 sp and in the foll dc, work 1 dc, 4 (5, 6) dc.
Row 10: 6 (7, 8) dc, ch 3, sk 3 sts, 1 dc in each of the foll 6 (7, 8) dc.
Row 11: 6 (7, 8) dc, 7 dc in the ch-3 sp of the previous row and around the centre ch-8 sp of the 5th row, 6 (7, 8) dc.
Row 12: 6 (7, 8) dc, ch 3, skip the fan st of the foll row, 6 (7, 8) dc.

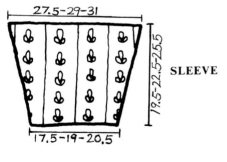

SLEEVE

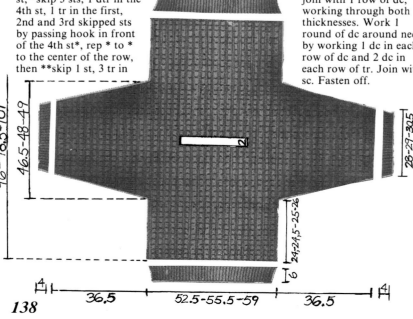

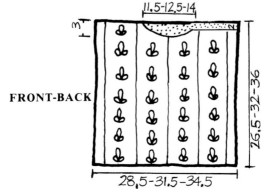

FRONT-BACK

Rep rows 1 to 12.
Half patent stitch: wrong side of work on an odd number of sts:
Row 1: right side of work: 1 border st, p1, *k1, p1*, rep * to *, end with 1 border st.
Row 2: 1 border st, k1, *sl the foll st purlwise, yo (wrap the yarn from front to back around needle), k1*, rep * to *, 1 border st.
Row 3: 1 border st, p1, *knit the foll st, dropping the yo, p1*, rep * to *, end with 1 border st.
Always rep rows 2 and 3.

BACK

With crochet hook ch 80 (88, 96) + ch 1 to beg first row. Work 1 dc in the 2nd ch from hook and dc in each ch across = 80 (88, 96) dc. Work as foll: 5 dc, 2 long sts, *15 (17, 19) sts in flower st, beg with the 2nd row, 2 long sts*, work * to * 4 times total, 5 dc. Work until piece measures 10¼ (12¾, 14¼) in. - 26.5 (32, 36) cm, fasten off.

FRONT

Work same as back until piece measures 9 (11½, 13) in. - 23.5 (29, 33) cm from beg. Mark the centre 18 (20, 24) sts. Work left shoulder as foll: work to first marker, turn, leave rem sts unworked. Sc over the first 5 sts once. Work to end of row, turn. Work to end of row, turn. Sc over first 2 sts and continue on rem 24 (27, 29) sts until piece measures 9½ (12, 13½) in. - 26.5 (32, 36) cm from beg. Fasten off. Work left shoulder by rev shapings, but work until piece measures 10¼ (12¾, 14¼) in. - 24.5 (30, 34) cm. Fasten off.

SLEEVES

Ch 49 (53, 57) + ch 1. Work 1 dc in the 2nd ch from hook and work 1 dc in each of the foll ch = 49 (53, 57) dc. Work as foll: 15 (16, 17) dc [the 15 (16, 17) sts of flower st], 2 long sts, 15 (17, 19) sts of flower st, 2 long sts, 15 (16, 17) dc [the first 15 (16, 17) sts of flower st]. Inc 1 st at each edge of every 4th row 10 (5, 1) time. Inc 1 st at each edge of every 6th row 3 (8, 12) times = 75 (79, 83) sts. (For each inc, work 2 sts in each edge st.) Work new sts in pattern sts. When piece measures 7¾ (8¾, 10) in. - 19.5

(22.5, 25.5) cm, fasten off.

FINISHING

Block pieces to indicated measurements. With knitting needles, pick up and knit 27 (29, 33) sts along the right shoulder of front and work in half patent st. When piece measures 1/3 in. (1 cm), make 2 buttonholes as foll: right side facing: work 7 (8, 9) sts in half patent st, cast off 3 sts, work 7 (7, 9) sts, cast off 3 sts, work 7 (8, 9) sts. On foll row, cast on 3 sts over cast off sts. Continue in half patent st until border measures 3/4 in. (2 cm). Cast off loosely. Work same on back shoulder omitting buttonholes. With knitting needles, pick up and knit 79 (83, 87) sts around neck and work in half patent st for 1/3 in. (1 cm). 3 sts from the right edge, cast off 3 sts. On foll row, cast on 3 sts over cast off sts. Continue until border measures 3/4 in. (2 cm). Cast off. With knitting needles, pick up and knit 77 (81, 87) sts and along lower edge of back and work in half patent st for 3/4 in. (2 cm). Cast off loosely. Make same border on front. With knitting needles, pick up and knit 43 (47, 51) sts along each sleeve edge and work in half patent st for 3/4 in. (2 cm). Bind off loosely. Lap front shoulder border over back and sew in place. Sew sleeves to side seams, matching centre of sleeve with shoulder seam. Sew side and sleeve seam. Sew on buttons.

BABY CABLE PULLOVER

SIZE

Child's size 1 (2, 3) years, chest 21 (22, 23) in. - 53.5 (56, 58.5) cm. Finished chest measurements: 23 (24½, 26½) in. - 57 (63, 69) cm, length: 11 (13½, 15) in. - 28.5 (34, 38) cm, sleeve seam: 8½ (9½, 10¾) in. - 21.5 (24.5, 27.5) cm.

MATERIALS

4 (5, 6) skeins fingering weight yarn (50 g skein) colour ecru.
Crochet hook U.S. size C/2 (U.K. size 11) (Metric size 3) or size

needed to obtain tension. Knitting needles U.S. size 2 (U.K. size 12) (Metric size 2.5). 3 buttons. **To save time, take time to check tension!**

TENSION

27 dc and 32 rows = 4 in. (10 cm). 11 sts of cable pat = 1½ in. (4 cm).

STITCHES

Chain (ch), single crochet (sc), double crochet (dc).
Pattern stitch: Alternately work vertical bands and cable bands. Beg each row with ch 1 to turn. Work 1 dc in the last st of the previous row. Insert hook in the back loop in each st of the previous row.
Cable pattern: Worked over 11 sts.
Row 1: Right side of work: 11 dc, work through the back loop, ch 1, turn.
Row 2: 4 dc, ch 3, skip 3, 4 dc, ch 1, turn.
Row 3: Insert hook in the foll st (work through both loops), yo and draw through 1 loop, then insert hook in the dc of the first row, yo and draw up a long loop, yo, draw through 2 loops, yo, draw through 2 loops (= 1 long st), 1 long st in the foll st, 2 dc, ch 3, skip 3, 2 dc, 1 long dc in foll 2 dc.
Rows 4, 6, 8, 10: 4 dc, ch 3, skip 3, 4 dc.
Row 5: 2 long sts, working both in the long st of the previous row, 2 dc, 1 bobble (insert hook in the first row in the ch-3 sp of the 2nd, 3rd and 4th row, yo, draw through a long loop, *yo, insert hook in the same dc and draw up a long loop*, work * to * twice, yo and draw through 6 loops, ch 1, make another bobble in the same dc, 1 dc in each of the foll 2 dc, 1 long st in each of the foll dc.
Row 7: 1 long st around each of the long sts of the previous row, 2 dc, ch 3, skip 3, 2 dc, 1 long st around each of the long sts of the previous row.
Row 9: 1 long st around each of the long sts of the previous row, 2 dc, 1 long st in the ch-3 sp by working around the ch between the bobble of the 5th row, 1 bobble, ch 1 and 1 bobble, 2 dc, 1 long st in each of the foll 2 long sts.
Always rep rows 7 to 10.
Half patent stitch: wrong

side of work on an odd number of sts:
Row 1: right side of work: 1 border st, p1, *k1, p1*, rep * to *, end with 1 border st.
Row 2: 1 border st, k1, *sl the foll st purlwise, yo (wrap the yarn from front to back around needle), k1*, rep * to *, 1 border st.
Row 3: 1 border st, p1, *knit the foll st, dropping the yo, p1*, rep * to *, end with 1 border st.
Always rep rows 2 and 3.

BACK

With crochet hook ch 79 (85, 93) + ch 1 to beg first row. Work 1 dc in the 2nd ch from hook and dc in each ch across = 79 (85, 93) dc. Work in pat as foll: 8 (9, 11) dc, 11 sts in cable pat (beg with 2nd row), 15 (17, 19) dc, 11 sts of cable pat, 15 (17, 19) dc, 11 sts of cable pat, 8 (9, 11) dc. Work until piece measures 10¼ (12¾, 14¼) in. - 26.5 (32, 36) cm, fasten off.

FRONT

Work same as back until piece measures 9 (11½, 13) in. - 23.5 (29, 33) cm from beg. Mark the centre 17 (19, 21) sts. Work left shoulder as foll: work to first marker, turn, leave rem sts unworked. Sc over the first 5 sts once. Work to end of row, turn. Work to end of row, turn. Sc over first 3 sts and continue on rem 23 (25, 28) sts until piece measures 9½ (12, 13½) in. - 26.5 (32, 36) cm from beg, fasten off. Work right shoulder by rev shapings, but work until piece measures 10¼ (12¾, 14¼) in. - 24.5 (30, 34) cm. Fasten off.

SLEEVES

Ch 51 (55, 59) + ch 1. Work 1 dc in the 2nd ch from hook and work 1 dc in each of the foll ch = 51 (55, 59) dc. Work in pat st as foll: 7 (8, 9) dc, 11 sts in cable pat, 15 (17, 19) dc, 11 sts in cable pat, 7 (8, 9) dc. Inc 1 st at each edge of every 4th row 10 (5, 1) time. Inc 1 st at each edge of every 6th row 3 (8, 12) times = 77 (81, 85) sts. (For each inc, work 2 sts in each edge st.) Work new sts in pat sts. When piece measures 7¾ (8¾, 10) in. - 19.5 (22.5, 25.5) cm, fasten off.

FINISHING

Block pieces to indicated

measurements. With knitting needles, pick up and knit 27 (29, 33) sts along the right shoulder of front and work in half patent st. When piece measures 1/3 in. (1 cm), make 2 buttonholes as foll: right side facing: work 7 (8, 9) sts in half patent st, cast off 3 sts, work 7 (7, 9) sts, cast off 3 sts, work 7 (8, 9) sts. On foll row, cast on 3 sts over cast off sts. Continue in half patent st until border measures 3/4 in. (2 cm). Cast off loosely. Work same on back shoulder omitting buttonholes. With knitting needles, pick up and knit 79 (83, 87) sts around neck and work in half patent st for 1/3 in. (1 cm). 3 sts from the right edge, cast off 3 sts. On foll row, cast on 3 sts over cast off sts. Continue until border measures 3/4 in. (2 cm). Cast off. With knitting needles, pick up and knit 77 (81, 87) sts and along lower edges of back and work in half patent st for 3/4 in. (2 cm). Cast off loosely. Make same border on front. With knitting needles, pick up and knit 43 (47, 51) sts from each sleeve edge and work in half patent st for 3/4 in. (2 cm). Cast off loosely. Lap front shoulder border over back and sew in place. Sew sleeves to side seams, matching centre of sleeve with shoulder seam. Sew side and sleeve seams. Sew on buttons.

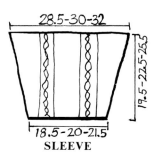

28.5-30-32
19.5-22.5-25.5
18.5-20-21.5
SLEEVE

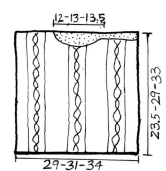

12-13-13.5
23.5-29-33
29-31-34
FRONT-BACK

139

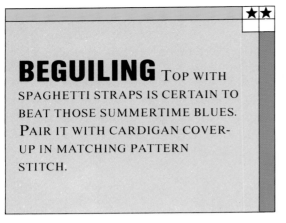

BEGUILING TOP WITH

SPAGHETTI STRAPS IS CERTAIN TO BEAT THOSE SUMMERTIME BLUES. PAIR IT WITH CARDIGAN COVER-UP IN MATCHING PATTERN STITCH.

CARDIGAN AND TOP

SIZE

Woman's Small (Medium, Large), bust 30-32 (33-35, 36-38) in. -76-81.5 (84-89, 91.5-97) cm. Cardigan: Finished bust measurements: 42½ (45, 47) in. -108 (114, 120) cm, length: 22½ in. (57 cm), sleeve seam: 18 in. (46 cm). Top: 33¾ (37, 40) in. - 86 (94, 102) cm. length 13¾ in. (35 cm).

MATERIALS

Cardigan: 12 (13, 13) skeins "Mayflower Cotton 8" (100% cotton - approx. 188 yds (171 m) per 50 g skein) colour blue. Top: 4 (5, 5) skeins colour blue. 5 buttons. Crochet hook U.S. size B/1 (U.K. size 12) (Metric size 2.5) or size needed to obtain tension. Knitting needles U.S. size 2 (U.K. size 12) (Metric size 2.5). **To save time, take time to check tension!**

TENSION

13 groups (= 2 crossed dc) x 12 rows = 4 in. (10 cm).

STITCHES

**Chain (ch),
single crochet (sc),
double crochet (dc),
treble crochet (tr).
1 group tog:** Work 1 tr in the 2nd st, until you have 2 loops on the hook, work 1 tr in the first st, until you have 3 loops on the hook, yo and draw through 3 loops on the hook.
Pattern stitch: Multiple of 2 + ch 3. Ch 1 at each edge of row.
Row 1: (right side of work): 1 tr in the 6th ch from the hook, 1 tr by passing the hook behind the 5th ch from the hook, *skip 1 ch, 1 tr in the foll tr, 1 tr in the skipped st by passing the hook behind the work = 1 group*, rep * to *, end 1 tr for the border st.
Row 2: (wrong side of work): Ch 3 (= border st), *1 tr in the 2nd st, 1 tr in the first st by passing the hook in front of the 2nd st, working from back to front of st*, rep * to *, end with 1 tr in the 3rd ch (= 1 border st).
Row 3: Ch 3 (= 1 border st), *1 tr in the 2nd st, 1 tr in the first st by passing the hook behind the 2nd st*, rep * to * across, end 1 tr (= 1 border st). Rep rows 2 and 3.
Shrimp stitch: Worked like a dc, but worked left to right instead of right to left.
1/1 ribbing: Row 1: *K1, p1*. Rep * to * across.
Row 2 and all foll rows: Work sts as established in previous row.

CARDIGAN: BACK

With crochet hook ch 142 (150, 158) + ch 3 to turn (counts as first st). Work in pat st = 70 (74, 78) groups + 2 border sts. Work until piece measures 20 in. (51 cm) from beg. Mark the centre 24 (26, 28) groups. Work to first marker. Fasten off. Beg after 2nd marker and work rem groups = 23 (24, 25) groups + 1 border st on each shoulder. Fasten off. The total height is 20½ in. (52 cm) from beg.

RIGHT FRONT

Ch 70 (74, 78) + ch 3 (counts as first st). Work in pat st = 34 (36, 38) groups + 2 border sts. Work until piece meaures 9¼ in. (24 cm) from beg. End with right side of work row. Shape neck:
Row 1: (wrong side of work): work to last group of sts on row, work 1 group tog, 1 border st.
Row 2: Ch 3, 1 group tog, work to end of row. Rep rows 1 and 2, 10 (11, 12) times. Work over rem 23 (24, 25) groups + 2 border sts until piece measures 20½ in. (52 cm) from beg. Fasten off.

LEFT FRONT

Work same as right front until piece measures 9¼ in. (24 cm) from beg. End with right side of work row. Shape neck:
Row 1: (right side of work) Ch 3, work 1 group tog, work to end of row.
Row 2: Work to last group of sts on row, work 1 group tog, 1 border st. Rep rows 1 and 2, 10 (11, 12) times. Work over rem 23 (24, 25) groups + 2 border sts until piece measures 20½ in. (52 cm) from beg. Fasten off.

SLEEVES

Ch 80 (82, 84) + ch 3 (= border st). Work in pat st = 39 (40, 41) groups + 2 border sts. On every 2nd row, work 2 tr in the st at each edge 20 (22, 24) times = 59 (62, 65) groups. After every 2nd inc, work these tr in pat st. When piece measures 16 in. (41 cm), fasten off.

FINISHING

Block pieces to indicated measurements. With knitting needles, pick up and knit 107 (113, 119) sts along lower edge of back and work 2 in. (5 cm) in 1/1 ribbing. Cast off loosely. With knitting needles, pick up and knit 51 (53, 55) sts along lower edge of each front and work 2 in. (5 cm) in 1/1 ribbing. Cast off loosely. With knitting needles, pick up and knit 46 (48, 50) sts along lower edge of each sleeve and work 2 in. (5 cm) in 1/1 ribbing. Cast off loosely. Sew shoulder seams. Along the front and back neck edges, work as foll: **Row 1:** (right side of work): Beg at lower edge of right front: With crochet hook work 1 dc in every 2 rows of the knitted border, then 2 dc in every row along the edges of front, (2 dc in the first neck dec), 1 dc in every st of the back neck, 2 dc in every row along edges of left front (2 dc in first neck dec). **Row 2:** Along the straight edge of the right front, make 5 buttonholes spaced as foll: 10¼, 8, 5½, 3¼, 3/4 in. (26, 20, 14, 8, 2 cm) from lower edge. For each buttonhole: ch 3, skip 3 dc. **Row 3:** 1 dc in each dc, 3 dc in each ch-3 sp over the buttonholes. **Row 4:** Work in shrimp st. Fasten off. Reinforce buttonholes. Sew on buttons. Sew sleeves to side seams, matching centre of sleeve with shoulder seams. Sew side and sleeve seams.

TOP: BACK

With crochet hook ch 114 (124, 134) + ch 3 to turn (= 1 border st). Work in pat st = 56 (61, 66) groups + 2 border sts. Work until piece measures 11¾ in. (30 cm). Fasten off.

FRONT

Work same as back. Block piece to indicated measurements. With knitting needles, pick up and knit 104 (110, 116) sts along lower edge of each piece and work 2 in. (5 cm) in 1/1 ribbing. Cast off loosely. Sew side seams. Along the top edge, join yarn and with crochet hook ch 1 in first st at 1 side seam. Work 1 round in dc, then sc to join and work 1 round of shrimp st. Fasten off.
Straps: Make 2 chains about 15¾ in. (40 cm) long. Work 1 dc in the 3rd ch from hook, then work 1 dc in each ch across. Fasten off. Sew chain straps to top of front about 7½ (8, 8¼) in. - 19 (20, 21) cm from side seams of front and 9 (9¼, 9¾) in. - 23 (24, 25) cm from side seams of back.

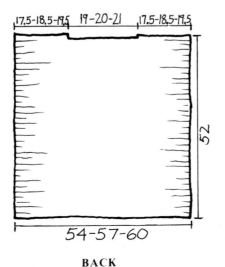

17.5-18.5-19.5 19-20-21 17.5-18.5-19.5

52

54-57-60

BACK

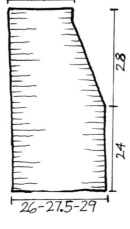

17.5-18.5-19.5

28

24

26-27.5-29

1/2 FRONT

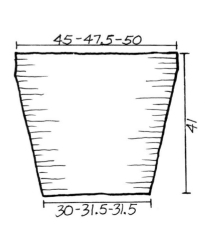

45-47.5-50

41

30-31.5-31.5

SLEEVE

INDEX